SHOOT, LUKE!
THE AIR IS FULL
OF PIGEONS

OTHER BOOKS BY JAMES "DOC" BLAKELY

Handbook of Wit and Pugent Humor, Rich Publishing

Push Button Wit, Rich Publishing

How The Platform Professionals
"KEEP 'EM LAUGHIN'", (with J. Robertson, J. Griffith,
R. Henry), Rich Publishing

Science of Animal Husbandry (with David H. Bade),
Prentice Hall

The Brass Tacks of Animal Health (with Dwight D. King),
Doan Publishing

Horses and Horse Sense, Prentice Hall

SHOOT, LUKE!
THE AIR IS FULL OF PIGEONS

JAMES "DOC" BLAKELY

———— ◆ ————

RICH PUBLISHING COMPANY

10611 CREEKTREE
HOUSTON, TEXAS 77070

Cover artwork and illustrations by Rebecca Blakely.

First Printed 1990
Library of Congress Catalog No. 88-63656
ISBN 0-9607256-7-9
Printed in the United States of America

FOREWORD

Not since Will Rogers has anybody manipulated America's funny bone with the gentle dexterity of Doc Blakely.

I say "gentle" because Doc, for all his pokin' fun at everybody never hurt anybody.

Daily, I necessarily deal with the mud and the blood called "news." Nightly, in just a page or two — or three — before lights out, I peruse some Blakely prose and sleep smiling.

"Push Button Wit" made any subject under the sun less grim.

Now, along comes "Pigeons" — fun-fact, fun-fiction plus a diary of this perceptive man's many encounters with names and places you may know. Yet, I'll bet you've neither seen them nor seen through them as you will through the eyes of this astute observer.

Superficially, Blakely seems to take nothing seriously. Don't you believe it.

I've shared enough public platforms with Doc to recognize his diligence. He <u>works</u> at his craft of keeping you and me entertained.

It's often been fun to include his observations in my own broadcasts; his salt, pepper and sugar makes the grim news more palatable.
Now, sit back — or lie back — and enjoy yourself. Read slowly; in few words Doc sometimes makes sharp points.

Paul Harvey

Good Day!

To all the

strange birds

that have roosted

in my mind.

BIOGRAPHY

JAMES "DOC" BLAKELY

Humorous, witty, down-to-earth. These are just a few of the words that describe Dr. James Blakely of Wharton, Texas. Doc Blakely is a full-time professional speaker and writer with over two decades of experience and success behind him. He has traveled to Australia, New Zealand, Canada, Mexico, Bermuda, the Caribbean, and throughout the United States delivering messages of inspiration and success, riddled with his brand of good, clean humor.

Dr. Blakely quips, "If I tell you anything important, it will be purely by accident," but a program chairman recently gave another view when he said, "Doc Blakely did a superb job on a very difficult assignment of mixing humor and a specifically tailored message to our management team. We came away from a three-hour seminar laughing and learning. He has been so effective with us because he cares about people. That is why we have had him back for the fifth time." In addition, Doc's value as a humorous keynoter, after-dinner, or professional entertainer has brought him recognition throughout the world. The Fortune 500 companies and associations of every sort have benefitted from his thought provoking, yet humorous teaching formula on human relations, communications, and personal development. He is a frequent guest on national TV and radio talk shows because of his wit and humor.

In 1984 the Nightingale-Conant Corporation released a two-volume album entitled "The Executive Treasury of Humor" featuring Doc Blakely as one of the top twelve humorists in America. Considered an authority on the creative use of humor, he is frequently quoted by newspaper columnists and radio commentator Paul Harvey.

Dr. Blakely holds a Bachelor's Degree from Sam Houston State University in Texas, also Master's and Doctor of Philosophy Degrees from the University of Missouri. He is a private pilot, and a consulting editor for Prentice Hall. He writes a weekly syndicated humor column entitled "Pokin' Fun." In 1978 he was elected by his peers to the 3,000 member National Speakers Association Hall of Fame. In 1987, he became the ninth recipient of the highest award, equivalent to the Oscar, given by the Association—the Cavett.

TABLE OF SHOTS

For additional books and products see pages 238–239.

INTRODUCTION

Not so many years ago, pigeons were so numerous in this country that they were hunted for food. About all one needed for a meal from the sky was a dead aim, a dead shot, and a dead pigeon. However, if you shot where the pigeon was going to be or had just been, the odds were greatly in favor of the pigeon. Confidence, experience, and opportunity are key factors in this sport. It's like the guy who was teaching his young son how to hunt. With a double-barreled, 12-gauge shot gun in hand, the elder sportsman was explaining his "never miss" technique when two pigeons flew directly overhead at super-sonic speed. The man fired both barrels and they disappeared as a dot on the horizon. Taking his hat off, in a soft voice, he said, "Son, you have just witnessed a miracle. There goes two dead pigeons and they're still flying."

You see, the opportunity was there, but like anything else in life, hitting the mark is not always as easy as it may seem. A man was on safari hunting birds in India. His gun bearer was a pleasant, little fellow who guided him time after time to places of opportunity. Birds would flush into the air, but the hunter was unsuccessful in bringing down his prey. He turned to the gun bearer and remarked, "I can't hit a thing. I must be the worst shot in the country."

His guide tactfully replied, "It is not that Sahib is such a bad shot. It is just that this day Allah was merciful to the birds."

It stands to reason then that if one is a poor shot, the best time to pull the trigger is when there are more targets to hit. It's like Luke the hillbilly who never seemed prepared for the opportunity when it came up. Quite by accident, he stumbled onto the roost area with his double-barrel breech open and empty. With birds darkening the sky, his friend yelled out, "Shoot, Luke! The air is full of pigeons."

Or, as a friend of mine once remarked, "Some people fail to see an opportunity until it ceases to be one." What do you do in a situation like that? Usually you laugh about it. You better laugh about it because all your friends are going to lie, exaggerate, stretch the truth, and retell the story at every opportunity. This custom is referred to in some parts of the country as "pokin' fun."

Using the pigeons as symbols of missed opportunities, let me ex-

ix

plain how this book almost didn't happen. As a professional speaker, I've been privileged to travel and speak all over the United States and seven foreign countries. Ten years ago, I was hired as an after-dinner speaker by the publisher of a large Florida newspaper. He had an annual appreciation day for all the advertisers who did business with his newspaper. At the luncheon for this annual gala affair, it was my job to entertain the crowd.

Just the day before, a bunch of kids had asked me if I knew what was black and white and read all over. I said, "Sure, a newspaper." One of the kids shot back, "Nope. A wounded nun."

I retold that story and several hundred more to a very appreciative audience. I even got a standing ovation. At least I think it was a standing ovation. As soon as I finished, everybody got up and left.

Anyway, the publisher who was a very influential man in the newspaper business had a great sense of humor. He not only paid my fee, but quipped, "I'd sure like to know who writes your material."

I fired back, "I'll divulge that information if you'll tell me who's going to read it to you."

"Do you think you could write a humor column?" he continued in a serious vein.

"I'm a speaker, not a writer," I replied. "I'm not supposed to think."

"Well, if you can write as well as you can talk, I think I could get you syndicated in the newspapers and we could make you rich and famous."

"I'm not one bit interested in being famous," I replied. "Let's just concentrate on getting rich."

Well, the publisher went on to explain that if I could write three columns per week and could stand the pace of that level of production, he would personally see to it that the big syndicates would be all over me like a duck on a June bug.

"Write thirty columns in thirty days to see if you can stand the pace," was the challenge he hurled at me as we parted company.

I filled both chambers of my double-barreled mind and pulled the trigger by shooting off my mouth with, "I'll do better than that. I'll write 45 columns in 30 days so I can rest for a couple of weeks before I start on my new job."

I returned to my private study headquartered in Wharton, Texas at the Loose Goose Saloon and wrote the 45 columns in 30 days. I sent them to the publisher and waited for the announcement that not only had my material been received, but that I had been nominated for the Nobel Peace Prize for humorous literature.

About a month later, a package arrived. It contained a cover letter from the publisher rejecting my material. It was like the two editors with a flat tire. A motorist stopped to help and out of habit, they said, "Your offer does not meet our requirements at this time." In leafing through the material, I found a couple of notes that a secretary had obviously forgotten to take out of the material. One was a note from the publisher to his senior editor asking him to evaluate the quality of writing. The other was a note from the senior editor to his boss. It read, "Dear Boss: I don't know what you expect me to do with this. It is obviously copied from other sources and we would be up to our neck in lawsuits for plagiarism if we used any of it. Dump this guy quick."

Since all of the material I had sent was totally original with me, that remark made my blood boil. Ask any doctor, he'll tell you—boiled blood is not conducive to one's good health. I might have died then and there if I had not had ice water in my veins.

It eventually dawned on me that maybe the material was good enough that the senior editor just thought it had to have been copied from other published sources. I retold the story of this gross miscarriage of justice to a number of people. One of my listeners who had a sympathetic ear, and maybe a cast-iron brain, suggested I contact a personal friend of his for a second opinion. I figured the second opinion would probably be something like, "You can't spell either." But, I decided to follow up the lead and called Editor Stanley Frank of *The Livestock Weekly,* San Angelo, Texas. As Luke might have reasoned, "If you're gonna look for pigeons, the livestock yard is as good a place as any."

Stanley Frank seemed like a nice sort of guy for a newspaper man. On the phone, he sounded sort of like a nap just waiting for a place to happen. He mumbled the standard, "Send me a sample of your work and I'll see what we can do." I sent Mr. Frank one column, not the 45 I had stored away, but one column. He called back in a few days and said, "I like this stuff. When can we start?" I assured him that we could start right away. Since his paper was a weekly, I figured I had almost a year's worth of work already in the hopper.

"What do you want to call this column?" he asked.

"I've given that a great deal of thought," I answered while I stalled for time to think. "How do you like 'Pokin' Fun'?"

Shortly afterwards, I syndicated the column myself. Excerpts from it have been printed in *Reader's Digest* and are frequently quoted over the 900-station Paul Harvey radio broadcast. What you will read in this book is what my own publisher and editors consider to be the best of Doc Blakely's Pokin' Fun, with subjects arranged to make them fly in formation. In the next few hundred pages, you're going to have lots of opportunities to get high on life. You can't miss. I guarantee it. And if you don't have ammunition, you can still enjoy the hunt. You can be like Zeke, who was asked by Luke to be a decoy on a pigeon hunt.

"How do you do that?" asked Zeke.

"Stand still," said Luke, "and pretend you're a statue."

BIG SHOTS 1

You are never famous until what you did in private is of interest to the public.

FAMOUS PEOPLE

Fame is a relative thing. I've had it and lost it several hundred times each year. As a professional speaker, it is my job to entertain a crowd, many of whom would rather be someplace else at the time. Virtually no one in the audience knows, or cares, who I am before I speak. When the talk is a success, I become an immediate celebrity. People want me to autograph my book, a napkin, or once even a banana. The fame, however, lasts as long as the banana peel. I can walk across the street to another hotel and instantly lose my celebrity status. Not so with people who have had national or international exposure. I marvel at their ability to handle the constant attention.

George Bush and I were on an airplane once and exchanged business cards. You'd think a fellow with that kind of fame would be doing all right, but everytime I hear from him now, he still asks me for money.

On a television program with famed singer Roger Miller, I asked if he would pose for a photograph of the two of us. He's such a nice guy. He threw his arm around my shoulder and as we both smiled broadly at the cameraman, he remarked, "Boy, this will be good for the ol' career, huh, Doc?"

I replied, "Yeah, I sure hope it helps you, Roger."

On an airplane, I was seated next to Julian Bond, the black legislator from Georgia. I recognized him instantly, but his name didn't come to mind quite as readily. I said, "Hey, I know you. You're. . . ." At that point, he actually rolled his eyes around a little and I could tell he was a bit annoyed at being recognized. I continued, "Wait, don't tell me your name. I know it. I'll get it in a minute. It's . . . Billy Carter." He laughed heartily and we had a wonderful time making references about his dull brother, Jimmy.

Visiting in the home of Erma Bombeck, through the invitation of a mutual friend, I found her to be a pure delight. Not only can she produce great humor, but she appreciates it as well. An interesting thing that surprised me about Erma is that she talks to herself and mumbles a lot. She asked me a few personal questions, and to my surprise, seemed genuinely interested in the answers. She asked, "Where is your hometown, Wharton, Texas?"

I replied, "It's between Houston. . . ."

She mumbles, "Houston . . . Houston . . . along the east coast of Texas. . . ."

With only a slight pause, I added, ". . . and Buenos Aires."

She burst into hearty laughter. I wasn't laughing. She poured tea in my lap.

In 1984, I was privileged to be a featured speaker at the Lombardi Awards, along with legendary quarterback, and former coach of the Green Bay Packers, Bart Starr. Since I was his warm-up speaker, I poked a little good-natured fun at him. One of the lines I used was, "Bart Starr is a master of the two-minute drill. I think he uses a Black & Decker."

When I introduced him, his opening line was, "Doc, most of your material is like most of my passes . . . over the heads of the receivers."

One of the finalists that night, one who did not receive the Lombardi Award, was a huge, young, black athlete who weighed about 350 pounds. He had a large gap between his two front teeth, a huge smile, and a great sense of humor. Some of the experts there said he would never make it in professional football because of his weight problem. I asked if he expected to make it and he replied, "I'm gonna be there if I have to get back down to my original weight."

I asked, "What was that?"

He replied, "Nine pounds, six ounces."

None of us knew it at that moment, but William Perry, the "Refrigerator," was to become one of today's most famous athletes. I think his sense of humor had a lot to do with his phenomenal success.

Famous people are just like all the rest of us. The only advantage we have over them is that we don't have to put up with us. Waiting in line to get on an airplane, I recognized John Connally, former Vice President, Secretary of Navy, former Governor of Texas, and bankrupt millionaire. Everyone around me was whispering, "There's John Connally."

"There's John Connally." But they were afraid to say anything to him.

I extended my hand to him, introduced myself, and said, "Glad to meet you."

He shook my hand, but only nodded at me and grunted something that sounded like, "Umhhh."

At that point, a lovely lady on the opposite side with a beautiful smile extended her hand and said, "I'm Nellie Connally. John's wife. And John is so glad to meet you. Aren't you, honey?"

He nodded again and replied, "Umhhh."

"What do you think of the way things are going in the Republican party?" I asked.

"Umhhh," he replied.

Again, Nellie sprang into action, leaned around him, smiled broadly, and said, "Oh, John thinks the leadership in the Republican party is extraordinary. Don't you, honey?"

He mumbled, "Umhhh," again.

Well, John may not have the most sparkling personality, but he is a very famous person that proves, in my eyes, the old adage that behind every successful, famous person, there stands a surprised mother-in-law. I fell in love with Nellie that day. I don't care if John does know about it. I know the only thing he would say to me would be, "Umhhh."

The point is that all fame depends on what you have done and who knows about it. Most of us can get along quite well without being famous if we have a great sense of humor and self-esteem.

My friend, Gene Perret, is a comedy writer. He was working with Jerry Lewis on a project once that required them to get up at 5:00 A.M. One morning on the way to the studio, Jerry saw a donut shop that appeared to be open. He suggested that Gene go inside and pick up coffee and donuts. When Gene tried the door, he found it was still locked, but could see people moving around inside as if they were about ready to open. Gene yelled back to the car, "Jerry, they're still closed."

Jerry, hoping to capitalize on his influence and his level of fame, yelled back, "Well, tell them who it is. Maybe they'll open up."

Gene shrugged his shoulders, cupped his hands around his mouth, and yelled at the top of his voice through the glass, "It's Gene Perret."

For an insight into the humorous side of the lifestyles of the rich and famous, the following observations are offered.

A TOUCH OF SHOW BIZ

On the "pellet pea" circuit, you get to hear lots of introductions of speakers who are close to becoming great and likely would if they would do one little thing—stay home.

People with a national reputation, like Ralph Nader, for instance, used to drive all over the country complaining about how dangerous it was to drive. Other people would take their lives into their own hands, drive down to hear him and pay good money so they could be afraid to drive back home.

Well, because so much of this is just show biz, I've made a list of some of the claims about famous people that some advertising man dreamed up. One major exception is that I've followed each glowing introductory line with the most likely explanation for someone having made this remark in the first place. Here's the list:

Intellectual athlete: "He has a fabulous command of the English language." (He coined the phrase, "More better," "Right on," and "Y'know.")

Corporate trainer: "Star of numerous training films." (Some of which are still being used by the U. S. Navy just before sailors get shore leave.)

Advertising Executive: "Consultant to the stars." (Pluto, Mickey Mouse, and Daffy Duck.)

Aging actor: "Can hold an audience in the palm of his hand. . . ." (for sometimes SECONDS at a time.)

Scientist: "The world's leading authority, without a doubt." (Without proof either. Also without foundation.)

Philosopher: "He is known for his sage advice. . . ." (He once said to a struggling young female, "Don't struggle!")

Writer: "Author of five books. . . ." (One of which may actually be published, tentatively titled "How To Avoid Procrastination and Get Published Quick.")

Boy Wonder: "A millionaire by the time he was 30." (He was born a multi-millionaire.)

Girl Wonder: "Her reputation is sterling. . . ." (It's her character that is tarnished.)

Boss's son: "Listed by 'Who's Who.'" (Even though he doesn't know "What's What," or "How Come.")

Politician: "Never makes the same speech twice." (He can't remember his lines.)

Ex-Politician: "His name is recognized throughout the nation." (His photograph is in all the post offices.)

Consultant: "He has offices in three cities." (He started with an office in only one place but the water heater exploded.)

Mayor: "His style is difficult to describe." (How about MONOTONOUS?)

Playboy: "He numbers numerous world figures among his acquaintances." (He's especially fond of the figure 10.)

Playgirl: "She is a frequent visitor in the homes of Hollywood stars." (Not when their wives are there, of course.)

TV announcer: "Recipient of numerous awards." (He was delivery-man for a trophy company.)

Humorist: "America's top speaker in his field." (Which is pork belly futures, bull, and bologna.)

Amateur: "Turns down twice as many speaking engagements as he accepts." (Which last year amounted to one, which is now in court.)

Retired President: "The only human in history to have received the Equus award." (It usually goes to a mule.)

Chairman of the Board: "Makes over 250 speeches per year." (Most of them begin with "Now, honey, be reasonable.")

CPA: "A creative genius." (If you don't believe that, just look at his expense account reports.)

Minister: "A trend setter in religious views." (He no longer believes he's God.)

Society Leader: "Annually speaks to over one million people." (Few of whom ever speak back.)

Economist: "Respected by colleagues and friends." (Both of 'em.)

Lawyer: "One client has consulted him 23 times." (The IRS, fol-lowed closely by the FBI.)

School Superintendent: "He does the work of three men." (Harpo, Groucho, and Chico.)

Small Businessman: "Has a staff of five." (All in the family; how-ever, his manager just turned six and graduated from kindergarten.)

Columnist: "Perhaps the best known personality in America to-day." (He's also wanted in 16 other countries.)

Editor: "His associates are active in three areas." (Unemployment, uninformed, and unimportant.)

Publisher: "His leadership ability has never been questioned." (In fact, it's never even been mentioned.)

Just joking folks, so don't get tense. I once asked a chairperson of a meeting what important words of wisdom she expected me to leave with the crowd. She replied, "Thank you . . . and good night."

SCHNOZZ HAD CLASS

One of my favorite characters of yesteryear was Jimmy Durante, the "Schnozz" had a gravel voice, an oversized nose, and a balding pate. "Just another pretty face," he used to joke.

How many people do you know who have actually coined such notable words in the English language as "Ink-a-dink-a-doo?"

In reminiscing about Durante, I recall that he never seemed to finish a song without yelling, "Stop da musik." That same phrase is still being used today by parents of teenagers.

Some of my favorite Durante lines are:

"What this country needs is a tailpipe and muffler that will last as long as a beer can."

"My children tell me everything. I'm a nervous wreck."

"Know what you call a Mexican cowboy on a white horse? Roy Rodriquez."

"Once I gave up drinking, smoking, and chasing women all at once. It was the worst 20 minutes of my life."

"A zebra is just a horse whose mother was scared by a venetian blind."

"I went out with an older girl, but her hair wasn't even gray. It was because she had more chemicals in her hair than Lake Erie."

"I just had this terrible thought. I just realized that I'm too old to die young."

"I once knew a rooster who was so lazy that when the other roosters crowed, he would just nod his head in agreement."

"My aunt married so late in life that Social Security picked up 80 percent of the honeymoon."

"This is still the land of opportunity. My parents immigrated to this country over 50 years ago. Today they owe over $261,000."

UNFLUSTERED LINES

Groucho Marx was a total comedian. He was funny to watch, listen to, and to read about. His walk, his talk, his physical appearance was uniquely his. So was his way of thinking.

His daughter was once denied admittance to an exclusive country club swimming pool, with her friends, because the Marx family were non-members. When red-faced officials apologized and sent an application to Groucho, he declined with the comment, "I wouldn't want to belong to any club that would have me as a member."

Still, someone tried to smooth over the conflict and got Groucho to let an application be submitted, only to be further embarrassed when it was turned down for another reason. The club was "restricted" which meant no Jewish members.

Unflustered, Groucho wrote back, "My wife is not Jewish. Can she go swimming and let our daughter wade up to her waist?"

A few more random comments from the great mirthmaker:

"If evolution works, how come mothers still have only two hands?"

"Misers aren't fun to live with—but they make wonderful ancestors."

"He's so heavily in debt that he's known as the Leaning Tower of Visa."

"Live each day as if it were the first day of your marriage and the last day of your vacation."

"I can remember when you had to ask if a gas station could break a twenty. Now they can fracture a fifty."

"September is when millions of bright, shining, happy, laughing faces turn toward school. They belong to mothers."

"There's nothing like a dish towel for wiping that contented look off a married man's face."

"There was a time when a fool and his money were soon parted. Now it happens to everybody."

"A fool and his money are the first two things a girl looks for."

"Ex-wives make great housekeepers; when they get divorced, they keep the house."

Right up to the end, Groucho kept his wit ready for any occasion. When he was ill and hospitalized, a nurse tried to cheer him up. "If I have to keep looking after you this way, you're going to ruin my social life and I'll have to wind up an old maid," said this sweet young thing.

"Bring two of 'em in," wheezed Groucho, "and we'll wind 'em up together."

PRESIDENTIAL LINES

Few people are privileged to meet the President of the United States. I'm fortunate to have met several. Harry Truman was the first. I asked, "Why do they call you 'Give 'em Hell Harry'?" He smiled and shot back, "None of your business."

Then there was LBJ, a religious experience. When he took over, several thousand close associates simultaneously said, "Oh, God."

Lyndon "pressed my flesh" but looked in the eyes of the next guy in line, I guess he had a lot on his mind, what with Lady Bird, Linda Bird, Luci Bird, and his opponent Dirty Bird.

I had the chance to meet Past President Gerald Ford at a convention. But I passed it up because I heard that it was his intention to pardon Woody Hayes.

Truman said, "When things get tough, I retreat into a mental foxhole." LBJ retreated to the Pedernales River, Nixon to San Clemente, Reagan to an old studio, but Ford goes to a Model A museum.

Ford was to speak on the state of the economy, which he thought was a new foreign power, but he was a good sport and didn't seem to mind the jokes making the rounds . . . like:

"This old football player is such a nice guy, but he has played too many games without a helmet. He kept talking about Mediocrity, who he thought was a Greek philosopher."

Security guards for most Presidents are armed with the latest electronic devices, automatic weapons, and two-way communications. The Ford security was a megaphone, two linebackers, and a rubber knife.

The man sure had a sense of humor. During the question and answer session, he was asked to comment on the Communist bloc. He said it would eventually be outlawed in the NFL.

Asked about the ICBM, he said he was not at liberty to discuss his golf game.

He did claim that the Republican trickle down theory can be credited to a Democrat. "We got the idea watching Tip O'Neill eat soup."

Asked to name his three top advisers, he quickly gave credit to Grumpy, Sleepy, and Dopey.

"What do you think of the First Lady, Mr. President?"

His comment, "Martha Washington or Eve?"

His suggestion for a simplified Presidential oath of office was a real classic. The last sentence was "cross my heart and hope to die."

The mass transit system would be a fleet of golf carts.

Laugh at him if you will, he's smarter than all the others put together. He got $15,000 for talking 30 minutes then stumbled down the steps and ran smack into the bank.

BEN'S PHILOSOPHY

Benjamin Franklin became a philosopher during a rain storm. Somebody read his almanac which predicted a hot, dry day and when it started to rain the reader personally came over and told him to go fly a kite.

He put a metal key on the string and flew the kite into a thunderstorm. That's when his philosophy struck him . . . about the same time as a bolt of lightning. Old Ben got a real charge out of the whole experience. That jolt cleared out his sinuses, melted the gold in his teeth, and magnetized those little buckles on his shoes. He was lucky that the zipper had not yet been invented because it would have melted, making him a genius—if he'd figured how to get his pants off over his head.

Instead, he just became a philosopher. He decided to quit living dangerously, but then he got married to a redheaded widow. Which made him even more philosophical.

Other great men were famous for some reason and are remembered for it. George Washington got married and became the Father of our Country.

Patrick Henry married and became famous for his cry of, "Give me liberty or give me death."

But old Ben Franklin was a real philosopher. Like a bolt out of the blue, he married a redheaded widow and discovered electricity.

Now that we are on the subject of historical nostalgia, who was it that uttered the most famous phrase, "Ask not what your country can give to you, but what you can give to your country?"

That's right. The IRS.

HI YO HOP SING

Recent entertainment news is that Buck Owens and his Buckeroos are to tour Red China, part of a cultural exchange program. A little barnyard ballet, that ought to do it.

The translators are sure to have a time understanding corn squeezins, white lightning, humdinger, and "aw, shucks."

Buck may have to change his style a little to conform to the Chinese taste for ballet type productions. Can't you just see Buck and the boys in red, white, and blue leotards, whirling, leaping through the air while playing a tune on a washtub and a standard pitchfork? These are items that every commune has but probably never thought of as an instrument of fun.

It may change their whole attitude; a fellow is reluctant to wash clothes or pitch hay with his musical instrument.

Why, I wouldn't be surprised to see Grandpa Jones appoint Minnie Pearl (a natural Chinese name) as Secretary of Culture. A new chapter in Chairman Mao's thoughts could start out with HOW-DEE. That would really be passing the Buck, Chinese style.

A PROFIT WITHOUT HONOR

At a meeting in Atlanta for people who make a living pokin' fun at life, I chanced to meet the chief writer for Joan Rivers and Phyllis Diller. Her name is Mary McBride. Mary is not pushing 40, she admits to dragging it behind her. She looks a lot like Erma Bombeck, thinks like Flip Wilson, and absorbs quips like Einstein did relativity.

Mary claims that most of her material comes from insults from her children. "They are allowed to be insubordinate as long as it turns a profit." Examples:

"Oh, darn. These panty hose are baggy at the knees."

"That's O. K. Mom. At least it gives some shape to your legs."

"I got a ticket for running through a red light."

"Yeah, we saw it still hanging on the back bumper."

"Do any of you know if our car has a title?"

"No, Mom. We just call it 'Car'."

"I want to take a peek at the engine before you kids take the car."

"O. K. Try looking through the keyhole in the ignition."

"Your Father has to call in sick this morning and he's afraid the company won't believe him."

"Tell him to call in dead."

"I'm getting old and wrinkled."

"Look at the neat places you'll have to hide your hearing aid."

I decided to try the system myself so I remarked to my son. "You can insult me all you want for a dollar."

"Good, I'll take two dollars worth."

No wonder I haven't hit the big time. What a dumb kid, I thought, as I put his two dollars worth of insults on his charge account and advanced him a five.

EQUALITY AIN'T FAIR

"That's the trouble with equality," said a recent acquaintance, "it ain't fair."

That doesn't seem to keep everyone from searching for it. Parents want equality with their children, kids want it with adults, and other grown-ups want it from each other. We've got more sensitive fragments than a runaway chainsaw in a glass factory.

Like one woman asked another, "Do you ever wake up grouchy?" She answered, "Only if he's late for work. He's so sensitive."

And to make this equality thing even, there's the fellow who says his wife verbalizes so much that when she gets laryngitis, she can't think.

The plain truth is that both men and women are fairly stable. They're paranoid all the time.

James Watt, former Secretary of the Interior, offended nearly everybody in the name of equality, specifically mentioning women, blacks, Jews, and the handicapped. He drafted an apology but frankly admitted, "I don't think they'll accept. I don't have a Chinaman's chance."

As one of his critics said, "There but for the grace of God . . . goes God."

"The difference between genius and stupidity," said another, "is that there is a limit to genius."

Well, there's a limit to equality, too. We've gone too far. A big flap was made over Justice O'Connor being appointed to the Supreme Court. Big deal. She just happened to be the best man for the job, that's all.

How about equal pay for equal work? Sounds good but let's face it, there are always going to be differences. I'm willing to do anything Burt Reynolds can do, maybe even for a little less than he gets paid. There should be no discrimination against me taking his place with Dolly Parton just because I look like Don Knotts after six weeks in a Turkish prison.

Come to think of it, I'm getting a little steamed about this business myself. I think us minorities have a right to complain.

I saw a cab driver make the point very well recently. A well-healed customer paid the $2.50 cab fare and tipped him 25 cents. The cabbie stared at it in obvious disappointment. "Ten percent. Isn't that correct?" quizzed Mr. Wealth.

"Yeah," replied the cabbie, "it's correct. But it ain't right."

INNOCENT INFLUENCE

Did you hear about the tough patrolman who caught a celebrity? Turned out to be Mickey Rooney, who tried to use his influence. For getting smart with an officer of the law, Mickey got two tickets—one for speeding and one for being too short.

Another interesting idea to combat crime is a new burglar deterrent. It's a cardboard sign that costs only 75 cents. It reads "This house is protected by a silent burglar alarm connected directly to police headquarters." An additional note at the bottom states "P.S.: The house next door is a pushover."

Then there is the story of the field hand who was given a nice pair of white pants and promptly got a spot of some dark, unknown substance on them. He brought them back to his employer and asked how to remove the spot.

"Did you put gasoline on it?" asked the boss.

"Yep, didn't do nothin'."

"How about pure alcohol?"

"Didn't work."

"Have you tried ammonia yet?"

"Yes sir, I did and they fit real nice."

Then there was the bank president who had a policy of giving stock certificates for Christmas presents. Turns out that one of his employees was an elderly maintenance man who couldn't read. There was a merge, the stock split and the company sold. Notices were sent out that new certificates would be issued and stockholders had to sign new papers and cash in or get new paperwork.

The chief executive explained this to his faithful employee of 30 years. "Just sign here and I'll take care of this for you. You tell me what you want to do."

"If I sign, does that mean I'm fired?"

"My goodness, no," said the President, "this means you have more money in your stock and you can save it and let it grow or cash it."

"How much would I get if I cashed it?"

"Well, offhand, I'd say about $1100."

The old fellow slowly signed his name and remarked, "In that case I quit."

"Why on earth would you want to do that?"

"Well, sir," drawled the troubleshooter, "there ain't no sense in one rich man workin' for another."

WHY BULLETS FLY IN TEXAS SKY

Since everybody has watched "Dallas" on TV, worried sick about who shot J.R., Willie Nelson has hit records about Luckenbach, everybody is dressing western and dancing to fiddle music again, I think it's high time to release this story. It's about the true Wild West and one of its legendary characters.

His name was Dr. Toxy Davidson and unlike Doc Holliday, he was not a dentist or gunfighter. He was a real medical doctor, a true professional, who used a scalpel to extract money from the bankers.

Unable to lose money in the art of healing, he became overconfident and entered the cattle business where he hit upon an artful combination of making a fortune in one field only to spend every dime of it in another. This balanced his life and checkbook so that he left this world as he entered it—with nothing. However, this grand old gentleman single-handedly supported a western clothing shop, feed store, several veterinarians, tractor dealership, blacksmith, livestock auction, coffee shop, automobile agency, meat packing plant, fertilizer company, trucking firm, utility company, and hired every high school kid from the moment of conception.

"Think we'll have another child, Dr. Toxy. What do you think?"

"We'll start him out hauling hay. Maybe he'll pay for his brothers you still owe me for."

With this kind of tremendous stress on his life, Dr. Toxy could have become a scoundrel like J.R., but he didn't. To relax, he used to go out to the ranch on his day off and "build fence."

One day a couple of feed salesmen looking for new territory traced him down to the ranch. Bouncing across the rough terrain, they came across a group of wetbacks and high school boys working on a corral.

"Looking for Dr. Toxy, boys. Where is he?"

"Building fence," they snickered, "down yonder." They pointed to the river.

The two salesmen finally spotted a pickup under a big pecan tree, both doors wide open. Dr. Toxy was sprawled all over the seat, boots on the dashboard, hat over his eyes, not a fence within a thousand yards.

A little while later the two salesmen passed the work crew in hasty retreat, bullets still flying from the direction of the river.

"Oh, we forgot to tell you," yelled one of the boys, "Dr. Toxy don't like to be disturbed when he's building fence."

Eat your heart out, J.R. That's the real Texas!

GOLF LEGENDS

Byron Nelson is a name readily recognized in the golfing world. Many have described him as a "machine" when it comes to cow pasture pool.

Although I don't play the game very well, I sure have developed a respect for Louise and her handicap, Byron. Fate deemed that our paths should cross, and unlike many well known names, they are not machines who shun the public, but just nice folks. Byron says he was turned out of some of the finest schools in Texas. When I asked where he graduated I found he didn't graduate, he was turned out.

But he learned something that isn't taught in schools. He learned how to think. He nearly thought himself into poverty until he developed the swinging style that is now taught in schools and colleges around the world.

He gave me a few tips. Tapping his temple with his index finger he said, "Golf is mostly played up here." I tried it. Out I went with a bucket of balls and everytime I swung I would say out loud, "I'm a golfer, I'm a golfer, I'm a golfer." Would you believe it? I attracted another great golfer with my outstanding performance.

Arnold Palmer took up the position next to me on the driving range. He watched my strokes with obvious envy as he would shake his head and smile. At least I think it was Arnold Palmer because when I quit for the day he told me, "If you're a golfer, I'm Arnold Palmer."

I may not be as great as the pros but I'm the most economical golfer in the world, so I ought to lay some claim to distinction. I've never hit a ball hard enough to hurt it or far enough to lose it.

Byron Nelson likes to tell the story on Arnie and Charley Boswell. Charley is an amazingly talented golfer. He is blind. A caddie describes each shot to him and he putts according to the sound of the flag which is rattled in the hole. Byron adds, more philosophically, "There can be no negative thoughts when a critical putt is planned." Boswell agrees, which is why he regularly shoots under par to frustrate many sighted opponents.

Once, at a golf exhibition match for the blind, Charley won with a blistering pace of precision. Arnold Palmer was there to see it, this time as a spectator. When he was introduced to Arnie, Charley said, "Mr. Palmer, I've been wanting to meet you. I'm a better golfer than you and would like a chance to prove it."

The old pro, his confidence unshaken, asked, "When do you want to play?"

"Just any dark night," replied Charlie, "Just any dark night."

TALKING TO YOURSELF

Writing a book that becomes a best seller has to be a great thrill. Making it a best seller has to be a great chore. I recently made the acquaintance of a fascinating writer of best sellers with the unusual name of Og Mandino, who wrote such classics as *The Greatest Salesman in the World* and its companion *Part II, The End of the Story,* and *The Christ Commission.*

Og now lives in Phoenix and except for an occasional tour to promote his latest book, lives a rather sedate life. But about every 18 months he hits the road, making the talk show rounds of TV and radio. In spite of the fact that his books have sold in the millions and a 200-acre pine forest was recently planted just to provide the paper for his future books, Og is basically a "good ol' boy." He claims that the talk show circuit helps to keep you humble and illustrates that fact with the example of a television show in a rather small community.

The talk show was narrated by a character known as Reverend John. This was a low budget show and consisted of a board fitted over two sawhorses, with close-up shots of the interviewer and Og. Reverend John had a series of 25 or 30 questions on a clipboard, but this could not be seen by the audience. When the television sets signaled that the show was on the air, Reverend John asked a question after which the TV camera swung to Og for the answer.

After about 10 or 15 minutes of this question-answer session, Og suddenly became aware that only three people were in the entire studio: Reverend John, the cameraman, and Og.

In the middle of an answer to one of the questions that Reverend John had asked, the telephone began to ring. After several rings, Reverend John slipped off the board and went back to answer the telephone. Mandino, aware of the situation, stretched his answer as long as possible, but soon ran out of words and Reverend John continued to talk on the telephone.

Mandino claims that it is situations like this that make a writer earn his keep. He merely eased his hand over to the other side of the board, picked up Reverend John's clipboard, saw what the next question was, and remarked, "Reverend John, you're probably wondering about how I. . . ."

For the next 12 minutes, Mandino interviewed himself, while the long-winded Reverend John continued to talk on the telephone. Just minutes before the station went off the air, Reverend John slipped back in his slot, the television cameraman panned from Og to Reverend John, and the sign-off for the program was complete.

Sensing that it must have been an urgent telephone message, Og asked Reverend John if everything was all right.

"Oh, things are just fine." he replied, "It was my mother. She promised to give me her recipe for carrot cake and I wanted to be sure I got it right."

Events like that, Mandino claims, help to keep an author humble.

MOON OVER MIND

Jeanne Robertson is an unusual lady in many respects. A former Miss North Carolina and Miss America contestant, she now travels about the country pokin' fun at the way she looks. She looks great, but she is not an ordinary beauty contestant. At 6 feet, 2 inches in height, and 160 pounds in weight, wearing a size 11-B shoe, she is hard not to notice.

Although Jeanne is a beautiful woman, these attributes were not altogether evident when she was 12 years old and was the same size as she is now. This could have been a very traumatic situation for a young lady who towered two feet or so above most of her peers. Her sense of humor, instilled by her mother, was the guiding element in producing a well-adjusted individual and the chief factor in her current popularity as a popular speaker on the professional platform circuit.

Jeanne has a thing about collecting original humor and draws greatly on her own personal background for stories and material.

She also claims that cab drivers are one of the best sources for original stories. All you have to ask them is "What is the funniest thing that ever happened to you in a cab?"

I decided I would put the theory to use. I jumped into a cab in New Orleans and asked that question of the driver.

He replied, "Man, ain't nuthin' funny ever happens in these cabs."

"Well," I asked, "Anything exciting ever happen?"

"Nope."

I was about to give up on the theory when I asked if he had ever met any famous people. He turned to me and asked, "Are you somebody?" I figured if I had to explain, I wasn't. So, I brushed off the answer by dropping the issue.

After about 10 minutes of silence, he suddenly brightened up and said, "Oh, yeah, there was one interesting thing that happened in this cab once. I had an astronaut and his mother ride with me to the airport." When I asked which one, he said he couldn't recall.

"Was it Neal Armstrong?" I asked.

"Yeah, that's the one."

"Did you recognize Neal Armstrong as an astronaut?"

"No, I didn't."

"Then how did you know it was him? Did he have to tell you?"

"No sir, he didn't say nuthin'. His mother told me."

Jeanne's philosophy may be right, but the next time I ride in a cab, I'm gonna carry along a note from my mother telling folks just who I am.

FORGETTING TO REMEMBER

What's in a name? People have a tendency to forget even famous people unless they have a memorable name. Few can recall the deeds of Alf Landon or Millard Fillmore and yet they were famous men at one time.

It's just an old custom to give everybody and everything a name. People are so important they have several of 'em. Some have exciting names like April Showers, Tab Hunter, Rip Torn. Others have names like Napoleon Schultz, Fensterwald O'Hoolihan, or O. J. (Orange Juice) Simpson. Some of those guys had it as tough as a boy named Sue. So you have to do something really great or have a catchy name to be remembered.

Remember "Crazy Legs" Hirsch? Well, he married a girl named "Swivel Hips" Johnson, according to rumor. Imagine what the kids would be called if they inherited characteristics from their parents. How about "Stumbling Sam," "Wild Walkin' Willie," or "Jellyfish Jack."

Doctors especially like names. There is not a spot on the body that you can point to that a doctor doesn't have a name for or can become famous for making up one. Just ask one what's wrong with you and you'll see. "Well, you have acute gammoglobulinosis with complications of enemic dermetitus which is separating your uvula from your Gluteus maximus."

"What does that mean in laymen's terms, doctor?"

"Your shorts are too tight."

There would be a lot less trouble and misunderstanding in the world if people could just remember more names of things and people.

For example, two guys were walking along the street in Houston recently behind a famous person and this was the conversation:

"Hey, see that fellow just in front of us. That's Alan Shepherd."

"Yeah, so who is Alan Shepherd?"

"You don't know who Alan Shepherd is? That's the guy who got the Coors distributorship in Baytown."

How quickly they forget. Does anybody remember _____? (Fill in the loser of the national election).

KISS AND TELL

Henry Kissinger negotiated with fear tactics. I'm surprised that nobody has reported this fact before. If you watched the TV coverage of his meeting with Sadat you saw him place his hands on Anwar Sadat's shoulders and give him a little kiss on each cheek. Why, he would get slapped silly if he pulled a stunt like that down at the livestock auction.

I suppose that should be expected from anyone having an obvious name like Kissinger or Kissinghim. No wonder a peace settlement was arranged between Israel and Egypt. Anything to stop all that kissing and hugging with Henry.

Henry is good at getting peace settlements because he strikes fear into the hearts of people. He uses the old "Yes, Yes. Technique" to get his way. It goes like this:

"Shiek, you have a beautiful country."

"Yes."

"You have a great government."

"Yes."

"Send us some oil."

No answer.

"If you don't say yes, I vil giv you annudder kiss."

"Yes."

With that kind of strategy, Dr. Kiss-Kiss got Israel to give up some territory and Egypt to promise not to build a pyramid in the middle of the Suez Canal.

A team of U.S. volunteers will supervise the program. Volunteers must be open-minded, neither Jewish nor Moslem, and completely impartial in their political views.

The first two volunteers were typical of the dedicated group being assembled. According to their applications they were Buddists, non-political and non-violent: Solomon Levine and Abe Levenson. Sol and Abe were asked what they would do if Henry gave them the traditional Mid-East kiss. We'll never get the answer because Sol beat up the reporter and Abe asked to be interviewed in a neutral place like Tel-Aviv.

Henry was advised of the incident but could not be reached for comment. The fearless negotiator was practicing his pucker and getting ready for another round of Kissing-er style talks.

HOT SHOTS **2**

Don't ever play poker with a man who has the
first name of any city.

CHARACTERS

If you were asked to name the characters in your circle of friends, how many names would come to mind and what would be their characteristics? If the ones that come to your mind are like mine, invariably they will be outgoing, uninhibited, great storytellers, and the life of the party. Women characters follow the same pattern of Carol Burnett and Lucille Ball. Men characters might closely resemble Robin Williams and Richard Pryor.

Although characters make up a small percentage of the population, they are always there. Once after I had just completed an after-dinner speaking engagement, a lady rushed to me, bubbling over with enthusiasm and said, "Oh, you're just the funniest thing. You remind me so much of that movie star . . . I forget his name."

Trying to make it totally absurd, I replied, "Oh, you probably have me mixed up with Robert Redford."

She shot back, "No, no, I remember now. It's Flip Wilson."

Now that's what I call a character.

My friend and colleague, Jeanne Robertson, is a character. She is a beautiful, perfectly proportioned lady who stands 6 feet, 2 inches tall. She won the title of Miss North Carolina and went on to compete in the Miss America contest. She always manages to stretch a point.

She jokingly claims two distinctions to this day. "I'm the tallest

22

Miss America contestant to ever compete . . . I'm also the tallest Miss America contestant to ever lose the contest."

Jack Benny and George Burns are a couple of well known characters. One story that Mr. Burns tells concerns the crazy things these two jokesters used to do to try to make the other laugh. Invariably, George Burns would crack up Jack Benny with his antics, but Jack had a hard time making George, the master of the poker face, break out in laughter. Both of them were in the same hotel, but Jack Benny had checked in first and already had a room. George called his friend and Jack asked him to come up to the room right away. Mr. Benny claimed that some urgent contract negotiations had to be ironed out with their agent. Then Jack Benny took off all his clothes, stood in the middle of the bed, and struck a pose like "The Thinker," holding a glass of water in his hand. He thought this would shock George into uncontrollable fits of laughter.

George says, "I thought he might try something silly like that, so I sent the maid in ahead of me."

In retelling the story, he claims, "What really made Jack mad was that the maid came in, took one look, drank the glass of water, and left."

However, not all characters are as well known as some of those just mentioned. I've met and enjoyed them all over the country. Carl Shannon, a local friend now gone to glory, exemplifies the kind of character I'm talking about. Carl always had a story. In the area where we live, there are a lot of Czechoslavakian people. Most often, they refer to themselves, rightly or wrongly, as Bohemians. There is a delightful little Czech pastry known as a kolache. Although it may be filled with cherries, pineapple, or some other fruit, the most popular one simply has poppy seeds sprinkled on the outside. I've never heard anyone else tell the story, so I assume it must have been an original with Carl. It seems that a Bohemian boy from our part of the country was drafted during World War II and had his ship torpedoed. He was stranded alone on a desert isle for two years. One day he saw another ship on the horizon and thought he was about to be rescued. To his dismay, a submarine sank the ship and one lone survivor washed up on shore. She was a beautiful, show-girl type blonde, who had lost all her clothes in the explosion, and was wearing only a wooden barrel. The sailor met her on the shore with his mouth open and his eyes wide open in astonishment. Sexily, she cooed, "How long have you been on this island, sailor?"

He replied, "Two years, ma'am. It's totally uninhabited. You and I are alone."

She said, "Well, then. I've got something inside this barrel I know you've just been yearning for, for the last two years."

Wild with excitement, he blurted out, "Don't tell me, ma'am, that inside that barrel you've got a dozen of them poppy seed kolaches."

On the pages to follow, you'll find many more stories that have characters and characters who have stories.

CHARACTER SURVEY

Magazines are always running self analysis quizzes to let readers determine if they have the qualities which would classify them as a success, a gentleman, a lady, or some equally endearing title. The following test is to determine another side of your personality. See how you score and determine your character by scoring 10 points for each "yes" answer to the following questions:

1. Have you ever purchased a present for your spouse by telling the saleslady to "pick out something under $20 and gift wrap it?"

2. Have you ever written your name on a wall?

3. Have you ever felt rotten and answered "Fine" to the question "How are you?"

4. Have you ever called anyone a jerk?

5. Do you automatically take your foot off the accelerator when spotting a police car?

6. Do you look for yourself first in a group photograph?

7. Have you ever spent the night at a friend's house and peeked in their medicine cabinet?

8. Have you ever thought about cheating on your income tax— again?

9. Have you ever taken the last biscuit at a Baptist brotherhood banquet?

10. Have you ever yelled "Shark" at an indoor swimming pool?

If you scored 0 to 30 you are a miserable wretch not worth knowing; 40 to 60 you are too dull to invite to a party; 70 to 100 you are normal —a typical American jerk.

The high scoring testee is also fond of saying "I could have done that," "I told you so," and "If I knew then what I know now. . . . "

So which had you rather be, miserable, dull, or a normal jerk? The jerks get invited to parties where they say things like, "I believe in the two party system. Party all day and party all night."

So to all of you who qualify welcome to the party.

SMALL TOWN CHARACTER

San Saba, Texas has a population of only about 2800 but what it lacks in population, it makes up for in "characters." I was invited to speak to the annual Production Credit Assn. meeting. I flew my single engine Cherokee into the local airport and the next morning I was having breakfast at the only cafe open at that early hour . . . before noon. The cattlemen were dropping by to coffee down and discuss world politics.

"Mexicans devalued the peso again. Know what that means?"

"It means it costs twice as many pesos to buy a pound of beans."

"Frenchmen don't drink coffee. They drink wine and that's what's ruining their economy."

"How could that ruin the economy?"

"'Cause they don't get up and go to work."

The conversation took a more serious turn when the subject of the arms race and the H-bomb came up. "That reminds me," said one, "I'm sure getting anxious to seine, trap, telephone, or blow out some catfish."

When I asked some of the locals what San Saba meant, they shrugged their shoulders and said the town was named for an old mission by that name.

"What was the mission named for?" I asked.

"The San Saba river," they replied.

"And the river?"

"It was named for the town." Everybody nodded their heads in agreement that the puzzle was solved.

Out at the Junior High cafeteria, a reception was in full swing by 10 A.M., more coffee and conversation. I was discussing the powers of goal setting with a couple named Red and Ivy and they told me of a skinny kid they knew who sent off for a Charles Atlas course. "Every morning he'd open a window, take deep breaths and exercise, determined to be big and strong."

"Whatever happened to him," I asked.

"Oh, he grew up big and strong, moved over to Lubbock and went bankrupt."

Steve, the emcee, called the meeting to order and then related how the Wall Street terms "Bear" and "Bull" markets came about.

"A bear strikes down with his paw, a bull hooks up. Thus, a bear market is declining and a bull market is rising."

"I never knew that," I whispered to a new found companion. "He's just making that up so he can tell a joke about a bear and a bull," he whispered back. Maybe so, but it makes sense to me . . . and so did the joke.

Many laughs later, leaving the meeting, an older fellow was fussed at a bit by a friend for leaving his keys in his car. "Always leave 'em in the car, no matter where I go," he replied.

"Why?" asked his buddy.

"Cause I'd rather look for my car than my keys."

SOUTHWEST CHARACTERS

The great Southwest has had more than its share of characters. People like Bigfoot Wallace, Calamity Jane, and Kit Carson are legends. Of course, they are not the only heroes. A fellow in Albuquerque told me his favorite was Adolph Coors.

Legends may not be in the making today but characters still abound. A visitor from Connecticut was being shown around Midland-Odessa, Texas. After hours of looking at miles and miles of nothing but miles and miles, he asked his host, "If you didn't intend to build, why on earth did you clear so much of it?"

Not to be outdone, the host explained, "Son, we're talkin' mega-shopping mall here. We've spent hundreds of years perfecting a wind-solar system just to transport our sand and gravel."

A flatlander from the Brush Country went out to Seattle. Doing some jogging past his buddies, he was huffing and puffing but explained he wasn't used to the altitude. At the time, he was running through a tunnel that was 50 feet below sea level.

Another cowboy-type Texas oilman always wore a $100 Stetson. Since his hat size was an unusual long-oval, it was hard to find and seldom fit anyone else. One day while traveling through another state, a gas station attendant cast a covetous eye on the cowboy hat. In a fit of generosity, the oil baron said he would give the hat to the man if it fit. It did. Several weeks later, he spotted a new man at the station wearing his old hat. He was mighty proud of it, said he bought it from the previous attendant for $15.

Perhaps the most memorable Southwest character story is the supposedly true tale of the old cattle baron who, on his death bed, called for a pastor. The preacher asked, "Brother, do you accept the word of Almighty God as represented in the Holy Bible to be true?"

"Yes," wheezed the old cowman.

"Do you repent of your sins, ask forgiveness, and accept the teaching of the Holy Church?"

"Yes," gasped the baron.

"And do you reject Satan, his doctrine, and all his angels of darkness?"

The old character opened one eye and rasped, "Reverend, this is no time to be alienating ANYONE."

ONE OF A KIND

There are some fascinating characters in the world and Joe Calley is one of them. Raised in the slum of a city in Pennsylvania, he "mentally left at 12 and physically left at 14" for Texas. For years he roamed the world as a consultant to corporations, then at age 45, with no training, decided to take up rural life by managing a 3000-acre ranch near Campbellton, Texas. He speaks no Spanish, yet works totally with Mexicans who speak no English. In partnership with the ranch owners, he is building a conference center in the Brush Country almost 100 miles from civilization.

We first met at a Farm Bureau meeting in Jackson, Mississippi, where both of us were appearing on the program for Southern Farm Bureau Casualty Insurance Company. Joe "busts out of the brush" to conduct training seminars frequently and I was privileged to sit in on one.

I liked the man immediately. He wears his hair slightly long, with a mustache and a goatee. With a deeply tanned face, squinty eyes, and a mischievous smile, he reminds me of Wild Bill Cody, at least the wild part. He conducts self-esteem and success type seminars and believes nobody should work at a job unless he or she has fun doing it, feels good about it, and develops self-confidence. To teach, he asks lots of questions, getting feedback from the audience.

"Be proud, learn to accept a compliment, take credit or blame," he lectures, "has anyone here ever won a beauty contest of any type?" Only one lady raised her hand.

"What was the title?" he asks.

Without taking a breath or using a comma, she blurts out, "Most Beautiful Franklin Junior High School. I was the only girl in the class."

"Hmmmm, obviously room for growth here. Accept our honors graciously and don't volunteer too much information."

By day's end, much improvement was noted; the class loosened up and continued to have fun, but with confidence.

"Have any of you men ever used a potato peeler?"

"I'm married to one," comes the reply.

One fellow got flustered and verbally stumbled over his answer. "I rented these lips," he cracked, "just washed my mouth today and can't do a thing with it."

This light-hearted banter goes on for several hours and gradually people get less sensitive, prouder, more success oriented . . . and wittier.

At the end of the day, Joe, myself, and Lt. Col. Robert Tufts, another speaker, were exchanging grins when an attractive young lady approached us to thank Joe for his session. With his squinty-eyed look and mischievous grin, Joe asks, "If the three of us invited you down to the bar for a drink, would you be happy, unhappy, or unaffected?"

Without a moment's hesitation, she replied, "Well, there's an answer for each of you."

No wonder he stays out in the brush. Students learn fast in the cities, but this character can match wits with the best. Down at the bar, over a glass of buttermilk, Joe explains his plans to import some exotics to his ranch.

"Game or women?" asks the lady.

"Yes," replies Joe.

CHICKEN SMITH

A fellow I know once stopped in a little country store to ask the where-abouts of a man he knew only as "Chicken" Smith. He asked if anyone knew him. An old-timer in overalls, whittling on an apple crate, his feet propped up on a pickle barrel seemed eager, in his own way, to help.

"Let's see now. Chicken Smith, that's a common name in these parts. I think he's the one that married the second cousin of Ben Twoshoes. No, it was the niece of his aunt's uncle by marriage, or did they call off that wedding altogether? It's coming to me now, wait a minute, that's the fellow who caused all the stir when he diluted that shipment of moonshine with kerosene by mistake. It made everybody's breath smell like Exxon with a double cross so they tried burning it in lanterns. But the lanterns hiccuped so bad they kept blowing themselves out. One blew up in Smith's henhouse, and the next day he was pedaling fried chicken along the side of the road, the place smelled like burned feathers for miles around. Why do you want to see him?"

"A relative of his died and left him quite an estate. Can you tell me how to find Chicken Smith?"

The oldtimer said, "Yep, I'm Chicken Smith."

A fellow can find out a lot if he asks the right questions and has the patience to hear out the whole answer.

BLOOD AND GUTS

Now that nostalgia is the big craze, everyone likes to tell about how it was with them in "the good old days." My friend, D. D. McWhistlebritches said he grew up wild, woolly and uncontrollable. He's still wild and woolly but marriage and controls sneaked up on him just in time to save him from a life of daring deeds.

During his younger, single days, D. D. ran with a rough crowd. The local toughs dared him to turn the corner in front of the police chief's house on two wheels. He did it on two wheels and turned over in the Chief's front yard. He was on his bicycle. The chief told him to get out of town and his yard because he hated to throw guys in jail who wore short pants.

So, D. D. went to see the Cagney and Bogart movies to learn how to be tough. He and some other fellows met in a cave where they had hidden a sack of Bull Durham. They wore floppy hats pulled down over one eye, let a cigarette dangle from a corner of the mouth, and kept a list of dirty words which they studied. Everybody would compare the words and add new ones to the list. They kept forgetting the words and had to meet once a week for a quick review. Times sure have changed. Now you can get the list from a government publication.

D. D. wanted most of all to belong to a secret club composed of three older boys. They made him wait two years before they led him through the padlocked door of Murphey's garage. The initiation ceremony included eating a live tadpole, walking barefoot in a tub of chicken innards, and signing his name in his own blood. After doing all that including the laborious task of getting enough blood from a pricked trigger finger to write "D. D. McWhistlebritches, Esquire," the fellows told him the club was disbanding. He was the only one who was ever dumb enough to do all that and was therefore the only member.

D. D. went back to the cave to get his list of names to call those fellows by proper terms and found somebody had smoked them, along with the last of the Bull Durham.

THE MEEK SHALL INHERIT THE MIRTH

Melvin was just a little fellow. Too short for basketball, and too light for football, he was told. Poor Melvin had to study violin and karate as an alternate sport. Karate was suggested so he could make it past the local toughs with his short pants and violin case.

Harold was big, the kind of guy that put on his suntan lotion with a paint roller. Harold played tackle on the local football team, ate raw meat for breakfast and delighted in the sound of leather popping, the smell of Absorbine jr., and the feel of a soft belly in his knee.

It was bound to happen. Harold picked a fight with Melvin when he was on his way to a music lesson.

"Hey, Punk," said Harold, as he lounged in front of the pool hall, "You ain't coming by here anymore with that sissy violin."

Melvin bowed to the rising sun, yelled "Kawasaki", drew his bow out of his violin case, scratched a line on the sidewalk and told Harold that if he stepped across that line he would get a violin down his throat.

Harold stepped over the line, snapped his fingers in Melvin's face and said, "Oh, yeah?"

When Harold woke up he was told that a team of Doctors worked over him for seven hours to remove a violin. At last report he was still coughing up splinters.

Melvin has worn his violin bow down to a nub trying to get others to fiddle around in his specialty sport, but all the football players say they are on strike. Melvin says they better not get out of line or step over one of his if they don't want to get struck.

SNOW BIRDS AND GREEN STUFF

It's getting worse every year. We've got the greatest influx of Yankees into the South since northern drummers caught a glimpse of Dolly Parton. It just sounds strange to hear a "Howdy, m'am" with a Brooklyn accent. "Snow birds" some call them, but even though they talk strange, there are three words that we understand perfectly—money, money, and money.

Where do they get it? Shucks, honey chile, they won the war—they run it off on their own presses.

The story is always the same when they come to Texas. Hat, boots, belt buckles, fake armadillo, country-western dance, Mexican food.

A friend of mine decided to capitalize on the new tourist trade and rake in some Union money. He contracted for western felt hats made in Yugoslavia, boots from Mexico, belt buckles with an outline of the Lone Star State from Japan, plaster armadillos made in Taiwan; he hired three hippies to play guitars, and converted his hay loft into a Mexican restaurant. Trying to hold down expenses, he hired some Iranians who had sided against the Ayatollah to do the cooking.

Then he sent out brochures and attracted his first customers who paid megabucks to see and experience an authentic Texas working ranch. First stop was the gift shop at ranch headquarters where all bought blue hats that were too big and green boots that were too small. They wore their belt buckles upside down. Each carried an armadillo under an arm, some two, while they drank the national brew of Texas and tried to wautusi to San Antonio Rose. After touring the ranch, the small crowd was allowed to pet and take pictures of a Longhorn steer and see the head of a striking rattlesnake pickled in a fruit jar.

That night, the group settled down to a fabulous Mexican food dinner. "What's that?" asked a guest. "Tamales," replied a ranch hand forced to serve as a waiter in this new venture. "What's that?" "Enchiladas." This went on with every dish. "What's that?" "Guacamole." "Cheez, fellows, this stuff is great." "Hey, pal, bring more of that green stuff."

After three servings, the Yankees were still sending the disgruntled ranch hand, who would prefer punching cows, back for more of this exotic new dish . . . guacamole.

Suddenly, a huge wood roach ran across the floor in full view of the dining guests. "What is THAT?" screamed a northern belle.

"Don't be alarmed, m'am," soothed the ranch hand, "that's just a Guacamole."

CALIFORNIA, WHERE ELSE?

I recently visited in San Jose, California. It is a beautiful place, but the tourists drive you nuts singing or whistling the tune "On my way to San Jose."

California is known as a rather unique state to say the least. People just do things differently out here. It's not unusual to see an executive going to work riding a skateboard. It does seem odd though when they stop to pick up a hitch-hiker.

One character lives on a hill and works in the valley below. He commuted by hang glider for a while, arriving wearing traditional California safety devices—helmet, goggles, and gas mask. Smog ate the fabric off his wings, though, and a weather-related accident grounded him for six weeks. The paper said a rain storm moved through and the cumulo-nimbus cloud build-ups slammed him into the cumulo-granite.

The whole place has a special air about it. The Goodyear blimp was filled with some of that air and made history—the first known case of a blimp coughing. A company doctor at a nearby Firestone plant answered the emergency call to treat a coughing blimp. He prescribed acupuncture. The dummies let him do it and set a world record for fastest time to Cleveland—backwards. Lost a lot of advertising potential, too, since the blimp turned inside out and the flashing sign on the side read RAEY-DOOG. Over 100,000 Californians inquired about how to smoke it.

This state started the drive-in church idea. It may sound strange, but some Californians are like the Hong Kong boat dwellers who live, work, eat, and sleep in their boats. The car people even go to church in them. Sure seems strange to see an Episcopal drive-in service marked PG, with a Jewish-Catholic choir singing "Ovey-Maria" and an express line confessional for those with three sins or less.

The sermon last Sunday was "The Four Commandments and Six Suggestions." Afterwards, literature was passed out and the membership voted their displeasure for the proposals by flashing their lights. Some weirdo had a raincoat over his headlights. Over 100 cars had to have a jump start.

Californians take a lot of kidding about their lifestyle but they are truly a gracious people and filled with creative ideas. And what a sense of humor. San Jose is one of the few places where they brag openly about their wealth. Have you ever seen a Salvation Army band with a string section?

They recently came up with an idea that could only originate out here. They propose a drive to collect money from the poor and give to the rich because they do a better job with it anyway. Believe it or not, they are halfway to their goal. The rich have all agreed to accept.

A FEW WORDS WITH A THOUSAND PICTURES

The male chauvinist pig is still around, but humor won't let him be much more than a ham. As John Wayne used to say, "A woman's place is in the home and she ought to go there just as soon as she gets off work."

I'm reminded of the elderly widow who said, "I had so much trouble collecting the money from my husband's estate—sometimes I wish he hadn't died."   •

Then there is the story of the dissatisfied husband: A man approached another man and said "I'll pay you one thousand dollars to kill my wife."

"A thousand dollars!" the other man replied. "Why should you want me to do that? Think of all the years you have spent with your wife. Think of what that woman has given you all those years."

"You're right," the man answered. "I'll make it two thousand dollars."

Another male chauvinist told his friend that his wife had recently gotten a mudpack to improve her beauty and his friend asked, "Did it?" The man replied, "It did for a couple of days and then the mud fell off."

Wife: "I thought you were going to the lodge meeting tonight."

Husband: "I was, but the wife of the Grand Exalted Invincible Supreme Potentate won't let him out."

A man and his wife drove through a red light and were stopped by a policeman. The man's replies to the officer's questions were somewhat surly. His wife, realizing he was becoming more involved every minute and thinking to help her husband out of the difficulty, spoke up and said, "Don't mind him, Officer, he's mad because he just failed his driver's test!"

Looking on the financial side of chauvinist pigs bringing home the bacon:

Wife to husband working on budget: "Perhaps we could borrow a little each month and set THAT aside."

Wife to husband: "All right, I admit I like to spend money—but name one other extravagance."

Wife, at desk with checkbook, to husband: "Well, it balances. The checks total up to exactly the amount I'm over-drawn."

Husband, looking up from newspaper, to wife: "What's happened between you and the retail merchants, dear? I see they say business is off 20 percent!"

Of course this works both ways. The females usually have the last word or two no matter what the situation. Sometimes it's pretty hard to top a well chosen couple of words. Like the fellow who asked the girl he had just met, "What would you say if I told you I can't live without you?" She replied, "Drop dead."

TWO RINGY DINGYS

Kingfisher, Oklahoma, sounds like a place where royalty might go to wet a hook, but such is not the case. The only connection that I could see with kings or fish was a princess telephone left off the hook at the Pioneer Telephone Co. That's a private company that tries harder even if they are the only dingalings in town. They have an annual stockholders meeting that draws people from the woods, lakes, farms, and reservations. Even the Redman has given up the smoke signal for a party line.

The first order of business was to read the minutes of the previous meeting. The company lawyer got up to do that and someone in the audience promptly suggested he phone it in—from the next county.

Another member suggested that if he did he would probably make the call collect.

"Good," says the first fellow, "We could at least refuse to accept the call and spare ourselves the agony of the report. This way we ain't got a choice."

"I move the minutes be approved as not read."

"That sounds unreasonable so I second the motion."

The motion carried, of course, so the lawyer took advantage of the opportunity to speak and told a joke which the crowd applauded.

"You ought to be on the stage," yelled an admirer.

"Yeah, there's one leaving in 15 minutes," cried another.

The crowd guffawed and poked each other in the ribs with good natured elbow jabs and looked forward to the entertainment that took place while the ballots were being counted for the new directors. Being the entertainment, I looked forward to it myself. It was the kind of crowd that would poke fun back at you.

"I have a way with strange crowds," I bragged.

"Yeah," said an oldtimer in overalls, "It's a strange way, but it's a way."

I can just hear them now in Kingfisher spreading the story, confidentially, person to person, over an eight party line. One hello, seven clicks, and group laughter. Ma Bell should have it so good.

LOW RESPECT AND HIGHER EDUCATION

A meeting of the Oklahoma School Administrators Association revealed some very interesting observations about the top brass of these men of cast iron stomachs and steel nerves. The stories you hear in the bull sessions center around true events in the lives of administrators.

"I had a student sent to my office with an attitude so hard that a cat couldn't scratch it. He finally broke down and told me that his problems were all related to the Home Economics class. One of their big projects is popping popcorn, and that faint odor goes all through the main building. He said he had been to so many X-rated movies that every time he smells that popcorn he goes wild."

"I love to fish and hunt when I get a chance. I went out to feed my dogs the other evening and while I was out decided to clean up my fishing rods so I set them on the front porch. One of my board members, a farmer, called to complain that I was overpaid. He said if you ever see a farmer with fishing poles in the front yard and coon dogs in the back you can bet he's behind in his crops or has come into an inheritance."

"We spent $100,000 on a new exercise plant for physical education classes, and I went in there the other day to see how they were using all that modern equipment. You know what they were doing? They were sailing lard bucket lids to one another. They said if our school system wasn't so cheap they'd have some frisbees to use."

The best tale I heard was by a fair minded, soft spoken superintendent who was new at his school. He called an assembly of all the students and told them, "Now this is your school. I know there has been some trouble here before and high handed tactics have been used to enforce strict discipline. You now have a chance to change all that, to be treated, as of this moment, as citizens of the community of education. This is your school."

Just then a staple was fired from a rubber band that parted the superintendent's hair as a spit ball whizzed past his left ear. He said, "By gosh, this was your school, but I'm taking it back."

SOUTHERN COMFORT

Norfolk, Virginia has it's share of southern gentlemen. A banker there told me of his trip to a farm, during the great depression, to foreclose on a $3900 mortgage, or get a payment.

The farmer was an enterprising fellow in bib overalls, a gap between his two front teeth, his face deeply tanned from the eyebrows down, a forehead paled from years of sun protection by a straw hat turned down in front and back. He removed his hat when shaking hands with the representative of the temple of the money changers.

"Eli," said the banker, "I just drove down from Norfolk for a little visit. How's your corn crop?"

"Oh, it ain't gonna make nothin'. Drouth and grasshoppers hardly left me more than a few nubbins."

"How about your cotton?"

"Naw, little old bumble-bee cotton was so bad the boll weevils had to pack a lunch to get across the field."

Eli hinted that he had been buying gasoline with an Oklahoma credit card (that's a siphon hose) but had plans to salvage the year with apples, which he got free from neighboring orchards because the bottom had fallen out of the fruit market. He had rigged up a press made from a chicken waterer and a bumper jack and was turning out apple brandy, which he claimed would analyze 120 proof.

Prohibition outlawed liquor, much less analysis. "Just take a swig, count to 120 and you'll have your proof," laughed Eli.

The banker took a gallon, gave Eli a $20 credit receipt for "Fruit and the spirit in which it was given," and spread the word. People who tasted it suddenly had a burning desire to visit that bumble-bee cotton farm.

Within 60 days Eli had paid off the entire note and was busy harvesting his nubbins and cotton stalks to be used as fodder to feed his bumper jack. He was producing apple brandy, corn whiskey, and cotton gin. Eli, with the help of an understanding banker and some southern gentlemen, had liquidated his assets.

A WORTHY EXCUSE

A bank president I recently met in Oklahoma City likes to call meetings and have everyone show up. He was fond of saying that he never heard a good excuse for missing one of his meetings. That was before he got the following note that was sent, not by registered mail, but by registered female nurse.

Dear Mr. President:

I was supervising a building job on our new bank wing this afternoon, prior to meeting time. I was standing on the ground, holding a rope that went through a pulley. The other end of the rope was attached to a barrel of bricks perched on the top edge of the building. I pulled on the rope to lower the bricks to the ground.

When the barrel descended, it was heavier than I was and pulled me up in the air. As I passed the barrel it hit me in the head, scraped my nose, tore my clothes, and injured both my feet. I was pulled further up and caught my fingers in the pulley at the top, but I managed to hang on to the rope.

When the barrel hit the bottom, it turned over, spilling the bricks. This made me heavier than the barrel. As I passed the barrel on the way down, my bottom and back were scraped by the barrel. When I finally reached the ground I did manage to do something significant to get out of this tense situation. I turned loose of the rope.

This released the barrel in a free fall, followed by a great deal of rope, and a pulley. In a desperate effort to evade this falling debris, I managed to jump just far enough for all three items to score a direct hit.

Since my hands are rope burned, I am dictating this to a nurse from the intensive care ward. I trust you will extend my apologies to members of the board. I hope you, and they will understand if I am a few minutes late.

Your Faithful Servant,
Mother

The president said he was almost moved enough by the sincerity of the appeal to grant a full day's sick leave.

A LIGHT RETIREMENT

You've seen the traditional retirement party where the executive director is honored for many years of faithful service to the association and mercifully forgiven for one or two questionable ones.

I recently attended one of these that was a little different. George was his name and each of his past presidents that held office for each year he had served came forward and made a 10-minute speech. Each one then stepped back a little and held up a card with a single letter on it. There were enough cards to spell out "We love you, George."

Then George came forward and was given the chance to tell why he was retiring. Pointing his cane at the 15 ex-presidents, he replied, "They made me."

"After listening to these birds for the past two hours, I am convinced that I am a wonderful fellow . . . which I suspected all along. I am further convinced that there is true wisdom in the old adage, 'Blessed is he who has nothing to say and cannot be persuaded to say it.'"

George received an immediate standing ovation.

"Sit down," he said, "I ain't through yet."

Of course, he was just joking. They presented him with a wrapped package which he could not open. He muttered, "I used to have a knife, but since I started working for these guys, I've lost so much weight that if I carry it, I can't keep my pants up."

Still fumbling with the small package, he added, "People want to know what I'm going to do now. First thing every morning when I wake up, if I don't smell roses and see candles, I'm going to get up."

"Then I'm gonna thumb through a copy of Joggers Magazine to get my heart started."

"Next, I'll take up cooking because by wife has had so little success at it. She sure did break our dog from begging at the table, though."

Finally, the package yielded its treasure of the traditional gold watch. With weak eyes, George strained to see the tiny face and asked, "What time does it say?"

The meeting closed with the story of George's near-sighted problem that prompted his retirement. It seems that one of his presidents got a speeding ticket. George parked behind the flashing red light of the policeman's car and waited. The president walked back to George and told him he could go on. "Oh no," replied George, "I ain't moving until that light turns green."

PUTTING ON THE RITZ

Years ago, when I was a kid, I was fascinated by the drifters who passed through. Most of them were running from something, from the law to a mother-in-law. All of them were interesting. Sooner or later, they landed at the Ritz Hotel. Society today would call it a flop house, but it had a character unknown to the modern version. The Ritz was covered totally with "tin." They call it corrugated metal today, but back then communications were simpler and more honest.

The Ritz was like an oven in summer, an icebox in winter. It was always full because of two endearing qualities that out-weighed all environmental discomforts—it was dirt cheap and nobody asked nosy questions. It was considered poor etiquette and a danger to the health of a stranger who asked a private question like "How are you?"

Because of this element of intrigue, a number of us kids used to wander into the lobby, listen to the rowdies tell stories and play music. There was no television to speak of then and radios didn't work inside a tin hotel, so the drifters made do with a guitar, harmonica, fiddle, and squeezebox. I've seen some play spoons, pots and pans, even a tire pump. They may have been wanted men elsewhere, but they were ever so gentle with us. They even let us "sit in" and try our hand with a spare instrument (I was once allowed to play a Packard hubcap).

"Ma," an understanding lady, owned and operated the Ritz and normally followed the code of silence on questions about the past. This day would be different. After several hours of spirited music, the mood turned melancholy with numerous tear jerking songs. As with most sessions, it was traditional to close with "Home Sweet Home." A dark wave of sad silence washed over the musicians as they drifted away like an outgoing tide.

One fellow stayed, sobbing softly, an empty bottle held limply in one hand.

"What's the matter, Joe?" asked Ma. "My father died," he sobbed.

Without hesitation, Ma slipped quickly away to return with a fresh bottle. After a long drink, Joe looked at her with red, swollen eyes.

"When did it happen, Joe?" asked Ma.

"Thirty years ago," he replied.

RAZORBACKS AND MUDBALLS

This country has produced a most peculiar citizen. It's the only place in the world where a man's goal is to work hard on the farm so he can get enough money together to move into town so he can get a job to make more money so he can go back and buy the farm.

This usually only happens after a lifetime of struggle and toil. Then about the time he is to retire something snaps. You can always tell when a man starts to lose his mind. He starts talking about "going back to the farm." Then he rolls his eyes around and looks like a dying calf in a hail storm.

Now, admittedly, the farm is a great place to be, but it is not always the romantic place the old-timers remembered from the days of their youth. We used to go to bed with the chickens, but now most of us roost on the slats while watching the late show on TV. We used to get the kids up at the crack of dawn, now we feel lucky if they are coming in by that time.

County agents used to come out and say, "Danged if I know what could be killing your cows," instead of mastering the difficult art of talking without saying anything. New diseases and problems are popping up so fast that veterinarians have special bumper stickers that are blank.

My friend Sidney Peoples, who retired from the school teaching profession and decided to go to work, went back to the family farm out on Route 1, Springdale, Ark. Sidney writes that he had planned to make a fortune raising razorbacks on some rich bottom land. He planted winter oats and put out supplemental feed to attract those porkers out of the hills. It really worked. He got more and more hogs coming down out of the hills to wallow in the bottoms.

He was already counting his money when suddenly hogs began to die off right and left. Obviously one of those new, modern diseases that strike at the pocketbook of the animal husbandman. The county agent, the extension service and local veterinarians waded through the gumbo turned to a sea of sticky mud by the hooves of thousands of razorbacks. Samples were taken and state laboratories spent thousands of hours to no avail. Absolutely no germ or organism could be found.

The only clue appeared to be a characteristic wide eyed stare on all departed swine.

Sidney said the mystery was finally solved by an old mountain man who never left the farm in the first place. He said the hogs just got to be gluttons when life got too easy, so they left the safety of a hard life in the hills for a free handout. When they wore out the grazing, a ball of mud started accumulating on their tails. The more they wallowed in the mud the bigger the ball got. Finally it got so big that it pulled the skin back so tight that they couldn't close their eyes and they all died from lack of sleep.

A SWITCH IN TIME

Bob Lyons of Ypisilanti, Michigan, tells a great story. Of course, coming from Ypisilanti, you can afford to have a loose tongue. Who can remember where you're from when you live in a place with a strange name like Michigan?

And Ypisilanti? Forget it. The rest of the world has.

Bob's chief claim to fame was serving as fundraiser for astronaut Col. Jack Lousma's unsuccessful campaign to be elected to Congress. His other great accomplishment was developing a miracle cure for which there is no known disease.

Bob was the master of ceremonies for the Distribution Contractors Assn., people mainly in the gas pipeline business. I think it was laughing gas.

He humiliated and belittled everyone in sight. But when he got to President Jim Donaldson, it was no more Mr. Nice Guy.

"Jim," said Bob, "is a second generation president, succeeding his father. The elder Donaldson gave Jim half the business when he graduated from college."

Then, as the story goes, the old boy asked Jim if he wanted to take over the accounting department.

"No, Dad," he replied, "I was never good at math, don't understand record keeping, and can't work computers."

He was offered several positions, including manual labor with the men out in the pipeline yard.

"No, Dad," he said, "that's not my cup of tea. I don't like dirt and can't stand to sweat."

"Well, son," asked the bewildered father, "have you thought about how you're going to make a living in this business?"

"Yes, Dad," he replied, "I've given it some serious thought. I'm thinking of selling my half of the business to you."

REDNECK SYNDROME

What's a Redneck? That's the burning question we must address. Is it a sunburned Caucasian in a cheap shirt? Are there any black, yellow, brown, or red rednecks? The question is too complex to concentrate only on the neck. We must go higher to get to the bottom of this.

After a good bit of research down at a quaint watering hole called "The Bloody Bucket," I discovered some basic facts about people that others call rednecks:

1. A redneck considers himself a cut above dumb ignorant jerks.

2. Rednecks are cultured people who listen to music by Bach, mostly Bach Owens, and his Bacheroos.

3. They all drive pickups and carry a dog in the back that weighs at least 40 pounds, trained to snarl and cut its eyes around at anyone who doesn't say, "Shut up, you heah!"

4. A redneck wears white socks but you never get to see them unless he goes swimming.

5. They wear pointed-toed boots so they can kill cockroaches up in a corner.

6. Most have big bellies and drink Lite beer.

7. Standard uniform is blue jeans, western shirt with snap buttons in case they have to quickly get ready to wrestle some barmaid, belt buckle the size of a No. 10 shovel, and hand-tooled leather belt. The belt usually has a nickname carved on the back in such a way that belt loops obscure every other letter of the name.

8. Memorize catchy phrases like "Nah, I ain't kiddin', I'd tell you the truth four or five ways before I'd lie to you."

9. Favorite sports to watch on TV are Rodeo, National Bird Dog Finals, and Championship Arm Wrestling.

10. Wear cowboy hats with a rolled brim . . . so they can ride three abreast in a pickup.

Basically, I found them to be a gentle, patriotic, proud group of people, not restricted to any certain category. One word of caution: Don't ever stick your head in a country-western joint and ask, "Are there any rednecks in here?" unless you are dressed right. It's the quickest way in the world to commit suicide.

MARCHING TO A DIFFERENT DRUM

In Mississippi, I recently met a colorful character named Jean (pronounced almost like John) Batreaux. When I asked what a Cajun fellow was doing in Mississippi, he casually explained that it happened years ago quite by accident. A man with a peg leg crossed over from Louisiana and Jean's ancestors followed him thinking they were following crawfish holes.

Jean is in the insurance business and it was my fortune that he had volunteered to drive me to the airport in Jackson after I spoke to an association to which he belonged. As we drove along behind a truck, Jean suddenly whipped sharply to the left, stomped on the accelerator, and declared, "I gonna switch to the show-off lane."

As we passed a burned out building, he remarked, "I used to hang out in that place when it was a lounge called the Kick and Yell Club."

"I thought you were a clean liver," I remarked with a grin, "being in insurance."

"I used to be," he said, "jogged and everything."

"What happened?" I asked.

"Oh, I got to drinkin' and smokin' and found out I liked that better."

Still further along, we passed his office building and Jean got to telling me about his facilities.

"I even got a picture of President Reagan on my wall."

He then explained that he approved of what the President was doing so he wrote him a note telling him so and asked for a photograph.

"All the guys in the office said I would never hear from the White House, much less get a photograph. Well, I showed them. About two weeks later, I got a letter and a large color photograph from Washington, D.C. I could hardly wait to show it off. I framed the letter and the photograph, hung them on my wall, and told everyone in my building about how much Ronnie appreciated my fine work in politics."

Impressed, I asked, "Was it a signed photograph?"

"It is now," he cackled.

COMMON INTERESTS - BANKING AND MINISTRY

The banking industry in Oklahoma, under the authority of the American Institute of Banking, called me recently. That's like the minister who was "called" to preach. When you are called by a banker, no matter where he is, you tend to listen and pay attention—or money.

The banking industry has a lot in common with the ministry. Just miss a loan installment and you get a glimpse of the hereafter. The loan officer will preach a sermon on why he is here and what he is after.

An "Okie" friend of mine says he has spent a little time observing his bank, worshipping at the shrine, and listening to the sermons, and he has noticed the following apprenticeship system:

The Junior Vice President unlocks the door to the money temple, has his keys to the washroom attached to his prayer beads (he is praying for a relative to be elected board member), looks as if he could walk on water, and thinks he can talk to God.

The Vice President has the door opened for him, blesses all the tellers, inspects the washroom, thinks he can walk on water, and claims to have been called by God.

The Senior Vice President glares at the door, which opens by itself, is never seen in the washroom, allows the tellers to kiss his ring, claims he has walked on water, and has seen God.

The President doesn't use doors. He walks through the wall, doesn't need a washroom, shoots bolts of lightning through the tellers, and during his morning stroll is often narrowly missed being run over by a sailboat. He is God.

So when the long distance phone rings and HE speaks to me, I feel "called" to tiptoe across the Red River myself to rub elbows with those who live in that other world. After all, a commoner doesn't get a glimpse of the here-after every day.

WIRE RIMS AND BELLS

My friend Charlie Willey is a collector of strange, unique, or amusing tales. Charlie claims his stories fall into three categories: true happenings, stories based on fact, or things that really could happen. These couple of stories are probably one of those.

It seems that a fellow who was not too terribly bright had just graduated from the local university and wanted to improve his appearance as well as his eyesight. He needed glasses, but had not taken the time to have a proper testing and fitting by an optometrist. This guy was so dumb he thought a dope ring was three or more of his relatives holding hands in a circle. The laws of inheritance had also not left him in probate as we shall see from this instance.

The fellow, whom we shall call Melvin, went to an optometrist and was asked to close one eye and identify the letters on a wall chart. He squinted, grimaced, and squirmed, but could not keep his right eye closed and his left one open. The eye doctor asked him to try the other eye. Same thing occurred. No matter how hard he tried, Melvin could not close one eye and keep the other one open.

The doctor, being an educated man, tried an unusual alternative. He put a paper sack over his head with one hole cut out and placed that opening over the right eye.

"That oughta' do it," he replied, "Let's see what we've got now."

There was a short silence, a lowering of the head towards the floor, and long, low, sobbing moans from inside the paper bag. "Is there a problem in there?" asked the doctor.

The patient replied in louder tones, "I really had hoped for wire rims."

The same guy, Willie claims, after hearing about the influx of wetbacks into this country, passed by a Taco Bell and muttered, "I'll be darned, there are so many of them over here they've set up their own telephone company!"

THE LIGHT CRUST DOUGH BOYS

My friend Walter Hailey, of Hunt, Texas is what is known as a "colorful character." Color him funny. Walter first gained fame as the marketing genius behind his little flour mill business. The mill and the flour became famous because of a group of country musicians he formed to promote his flour. They were called, "The Light Crust Doughboys" and Walter guided them and the company to fame and fortune.

"What instrument did you play?" I asked Hailey.

"Couldn't play anything, never could," he answered.

"Did you sing?"

"Nope. Couldn't sing, either. Can't carry a tune, so I just got the rest of the boys to play and sing. I moved my mouth at the right time but I never made a sound. Nobody ever knew the difference."

"So, what was your contribution of talent?"

"I was paying the bills so I didn't need to be overflowing with talent. Besides, I did the talking, promoting, and selling once we got people's attention."

Walter still has that colorful streak in him. Recently, when another friend of ours rubbed him the wrong way, Hailey, obviously fighting to hold down his temper, remarked, "I've got two personalities and you just nearly saw one of them."

A typical Haileyism: "My grandfather drank pretty heavy. He wouldn't even get out of bed unless there was a nip in the air."

Then there was the story he loves to tell to illustrate the difficult art of communications: A man called the home of his associate. The young son answered the phone.

"Is your Daddy there?"

"No."

"Can you tell him to call me when he comes home?"

"What is your name?"

"Jones. Are you old enough to write it down?"

"I'll try."

"Okay. Tell him to call Jones."

"How do you spell it?"

"J O N E S."

"How do you make a 'J'?"

Finally there is Walter's scoring system that corresponds to the popular movie "10" which relates to a perfect score for a beautiful woman. He has coined the sheepherder's 10. "That's a 4 with six million in oil" explains the crusty old doughboy.

LONG SHOTS 3

Politics is the art of finding out which way the
people are going and then jumping in front of
them to yell encouragement.

POLITICIANS

Although too young to remember this, I'm told by my parents that when I was just a child being held by my father, Lyndon Johnson took me in his arms. The thought of it still makes me shudder. He was an unknown then, running for his first elected political office. When he returned me to my father, he also handed me a nickel. My father told my mother, "Put that nickel away. This man is going to be President of the United States one day." I've still got the nickel somewhere and two-bit politicians are everywhere.

Politicians have to have the toughest hide and the greatest sense of humor of any profession I know. Once they enter the political arena, they know they are going to be asked every leading question and have every dirty trick pulled on them imaginable. It doesn't seem to bother the clever ones. President Reagan was one of the best. When he ran for a second term, Walter Mondale challenged him to a debate. The Mondale camp decided to attack the issue of the President's advanced age, implying that he was not qualified any longer to lead the nation. When Senator Mondale brought the issue direct to the President in the second debate, he asked, "Would you care to respond to the nation's concern over the age issue, Mr. President?"

The President should have won another Academy Award. He lowered his eyes as if he were ashamed, shook his head slightly from side to side, and answered, "Now, I'm not going to get into this age issue. I

46

will not exploit for political purposes my opponent's youth and inexperience." The crowd laughed, the nation laughed, and even Mondale couldn't keep a straight face.

I've been privileged to meet and become personally acquainted with governors of Arkansas, New Mexico, Oklahoma, and, of course, my home state of Texas. They all seem to realize the power of humor. For instance, I once appeared on a program in Arkansas with the then young Lieutenant Governor Bill Clinton. He had all the qualifications needed to become a great politician. He had youth, charm, good looks, a full head of hair, and what appeared to be his own teeth. He's a powerful orator, very persuasive, and eloquent. He was about to launch his campaign for Governor of Arkansas, so he was getting in a little oratorical practice at every opportunity. They gave him ten minutes just prior to my keynote presentation. He did a fine job, but there was no applause except the polite bit he received at the end of his presentation. To his credit, instead of excusing himself and dashing out to catch a plane, he stayed to hear my full-length keynote presentation, which was interrupted numerous times by applause and accompanied by lots of laughter. The next week, I received a letter from Lieutenant Governor Bill Clinton. It consisted of four words, "Doc: Send jokes. Bill" I did. The next letter I received was from Governor Bill Clinton, an invitation to his inaugural ball.

Speaking of inaugural balls, they tell the story in Texas of the time Lyndon Johnson was planning for his. He telephoned his chief organizer who answered, "Yes, Mr. President, I understand that you want a very special invocation. We'll need someone who can touch the hearts of people everywhere. I'd recommend Bishop Smith. . . . Sir? . . . Higher than a bishop? . . . Yes, sir, well . . . I could get in touch with Cardinal . . . Sir? . . . Higher than a cardinal? . . . Sir, you're not . . . you're not talking about the Holy Father in . . . Sir? Higher than the Pope? But that would be God Himself! . . . Sir? . . . Higher than that? . . . Oh, yes sir, I see. You're going to give the invocation yourself."

Well, it's obvious that most politicians have received every kind of barb and most are immune to the criticism. Some of them even take it with a grain of salt and rub it in their own wounds. Such was the case when I had the chance to meet President Harry Truman in his office at the Truman Library in Independence, Missouri. This was just a few months after President Truman had left office. I had been sent as a delegate from Sam Houston State Teachers College to the National Future Farmers of America convention along with our president, Hans Wimberly of Cranfils Gap, Texas. Hans and I were in our early 20's, both of us wearing blue FFA jackets, cowboy boots, and the traditional Stetsons. Wimberly was a great big Norwegian boy who had an outgoing personality. He marched right up to a guard outside President Truman's office and said, "We've come 2,000 miles to see the President." To my utter amazement, they let us in, along with about fifteen others who had been waiting for a couple of hours.

President Truman made a few remarks about how important politics were to the country, how glad he was to see young people taking an interest in it, and then asked if there were any questions. There was about five seconds of total silence. I spoke up, "Mr. President, I don't have a question, but Hans Wimberly here is the president of our collegiate FFA chapter back at Sam Houston State Teachers College in Huntsville, Texas. People are never going to believe that we got in to see you unless I have photographic proof. Would you mind if I took a picture of the two presidents shaking hands?"

Without missing a beat, Harry Truman replied, "No, I don't mind if you don't think it will ruin his reputation."

Whether the politics are on the local level, national, or international, somehow a sense of humor seems to put it all in perspective. The stories that follow in this chapter illustrate that point. The irony of it all is embodied in the comment made by a former governor of New Mexico who told me, "My opponent in the last election said the only way I could have done a worse job was to have learned a second language and become bi-ignorant." I suppose it just proves the old adage that everyone in America should be married. There are some things you just can't blame on the government.

DECISIONS BY HAIRS

Once in a while a really interesting and relevant difference between Presidential candidates is printed in the press . . . hair, or lack of it. It seems that some reporter got to looking back over past campaigns and found that when a candidate with a full head of hair was pitted against a bald one the hairy devil always won.

Think back for a moment. Can you remember any President from the past who was bald? If you thought of Eisenhower, you win a scalp treatment. So he's an exception, but who did Eisenhower run against? That's right, Adlai Stevenson, who had exactly three hairs more than Ike. The reason Ike won in spite of being balder than Adlai is that Stevenson also had a sense of humor. People always vote for the hairy serious guy. A bald guy with a sense of humor just can't be trusted . . . or elected.

I suppose it's just as well that I'm not running. Even though one of my New Year's resolutions was to grow more hair, I think I've started too late to catch the front runners. I've tried everything. Somebody told me to use hairoil with alum to shrink my sideburns up to fit. I think I used too much and they just changed sides.

Then there was the ad that claimed a substance had been discovered that would grow hair on a doorknob. It was even mailed in a plain brown wrapper. Didn't work on me but I've got the hairiest doorknobs you've ever seen.

Toupee? Not for this kid. I saw a politician at a party once who was wearing a rug that looked like a dead squirrel. We were all gathered around the buffet table when he leaned over and it fell into the avocado dip. It was the first time all night that there was a lull in the conversation. Then it got so quiet you could hear a ballot box being stuffed. People suddenly lost their appetite. The avocado futures market dropped 30 points.

Hair stylists claim there's an easy remedy. Just let the hair grow long in one place and comb it over the bald spot, part it high, part it low, sweep it over. One guy even had his parted crossways. That got to be very embarrassing because he was a Presidential candidate and his aides kept coming up to him to whisper in his nose.

All this means is that it's going to be a close race between Presidential candidates especially if both have hair . . . and neither have a ser.se of humor. Guess we'll have to choose on relatively minor points lil.e inflation, balancing the budget, big governmental spending, taxes, defense and whoever promises to bring back the crew cut.

LABELING A POLITICIAN

The Kansas City headlines just after the last national election read, "Liberals Find Little Joy at Polls." Little Joy was the stage name of a burlesque stripper. The liberals were mortified to find her there but had to recognize her presence because she knew them all by name: "Hi Cuddles, Hi Peaches, Hi Sweetie."

The situation was made even more tense because a liberal senator had promised several years ago to marry her after the next election . . . in Rome, but only if the Italians elected a Polish Pope.

Liberal campaign promises have a way of labeling a politician. Little Joy labeled him "A Dirty Rat," jumped in a voting booth, and voted conservative. She wasn't by herself. Several guys tried to get in there with her.

It appears that lots of people were pulling conservative levers. Texas, for instance, voted in the first Republican governor (labeled a conservative) since reconstruction. Fortunately, say some of the liberals, "There's enough graft left over to keep us going."

Two fellows were standing in the unemployment line after the election and one remarked to the other, "Frankly it worries me that the conservative element has taken over with such erratic, irresponsible policies when they are my sole source of support." The other guy nodded in agreement.

As they approached the desk of the unemployment clerk, they were recognized by the official who asked, "Aren't you two guys the ones who were defeated in that hotly contested race?"

"They told lies about us," said one.

"And then they got really dirty," replied the other, "they started backing up those lies with facts."

"Well," sighed the clerk, "I voted for you myself and look where it got me. Now I've got to go to work. This conservative governor gave me the job of finding employment for you guys instead of just giving you money. Governor Clements is willing to forgive and forget. You two have been appointed to a government job, as a part of his cleanup campaign."

"Doing what?" demanded the two.

"Taking down all the campaign posters."

"We're not taking down his posters."

"No, just yours. He ain't that conservative."

REPRESENTATIVE WOODY TAKEUS

Politics is a mystery to everyone, but a complete idiot. Apparently only politicians understand it.

Who can understand all this talk about left wing, right wing? It sounds like Colonel Sanders is running their finger licking campaign. One voter recently summed up his feelings by stating, "I don't worry about labels. Liberals, conservatives, or radicals, they are all about the same—rotten."

My elected representative, Woody Takeus, was accused of being a wild-eyed radical. He denied it and threw a brick at the guy who said it. Woody, with the help of a front end specialist, got his eyes realigned and continued his campaign with the slogan "Takeus Won't Break Us. Elect a Cheap Politician."

Elections will soon be coming up and all prospective candidates claim they are honest and would love to serve their country but under no circumstances would they be a candidate this year.

They all say the same thing, "I am not a candidate. If nominated, I will not accept. I will not, under any circumstances, run for office."

Then they get funds from loyal supporters and travel all over the country telling people they will not run . . . with a racing stripe on the side of their tongue.

But the right to vote should not be taken lightly. All voters are basically honest. They sell their vote to the candidate who promises them the most. I promised Woody Takeus that I would vote for him twice: once to put him in office and once to get him out. The rest of the time he is on his own.

BALANCING THE BUDGET

So the move is on to balance the budget is it? It seems simple enough until you discover that balancing is like a seesaw. Weight has to be fairly equal on each end, and the taxpayer is trying to teeter totter with some heavy weights whose plank runs all the way to Washington. Of course, we get the short end of the plank.

Or, for the mechanically minded, take this example: The U.S. budget is like a car. We all have a part in keeping it running. The chassis and engine are the Senate and the House. The steering mechanism is the President, useless accessories are the vice-president, the wheels are the politicians. The transmission, however, does belong to the voter. He usually gets the shaft.

This is the perfect time to gain a little leverage on our end of the plank. Your vote is most powerful, most sought after and it should be withheld until you get some assurance that your candidate will act on fiscal responsibility. Why not send all candidates an oath to sign and return to you? If you like this one, feel free to reproduce it and send it along to those who always claim to be anxious to hear from you.

Dear Voter (disregard as insincere if "Occupant" is substituted):

Yes, I am concerned about the high taxes, high inflation, excessive government spending, reduced productivity and a failure by politicians to balance the budget.

Yes, I understand that balancing the budget does not mean the interest rates on loans matching the annual inflation rate.

Yes, I understand that the printing of extra paper money by the government to cover its bills is called inflationary while its counterpart by the citizenry is called counterfeiting.

Yes, I reject the recessionary measures taken by other government officials to press upon the public brow the thorny thought of bureaucratic economists who forecast the doom of the private enterprise system with the funds generated by it. Yes, the spark of economic revolution has been struck and you have my support to fan the flames across the tinder box of tyranny from (your town) to Washington, from (your state) to tomorrow. I pledge not to participate in recessionary legislation, bigger government, higher taxes or terminal stupidity. To show my good faith, enclosed is a list of my top three priorities and a plain English explanation of how I plan to help balance the budget.

Signed: _____

Too strong? Are you man or mouse? Squeek up or speak out. And not just the males. All able bodied men and full bodied women need to come forward and be recognized.

Balancing the budget means what the term implies. The most respected accountant of thrift and wisdom, Benjamin Franklin, was and still is revered for budget balancing. Old Ben used to study a scrap of paper kept in a locked box just before working on his accounts. When he died, his successors tore open the box to get at his secret. The worn and tattered note contained eight words. "Debit on the left, credit on the right."

BEN'S POSTAL MALADY

Few people know that Ben Franklin invented the Postal System in the U.S. But every once in a while a postcard crops up that was mailed 200 years ago to prove it—still carrying his signature, riding that eternal zip code into immortality. Ben had a flair for writing and advertising. His cards and letters started out, "My Most Dear and Honorable Occupant," just one of his many ideas still in use today.

Old Ben was frugal (most postmasters are Protestant) and it still shows up in his postal ideas being carried on today. For example:

Make ye olde writing pens available, held by chains that are shorter than a politician's good intentions, to writing tables that are taller than the Olympic high jump record.

Make ye olde mail boxes big enough on the back side to stable a water buffalo sideways but small enough on the front side to look like the peep hole in a front door.

Display ye olde posters of the most wanted criminals alongside the current President and the former Postmaster. That way if anything ever goes wrong, the picture can stay and the word WANTED merely added.

Most postal employees labor behind bars, which teaches them respect for law and order—you have to lay down the law to order a roll of stamps. But the qualifications for Postmaster is the key to Ben Franklin's inexpensive system: there ain't any, except to be able to produce an evil grin whenever you hand him a package marked FRAGILE.

HAIL TO THE CHIEF

The Inn of the Mountain Gods, Ruidoso, always fascinates me. The U.S. government subdued the Mescalero Apaches over a hundred years ago. To punish them, the Apaches were banished to a 500,000 acre tract of useless wilderness. "We'll teach those savages a lesson," said the U.S. General in charge. In the early 1900s they struck oil and then really had a problem. Since Indians pay no taxes, by law, what do you do when the reservation gets littered with all that money?

In typical fashion, the U.S. defeats its enemies like the Apaches, Germans, Japanese, and punishes them by making them learn our ways. The Mescaleros learned well. They are all now paying no taxes and driving Mercedes and Toyotas.

But as clever people, they realized that oil and timber was not an infinite resource, so they opened a ski resort, built a huge lake, and stocked it with fish, put in a great golf course, and established a huge hotel on the reservation and named it the Inn of the Mountain Gods.

The dark-skinned bellboy greeted me, "Welcome White Eyes . . . and Greenbacks."

We used to greet Apaches with "How . . . Brother." That's all changed.

Now we say, "How . . . much?" And when they tell us, we say, "Oh Brother."

I got a room overlooking the lake but not my billfold.

Shell Oil Company had invited me to speak at a meeting there and the facilities were wonderful. When you check in at the desk, they give you a wooden nickel which entitles you to a free drink of firewater. Just think, we thought we were pulling a fast one when we got Manhattan Island for a string of beads.

We met in the Chief Navatille room. I asked an Indian security guard, "Who was Chief Navatille?"

He shrugged his shoulders and replied, Indian fashion, "Umhh, long time ago."

So much for history, but the guy was a philosopher. He told me, "You white eyes are always welcome here but you think funny. You say we were savages who beat the ground with clubs and yelled out curses. Now you come here and pay us to do the same, but you call it golf."

The logo of the Inn is a figure representing one of the Mountain Gods, dancing with both arms raised. In one hand, he holds a knife. I couldn't tell what was in the other hand, so I asked a beautiful maiden at the desk. She joked, "Credit Card."

"A credit card and a knife?" I asked, "What's that supposed to mean?"

Laughingly she replied, "Use a valid credit card if you value your scalp."

MISSILE MUSCLE

Now they're putting missiles around the White House. Why not? It's surrounded by hostile and aggressive people trying to take over the government, not to mention the Democrats.

If the Russians ever try to break down the gates at the White House, we'll set off our missiles. I wonder what the power setting is for a trajectory of 100 yards?

The reason for the missiles being in a ring encircling the Chief of State is that we can't miss. We have enemies everywhere. If we get attacked, we're bound to be able to hit somebody who doesn't like us even if we just chop the guy wires and let'em fall over.

Being President has got to be a real pain. Imagine having to explain to everyone that we aren't digging missile silos, but we're putting in a new sewer line. What a way to flush out Communists.

If you've ever been to the gates on Pennsylvania Avenue that surround our Chief Executive's home, you'll remember that people are standing, marching, carrying signs, trying to influence the President with their views. But enough about the vice president.

The theory is that if protective radar sees some unidentified flying object within seven miles of the White House, the missiles will be deployed. Imagine, some guy could start a war on a windy day by opening his umbrella.

Some kinky ultralight pilot could make his load even lighter with an ICBM through his tail section.

ICBM stands for "I Could Be Mistaken."

That in itself is enough to scare the Russians into staying home where they belong, tilling the soil to plant their spring missiles.

This whole episode is like the two kids who faced off on either side of a line drawn in the dirt. After much arguing, clenching of fists, and threatening body language, one kid yelled at the other, "My dad can whip your dad!"

The other yelled back, "Don't be ridiculous, my dad is your dad!"

FORGIVE THEM FATHER

Every time someone wants to describe a real desperate situation for somebody else, a phrase comes to mind like, "He doesn't have a prayer."

With the political debates we've endured many people feel that way about the taxpayer. Now if anybody needs a prayer during election time it's us. Keep the following handy and recite it together to ward off post-debate depression:

The Last Psalm

The government is my shepherd; I shall not want.

It sheareth my cloak and fleeceth my pockets for my own good. It giveth my back warm greetings and hot air to protect me from the cold war against economics.

It maketh me to lie down in green pastures because the finance company repossesseth my shelter; it leadeth me beside the still waters while it tries to thinketh of ways to cleaneth them up.

It restoreth my soul; the IRS sayeth it is of no value in this world; it leadeth me in the paths of righteousness for its name's sake. We calleth out that name daily when we raise our eyes toward Washington and bleat, "Baa."

Yea, though I walk through the valley of the shadow of death, I will fear no evil: for thou art with me, whether I wanteth thou or not; thy rod and thy staff they comfort me because my rod bleweth it's catalytic converter and my staff quiteth to go on welfare.

Thou preparest a table before me in the presence of mine enemies; this aideth not the digestion.

Thou anointest my head with oil; doth it asketh too much to greaseth my palm?

My cup runneth over: mainly because my cup shrinketh; I am underwhelmed.

Surely government and taxes shall follow me all the days of my life: and politicians shall dwell in the House and the Senate forever.

THE COURT JESTER

Commissioners Court has county authority to do just about everything but sit in session on Judgment Day. They would be willing to hear cases even then if they could find out when it was, but most commissioners agree that the county judge would probably veto paving the streets of gold when a load of gravel would do.

I heard a county judge in Montana give a civic club talk about his court. He was the court jester, apparently, and started his remarks by saying that he had been accused by the commissioners of "out of this world ideas." There was even a rumor that he was out taking his morning stroll, talking to God, when he was hit and run over by a surfer.

After a few giggles the judge got serious and talked about the most pressing problems facing local government: getting re-elected.

The question and answer session was almost over when a member of the club spoke up. "Judge," he said, "You have made light of yourself and joked with the boys here but I want you to know that commissioners court used to be a joke, but under your organization and leadership it has become a credit to good government. You deserve all that credit."

A long silence was followed by a lump in the judge's throat and a tear in his eye.

Then "one of the boys" added, "That's his opinion, Judge."

That led to the final story of the day that adjourned the good natured meeting. A club member said he dreamed he was St. Peter and on Judgment Day everyone seeking admittance had to come before commissioners court because they had set up just outside the Pearly Gates. St. Peter noticed them and asked what right they had to sit in judgment. They said when they came to office on earth the county was so broke it couldn't pay attention, but under their organization and leadership things were rearranged, budgets slashed and great economy realized and they ought to be allowed to continue their work, so heavenly were their deeds.

St. Peter went back in to check his records on this boast. When he came back the commissioners were gone.

And so were the Pearly Gates.

PLATFORM PLANKS OR PRANKS

Democrats and Republicans are very nervous this year. Experienced politicians are taking trips outside their home state. They know better than to stay home where people know their voting record.

There are some thinking that they should vote for the inexperienced first timer and then quit work because they've already been promised everything.

The planks in all their platforms appear to be wide enough to let the largest promise fall through.

As one candidate complained to his volunteer staff, "We have to redouble our efforts. Our opponents are telling vicious lies about us and proving half of them."

But I wouldn't want their job. It would be like blind dating by correspondence and then asking for your rating as a lover.

The voters are very fickle and a lot smarter than many politicians think. One candidate was so visibly impressed that a large crowd had gathered to hear his views on a touchy local issue that he remarked in his opening statement, "I'm surprised at this turnout."

A voice from the back yelled, "Your predecessor was surprised when we turned him out, too."

But let's face it, we voters are not exactly Einsteins on politics when we criticize our Mickey Mouse government. A man-in-the-street reporter asked a fellow once about his views on the FTC. He replied, "Greatest darn president we ever had."

"That was FDR," corrected the interviewer.

"I'm talking about our Rotary Club," replied the interviewee, "Fred T. Cook, promised he wouldn't do nothin' and then didn't do it."

"That made him great?"

"Yeah, 'cause nothin' was what we wanted done."

FDR once said, "There is nothing to fear but fear itself." Most politicians would be afraid to say that.

The reason is that the politician would be accused of practicing plagiarism and the average voter would think it was some kind of cult.

Can't you hear the crowds? "Devil worshipper," they cry in unison. Also in Pennsylvania, Texas, California . . . .

So give them a break folks and don't believe everything you hear. Find out all you can and then exercise your right to vote your convictions. Or suspicions. They will appreciate it, even if they are appointed. Like the lady who shook Henry Kissinger's hand and said, "Mr. Kissinger, I want to thank you for saving the world."

Henry replied, "You're welcome."

DIPLOMATIC DEFECT

The nation's capital has a strange mixture of opposites: city–country; wealthy–poor; intellectuals–politicians.

The hotels are filled with foreign accents. "Diplomats," I thought to myself when I entered the huge banquet hall of the Sheraton Hotel and heard a group of men in tuxedos, speaking alternately in six or seven languages.

"What embassy are you guys with?" I casually inquired. It was obvious I was the foreigner. They were all waiters.

"You only need two languages to be a diplomat," said one of the fellows who spoke seven, "just think of us as diplomats with brains."

The fact of the matter was that several of the waiters had defected to the U.S. A Russian defector named Rudolph told me it wasn't too hard. "To give you an idea of how smart they are," he told me, "a KGB agent came in here and tried to bribe me. He was carrying a sack. He said, 'Guess how many bottles of vodka are in this sack and I'll give you the other one.'"

He poured me a very tiny glass of a strange looking liquid which he said was a strong Russian drink. I asked, "Do you drink this all at once?"

"Nyet," he scoffed, "we're not Norwegians."

Rudolph said he got out of Russia in a very unusual way—in one piece.

"Rudolph make joke," he continued. "There are good people in Russian system. They're in Siberia, but they're there."

He told me that he could not yet afford a car, but he had traveled widely as a Russian anyway, "I took the subway to work, the train to see my girlfriend, and if I went abroad, the government sent me in a tank."

"We stayed for a year in a resort in Afghanistan. Big hotel, same number of rooms as this one . . . but without walls."

Rudolph told me that the main difference he saw in Russian and American politics was that if you got too involved in Russian politics, you could never be heard from again. "Over here," he said, "the only way that could happen is to become vice president."

C-SPAN SIT-COM

The latest thing on the floor of the Senate is a TV camera. It telecasts a new sit-com. Even the Japanese camera is a Yamaha-ha-ha.

The ratings are already so bad that Nielson has refused to watch it long enough to give it a score. So the job has been given to Knutsen who is studying English to become a citizen. Knutsen was ejected from the floor of the Senate. He snored so loud he woke up a Senator.

These guys are going Hollywood on us. All of a sudden Hart, Shaftner, and Marx are being replaced by Toupee, Mascara, and Rouge.

Senator John Glenn actually held up two ties and asked the people of Ohio if they preferred one color over another. Three people wrote. One wanted him to change ties, one wanted him to change his suit, and one wanted to change senators.

His make-up man said the pancake make-up made him come across a little flat.

Glenn is being encouraged to change his image for television. For years, he's been the clean cut astronaut type, but now he looks a bit like the Pillsbury doughboy. I think a nice Afro wig would do it.

One of the politicians, dressed to perfection, sprang to his feet in a burst of enthusiasm and for his opening remarks, flung his arms wildly and yelled, "Heeee-yahh!" Then he kicked violently several times while yelling, "Haaaa-yahhh!" The chairman asked, "Karate, Senator?" He replied, "No, tight girdle."

One can learn a lot about the show business of politics by watching the proceedings. I saw a senator making a speech. It was marvelous. He opened his mouth and a foot fell out.

It was a size 12½ EEE. Not surprising, since the parts are interchangeable.

I really think it's in bad taste to have Gramm-Rudman warming up the audience with their version of "Who's on first."

The Speaker from the House wanted the lead in "South Pacific" so, as usual, the Senate compromised. They let him be New Zealand.

What we have learned is fascinating. We always wondered what the vice president did besides preside over the Senate. Now we know he's also the one who goes out for doughnuts.

When you get right down to it, this show is not much different from the others. It is filled with bad actors, has no plot and can't hold a candle to the Bill Cosby Show.

There is one area where it really comes through. It has no canned laughter. Anything that costs billions and is directed by temporary amateurs doesn't need canned laughs. However, once in a while a real one comes along that gives the show hope.

A filibustering senator had droned on for hours. He suddenly stopped for a few seconds. The silence got attention. They thought he was through until he added, "I pause to ask myself a question."

An old opponent yelled out, "The intelligence of which will be exceeded only by its monotony."

THE TICS IN POLY

Someone once told me that Latin was good to know because you could study words and get at their root meaning. For instance, politics is taken from the Latin "poly" (many). I couldn't find "ticks" but everybody knows that is a little bug, so it stands to reason that ours is a system with many little bugs in it.

Politicians simplify and justify the system. They say politics is only a matter of two policies—getting in and getting even. Some of them also abuse their Latin training because quite often those who have been appointed think they have been annoited. For example, a high ranking national appointee was going through Senate confirmation hearings and a senator asked, "How do you possibly propose to turn the economy around when God himself has no plan for straightening out our system?"

The candidate replied, "Verily, verily, I say unto thee . . . ." Then he explained his plan, got up, and walked through a wall. He broke his nose in the process.

Yes, the Bush administration does sound like they have the answers and I hope they are right, but it's like the great political philosopher Bubba Smith once observed, "Don't expect nothin' too deep."

Who knows what we'll be expected to do next? The health department got so regulated in the last administration that some city drinking water was called unsafe because it had one part per million of some harmless, obscure substance in it. For perspective, that works out to be equivalent to one ounce of vermouth in 750,000 gallons of gin.

The house also passed a resolution forbidding the sale of wine bottled in cans. They completely overlooked the possibility that someone might put dogfood in bottles.

But the strangest proposal came when legislation backed by biologists tried to warn the public that nudism in sunny climates could be dangerous to your health, but nobody could agree on where to put the warning label.

Now with a government like that it's obvious that some fat can be trimmed, so the administration's consultants are hard at work. By the way, don't expect immediate miracles because a consultant has been described as a man who knows 49 ways to court women and has no women.

This epistle doesn't mean that I don't have faith in our system, because I do. I'm optimistic and thrilled with the administration. It's just the tics in politics that concerns me now. I'm like the college freshman, first day in Government 101. The instructor pointed at him and asked, "Quickly, what's the effect of the Gross National Product on Democracy versus Totalitarianism?" He replied, "Hell, Professor, I just came in."

HUMOR FROM AFAR

Emperor Hirohito was once in the U.S. for talks with the President. The two leaders exchanged presents. Our President gave the Emperor a shipload of rice and the Emperor repaired the White House Sony TV set even though the warranty was out.

The Emperor is forbidden, by Japanese law, to comment on politics. However, the shrewd little monarch did burst out in a regal laugh every time a political policy was explained.

"Our plan, Your Highness, is to cut taxes and increase government spending."

"Ah, so. You Amelicans. Ha, ha, ha. We love Johnny Carson."

"Emperor, Johnny Carson is an entertainer, not a politician."

"That why we love him."

"We also plan to send arms to Israel and Egypt. Then we place our noncombatants in between them to keep the peace."

"Oh, ha, ha, please no more. Royal sense of humor is strained to limit. We love Bob Hope."

Then they took the emperor to see a professional football game. Each side was hitting hard and threw numerous bombs that scored points as injured players were hauled off by the ton. The Emperor appeared very sad. In the fourth quarter, just after the announcer said another bomb was unleashed that scored in the end zone, the Emperor turned to the President and said, "Please, if this is World War III, I not take blame this time."

"No, Hirohito. This is a game. We do this for fun. The bomb we throw here makes people happy."

"Ah, so. You Amelicans velly clever. This big joke, yes? Like Big, Bad LeRoy Nagasaki . . . each December 7, he bomb Pearl Mesta?"

Now you know why the Japanese passed a law forbidding the Emperor from making public statements about politics. He might put those comedians in Washington out of business.

HISTORY WILL RECORD

"Lincoln's birthday is this month," I told a friend.

"Big deal," he said. "I drive a Mercury."

"No, I'm talking about Abraham," I replied.

"What kind of a car would have a name like Abraham?" he questioned. "Give me a macho name like 'Cougar'."

"Listen, dummy, I'm talking about the Abraham Lincoln of history . . . the man who freed the slaves."

"Thought that was Henry Ford."

"No," countered his wife. "It was the Big Three who freed the slaves."

"The Big Three?" I asked in amazement. "You mean Roosevelt, Churchill, and Stalin?"

"No I mean Betty Friedan, Gloria Steinham, and Jane Fonda," she cackled.

Well, however you perceive history, you have to admit Lincoln's birthday, February 12th, was a significant event. When Abe was born, Ronald Reagan was just a boy.

Lincoln had things named for him—Lincoln Center, Lincoln Tunnel, and NFL wide receivers.

Reagan will have things named for him, too—Reagonomics, Reagan Star Wars, even a presidential bush named George.

Both Lincoln and Reagan were shot, but it looks like they'll both live forever. One of them lives on in history books, the other on the late, late show.

If Abraham could talk to us today, I suspect he would have some very interesting things to say about the country. Probably things like: "I preserved the Union so all the Yankees could go south for the winter. So why is Miami full of Cubans?"

"Four score and seven years ago . . . . Wasn't that the last time the Houston Oilers won a wild card?"

"The west is finally settled . . . with the possible exception of California."

We don't have politicians like Lincoln around any more and that's too bad. Lawyer Lincoln was arguing a case once and the judge thought he was out of line. Fined him $10 for contempt of court. Honest Abe wanted to pay on the spot with a $20 piece. The judge said the court had no change for the twenty. "That's alright, Judge," said Honest Abe. "I'll just take the other ten out in contempt."

LITTLE SHOTS 4

I would have been a teacher except for class
and principles.

CHILDREN, SCHOOLS, TEACHERS, SCHOOL BOARDS

Education is usually in a logical sequence. Something like primary, secondary, and higher education. Of course, some of the smartest people I've ever known have had no formal education. You know the type. The millionaire who addresses the commencement exercise and says something like, "If only I had been able to get an education, I might have made something of myself." However, when the college president asked him to fund a $250,000 chair in humanities, he replies, "I may not have much education, but I'm smart enough not to lay out that kind of money for a piece of furniture."

A wino once told me, "People who complain that Americans spend more money on alcohol than they do on education just don't understand how much you can learn about life in a beer joint."

My friend, Bob Murphey of Nacogdoches, Texas, a lawyer and well-known after-dinner speaker, claims that when he started to school in the first grade, there was a rumor that his classmates set the school on fire. Bob says, "It ain't true. They set the teacher on fire and she ran in to the schoolhouse."

My first day in the first grade was an unforgettable experience. I literally had to learn a second language in order to defend myself. More than half of my classmates spoke Spanish, but no English. I grew up in a minority group, but I'm a fast learner. The first Spanish word I learned was "Si." A Latino classmate ran up to me and asked, "Quiere combate?" I smiled broadly and replied, "Si."

He hit me right in the mouth. It was my most unforgettable Spanish lesson. "Quiere combate?" means "Do you want to fight?" My father, on the other hand, is not such a fast learner. He is fond of saying, "When I first came to this part of Texas, the only Spanish word I could say was 'Si'. Now I've lived here for over forty years and I can say, 'Si, si'."

My primary education was marred by tragedy. The tragedy was that I skipped the third grade and nearly failed the fourth. At the time I was in school, there were only eleven grades. Some of the nation's top educators convinced the lawmakers that we needed twelve years of school, but as usual in order to appease the voters, the law stated that anyone who was in school at the time would simply be promoted to the next level thereby skipping one grade. I don't know what happened to the juniors in high school during this period, but I suspect they were way ahead of their time and were simply kicked out of school. Anyway, as I recall, my parents were quite happy about the fact that I would only be in school eleven years and then have to go out and support myself.

My senior year in high school was an anxious one. I thought they were going to add another year to make up for skipping the third grade, but the superintendent decided to let me graduate and the board voted six to five to wish me well.

At the time I graduated from high school, the most commonly accepted course of action was to go to work. Much to my surprise, I found that all my classmates were going to college. Since I always tried to keep up with the latest trend, I asked, "Where is it all of us are going to college?" When I arrived in Kingsville, Texas, on the campus of Texas A & I University, I found that I had joined the ranks of the "Fighting Javelinas." If you don't know what a javelina is, let me explain. It is a small, wild member, distantly related to swine, that looks like a cross between a hog and porcupine. It weighs about forty pounds at maturity, has tusks like an African boar, stiff hair, and no tail. I turned out to be a "Fighting Javelina" alright. I gnashed my teeth in English, bristled up at Biology, and lost my tail in Chemistry.

Before the end of the semester, the dean sent me a threatening letter. It said I should appear in his office immediately or suffer the consequences. I threw it in the trash. A few days later, the dean saw me on campus. He said, "Come in to my office, will you, boy? We need to talk about your future in education. It won't take long."

He was so right. I joined the work force the next day. My education had just begun. I thought about doing something exciting like joining the

French Foreign Legion. I didn't have to . . . before the year was over, I was drafted into the U.S. Army.

I've still got splinters under my fingernails where they drug me off the back porch. There were five of us that went all at the same time. Me and four MP's.

Even in the military, they kept stressing education. "You are so lucky to be in the army," they told me. "Because when you get out, you'll have the GI Bill and can go to college."

"I tried it once and didn't like it. What's more, they didn't like me," I told them.

"We don't like you either," said my First Sergeant. "We're going to march you till you drop, teach you to obey orders without question, and make you curse the day you were born. Then, no more Mr. Nice Guy."

Now that was an education. Six years after graduating from high school, I decided to take Uncle Sam up on his offer of sending me back to college. The second time around, I went to Sam Houston State Teachers College, Huntsville, Texas. I became a "Fighting Bearkat." The college later changed its name to Sam Houston State University, but the image and emphasis remained the same. I still found it amusing that a teacher's college had a mascot that nobody had ever seen, even knew what it was, and couldn't even spell "cat." It was my kind of university—one with a sense of humor. Other colleges made jokes about us. The most common was, "Any graduate of Sam Houston should be made by law to leave the state and get an education."

Although I didn't plan to leave the state, my mind was changed when I did my practice teaching at Madisonville, Texas, High School. I always will be grateful to that group of high school students. They drove me into higher education.

The University of Missouri in Columbia, Missouri, offered a graduate teaching assistantship so I could pursue a M.S. and Ph.D. in order to teach in college. Discipline was not so much of a problem there. Although I was a major in animal husbandry, my advisers placed me in a 5-hour course in human anatomy, alongside the medical students. The theory was that if you were not tough enough to make it in the most difficult courses, they wanted to find out about it now before they wasted too much money on you. We were gathered in this large auditorium, about 500 students. Being the friendly sort, I turned to the fellow on my left and asked, "Where are you from," thinking that he would say something like, "Boston."

With a smug look on his face, he replied, "Harvard."

I asked the guy on the right the same question.

"Yale," he answered.

Others around me volunteered, "Purdue" and "Rutgers."

At that precise moment, I knew I should have not started this line of questioning. Somehow I sensed that they were going to ask me that same burning question.

When I answered, "Sam Houston State Teachers College," it seemed that the whole room burst into laughter and I became an instant celebrity.

However, when the test papers from the first exam were handed back, I took a peek at the scores made by "Harvard," "Yale," "Purdue," and "Rutgers." Much to my surprise, I found that I had the highest score. They graded on the curve system. I don't like to brag, but I've never been more proud in my life of a 39.

After graduating from the University of Missouri, I returned to Texas to teach for ten years at Wharton County Junior College, Wharton, Texas. I left the college in 1974 to pursue a full time speaking career. The president of the college was kind enough to serve as a reference when educational groups invited me to speak. He always thought it was cute to write, "Dr. Blakely taught at our college for ten years and when he left, we were all very happy about it."

As one of my favorite college professors used to say, "An education is nothing more than knowing where to go to look for the answers that come up in life."

Brilliance is not measured by the number of degrees you can tack on to the end of your name or the number of diplomas you can accumulate to hang on your wall. But even those who don't have it seem to be the first ones to recognize the importance of it. Like the old mountaineer told his grandson, "Git a education, boy. You can't no more do what you ain't prepared for any more than you can come back from where you ain't been."

Our experience at all levels of education are reminders of the enjoyment, mischief, and struggles while searching for a role in life. Perhaps you will find some common ground in the stories that follow.

BRIBES AND YUCKY THINGS

Ever try to get a kid to eat something he doesn't like? The only sure fire method appears to be to convince him he can't have it because you want it. "If you eat all your ice cream then you can have some spinach," only works once and then you have to get more creative.

It would be much simpler if parents just threw all those greens and vegetables into a blender and drenched the kids like they do sheep and goats. It probably wouldn't hurt to de-worm them at the same time. Of course, that's not practical because there would be too many injuries

. . . to the parents. Kids get mean when it comes to eating yucky things. So we resort to gentle persuasion. "Eat all your carrots or I'll short-sheet your bed."

Or you can set a good example and show them how good this stuff is for you by eating lots of it yourself. I know a guy who has eaten so many carrots he has an orange tinge to his skin and insomnia. He sees right through his eyelids. He can't go into the woods without being attacked by rabbits. His breath attracts 37 varieties of beetles. His kids eat hostess twinkies and are healthy as hippos . . . which is plural for hippy.

So how do you get the little monsters to eat the right things to grow up big and strong? You use Christian principles, that's how.

You scare the liver out of them with horrible tales of what will happen if they don't eat fruit and vegetables. "Eat that asparagus or your navel will rupture, let all your air out and you'll go Pfttttt. There you'll be, lying limp as a burst balloon, too small to read the advertisement."

Sometimes we think all our efforts are being wasted, that the kids are not paying attention, but my friend Weldon Rackley, from Reston, Virginia, tells me of an interesting case he observed that may prove otherwise.

A lady who works for the same company saw Weldon and some of his friends at a restaurant. She came over to say hello, and met Weldon's friends, one of whom was a little girl about 5 years of age. This lady happened to be all of 4 feet 11 inches in high heels and could look everybody right in the eye even though she was standing and the others were seated. After she exchanged the customary pleasantries and left, this little girl quizzed her dad.

"What's the matter with her, daddy?"

"Nothing, dear. She's just small."

"Did God punish her for something?"

"No, of course not."

After a long, thoughtful pause the little one asked, "Daddy, was it the broccoli?"

CABBAGE PATCH PROGENIES

The cabbage patch kids have taken the nation by storm. The stork doesn't bring them anymore. I think it's all a publicity gimmick by the nurserymen.

These cabbage patch dolls are not born exactly. They are "harvested." We're soon going to lose the generations who played house. Parents will start to worry when their kids give those sly glances at a combine.

An unfit mother will probably just be made into a bowl of cole slaw.

Fathers, when they get old, will be turned into sauerkraut. But the cabbage patch kids will be sold to the highest bidder, complete with birth certificate from Neiman-Marcus and umbilical cord from Wells-Fargo.

A philosopher friend of mine put it all in perspective for me when he said, "The poor folks are the ones that keep driving up the price."

I can just hear it all now. "Mom, where did I come from?"

"Well, your father and I were out fertilizing the garden one day and there you were in the cabbage patch."

"Show me where."

"Right over there at Horticultural General between the broccoli and the spinach."

"Spinach? Yuk, no wonder nobody likes me at school."

"Now don't talk like that. You'll grow like a weed and leaf out beautifully. Besides, you've got a good head on your shoulders."

"What good does that do when you're built like a bowling ball?"

"Now, darling, be patient. You'll grow up just fine. Someday you'll meet a nice young person of the opposite sex and the two of you will put down roots."

"I want to travel. Sure hope he gets a good job and brings in lots of 10-20-10. Hey, maybe we can have cabbage patch kids of our own and make lots of 20's and 50's. Forget about the small stuff."

"That's the attitude, sweetheart. What will you name your cabbage patch kids?"

"How about rich and famous?"

"That's my girl. Just stay away from the fruits and nuts."

RENT - A - KID

The latest thing on the market is rent-a-kid. It makes sense. They are guaranteed for 100,000 miles, five minutes or until they drive you crazy, all of which occur remarkably close together. Then if you don't like the model, just have it recalled for modifications, like a latch on the lip.

Children should have to run for reelection every four years and stand on their platform of past performance. I know a kid who keeps his room so messy they can vacuum only after they've used a rake. The room was so cluttered that the family cat learned to walk on its hind legs.

Of course, the kids have their side of the story, too. Most of them suspect, at some time during their lives, that they are so superior to the genetic stock around them that they must be adopted. Some friends of mine had two children the old fashioned way and figured there must be a better way to commit hari kari, so they adopted a little girl. The three were normal—wild as Comanches. One day while visiting a neighbor, these three were stricken by a strange virus that made them appear sweet, kind, and loving. The grandmother of the neighbors, also visiting, remarked, "Oh, you Baker kids are so sweet. I think I'll just adopt all of you."

"Not me," said the youngest Baker.

"Why not?" asked the kindly lady.

"Because I've already tried it once," said the sweet adoptee, "and I'm not so sure I like it."

A few years later her older "brother" was applying for his driver's license at age 16. He was worried stiff, so Mom gave him a pep talk to bolster his confidence. She also advised that he practice some old fashioned public relations.

So when the big day came, Billy got up, bright and early (about 9 A.M.) and hustled off to take the driving exam, having earlier passed the written part. The highway patrolman was a huge, burly guy wearing a pistol the calibre of Mt. St. Helens. There he stood, cowboy hat pulled over the upper half of his eyebrows, feet placed in a stance similar to that used by the Dallas Cowboys, both hands resting on a clipboard that was supported on the other end by his ammunition belt, and handcuffs. The kid walked right up, lowered his voice, stuck out his hand, and said, "Hi, I'm Billy Baker."

The patrolman never moved a hand from the clipboard. With a penetrating, icy stare, he asked, "What'chu tryin' to do, boy, influence my decision?"

"No sir," said Billy, "my momma told me to try it."

He passed the exam, but now he's up for adoption through rent-a-kid!

COMMUNICATION PARODY

It's a wonder we ever learn anything from others because of communication, or lack of it, between humans.

For instance, a small Missouri town had a school board that advised the superintendent to "assemble the student body on the football field for observation of Haley's Comet, an event which happens every 75 years. In the event of rain, classes will dismiss to the gymnasium where they will be shown films on the subject."

The superintendent told the principal to "find a 75 year old football field where it doesn't rain, so the student body won't be dancing across the gym floor, upsetting the coach, watching movies of Haley's Comet."

The principal told the teachers to "accompany the student body to the football field because the 75 year old Haley's Comet is not fit as a film unless it rains. Classes will dismiss to the gym, but dancing will not be permitted by the coach."

The teachers told the students that, "because the student body has been dancing in the gym and possibly watching questionable movies, the coach will take the student body to the football field to listen to the 75 year old principal talk about Haley's Comet even if it rains."

The students spread the word that, "for 75 years the principal has been studying student's bodies and the coach is going to show a movie about it on the football field. If it rains, classes will dismiss to the gym for a dance by Bill Haley and the Comets."

One parent overheard the plan and spread the word that, "X-rated movies of dancing bodies in a gym are shown, by the coach, to football boys every time it rains. The principal dismisses any wrongdoing because the stars, Bill Haley and the Comets, are over 75."

When the word got back to the board, they met in called session and dealt decisively with the crisis. They fired the football coach, Will Bailey, for his comments on over-75 principals' bodies. The lesser charge of rain dancing was dismissed.

JOY AND PAIN IN EDUCATION

They say that education in America is going downhill, that students nowadays can't write, can't spell, and can't even speak the English language properly. I say it ain't never been no better.

What do educators expect when they butcher up a very easy word like "baloney" and spell it "bologna." It sounds like a town in Italy. No wonder nobody can spell it.

This is a strange country. You get an education in English, study in English and when you graduate, they give you a diploma and a Latin designation like "magna cum laude."

With all the foreign competition nowadays, we shouldn't be worrying about Latin. We should be studying Japanese and graduate "magna cum toyota."

I know some people will think I'm taking a shot at education, but the truth of the matter is that we have a funny language, a funny system, and until we see the humor in it we may never become fully educated.

For instance, a little girl shouted to her mother when she got home from school that "I've learned how to make babies."

Mustering all the emotional control at her command, the mother calmly asked, "How do you make babies?"

The little girl explained, "It's easy. You drop the 'y' and add 'ies'."

Isn't it true that we want to believe that we are a nation of dummies? It's the old bad news philosophy. Like these two women at a health club who saw a mutual acquaintance across the gym. "Do you believe that vicious rumor that's going around about her?" said one. "Yes," said the other. "What is it?"

Well, until we can make education fun again and not take ourselves so seriously, we are going to continue to have difficulty in making education attractive to the masses. Get with it, America. Today, teenagers think "the straight and narrow" is a style of jeans.

You know what I can't understand? Here's Adam and Eve. He's incredibly handsome and she's indescribably beautiful. Both of them were supposedly brilliant people. So where did all the ugly and dumb people come from?

People were smart during the time of Adam and Eve and they also had a sense of humor. When Adam bit into the apple, you could tell it was from the Tree of Knowledge. Adam looked at the apple, turned to Eve and said, "You call this dinner?"

Yes, education can be painful or it can be fun. We learn from our past mistakes, laugh it off, make the necessary corrections, and get back on track. For instance, if you were Adam or Eve in the Garden of Eden and you selected a fig leaf to hide your nakedness, you learned something. But you really got an education if you selected poison oak.

The tragedy of education is the painful awareness that past mistakes can't be laughed off and the future made more exciting.

IMAGINE THAT

It has come to my attention that many readers are young people of high school and college age. Classes have already started in both of those categories and nobody is ready except the old teachers who have spent all summer trying to figure out how to maintain an adequate level of poison in their system to sting a freshman into submission with a well placed tongue lashing.

Maybe it will help my young friends to know that education can be made more bearable if they try to think of these aging (some of them are over 25) instructors as they once were. Let your imagination wander back to the high school freshperson (things have changed) of your choice.

Your football coach was once a picture of health, a broad chest, and trim waist. He now suffers from the dread furniture disease: his chest has fallen into his drawers.

Your history teacher was a bookworm, now he or she has outgrown books, but still qualifies for part of the former title. But instead of reading about ancient history, they are now walking examples of it. They used to be the quiet type, skinny, with thick glasses that looked like the ends knocked out of coke bottles. Now they have contacts, especially those who have a relative on the board. They suffer from the tongue-tied disease. Their tongue is tied in the middle and loose on both ends.

The home economics teacher was once a one hundred and ten pound beauty with moving parts of great interest. Then she started eating her own cooking and her interests spread. When she goes to the beach she has to put her suntan lotion on with a paint roller. At one time she resembled the figure eight but that has now been reduced to nothing. When she laughs she looks like yogurt with a belt.

Your chemistry instructor was once a wild, silly, uncontrollable kid who couldn't make aspirin in the laboratory, but gave plenty of people a headache. He did learn how to make gunpowder that was sensitive to temperature changes. He hid it among the eggs in the hen house. The survivors of the explosion produced off-spring that set eggs with a frown and closed eyes.

So don't frown and close your eyes to education, my friends, just imagine in dull moments that your teacher is standing before you in thong sandals, long hair, and a beard . . . or maybe she is.

THERE HE IS . . .

Did you ever go to the local "Mr. and Miss Contest" for young-sters? There are more politics there than at the National Convention. Mothers trying to bribe the judges by yelling out little subtle hints like, "Smile and wave at the judge," "Open both eyes darling," or "Throw a little kiss." The girls are dressed up in blue eye shadow, high heels, and tailor made panty hose. They look kind of cute, like an unsanforized Raquel Welsh.

But the boys are boys, complete with freckles, missing teeth, and cowlicks. They wear those white pants, and carry their pet frog along for company. A nice handful of wet mud in the right front pocket makes a comfy home for him, and an ever growing circle on the white pants.

Those nice, new shoes with the fresh polish job are just right for turning the side of the sole so that a long mark can be made by walking backward. You can't be too careful about keeping your bearings. You can always follow that mark back to where you left your garden snake sealed in a coffee can under a seat in the auditorium.

On stage, freckles, cowlicks, stained pants, and scuffed shoes, the M.C. asking questions, is where the fun really starts. Those kids come up with some great answers. And philosophy.

"What did your Mother tell you not to do?"

"Don't scratch no matter where I itch."

The kids will probably never be as free, or honest, or lovable, or as unconcerned with public opinion again.

The only difference between men and boys is their choice of toys and a developed concern for how others will see them.

LIKE FATHER LIKE SON

Mark Twain once wrote, "When I was 14, my father was so stupid that I could hardly stand to be around the old man. When I turned 21, I was simply amazed at what this elderly gentleman had learned in only seven short years."

Everyone who has ever worked for their father probably recalls some incident that proved unsatisfactory to father, child, or both. Like the blacksmith who put one end of a red hot piece of iron on an anvil and told his son "When I nod my head, you hit it with a hammer." Yes, it was tempting but the kid hadn't been paid and it was his first day on the job, so he hit him on the thumb instead.

It was the first time he had ever seen his father walk on his tiptoes, a feat he soon found himself performing.

A bystander jokingly remarked to the kid, "Your father seems to suffer from a loss of temper."

"No," said the boy as he clasped both hands to his bottom, "he suffers from a loss of politeness."

From a father's point of view, the child is always expected to do a perfect job which he should have learned by osmosis. It's the old story of expecting too much too soon. A father can be a tough boss, a bit like the relationship between umpires and Billy Martin. As one young man recently told me, "I work for my father but usually not with him . . . if I'm lucky."

Of course, the youngsters recognize responsibility and usually evaluate their poor performance honestly . . . if it looks like they're going to get caught goofing off anyway. A man told his boy he would give him a dollar if he cleaned out the garage while he was gone for the day. Upon returning, he asked, "How well did you do? I'm not even going to look. If you deserve the dollar, I'll give it to you."

The boy shuffled his feet, shifted his weight, twisted up his face, and replied, "Gimme a dime."

From the son's point of view, the father is impatient, old fashioned, and unreasonable.

"You know what my father told me?" remarked a young friend.

"He said he hoped when I grew up and had kids that I'd have a son just like me. Now what kind of father would wish a kid like me off on his own son?"

BLOCKS AND BRAINS

Do you ever get the feeling that the world is being run by 'C' students?

I'm sure some teachers do. Communication is of extreme importance between teacher and student.

For example, a pupil looked at the examination question which read: "State the number of tons of coal shipped out of the U.S. in any year."

His answer: "1492, none."

He may have been a 'C' student when it came to teacher-student communication, but I'd give him an 'A' for inventiveness!

Sometimes the students misunderstand a bit, as illustrated by answers given to test questions:

"Where was the Declaration of Independence signed? At the bottom."

"Where is Houston? Last place in the American Football League."

"Denver is located just below the O in Colorado."

"The climate of Bombay is such that its inhabitants have to live elsewhere."

But the teaching goes on, and hopefully the communication. Some students drink from the fountain of knowledge while, unfortunately others just gargle. For example, the teacher asked, "Where's your pencil, Herschel?"

"I ain't got no pencil."

"How many times have I told you not to say that? Now listen. I haven't got a pencil. We haven't got a pencil. They haven't got a pencil . . . " explained the teacher.

Herschel said, "Gosh, they ain't nobody got no pencils?"

Another example of a lack in communication happened when the English teacher was trying to break her class of the "I seen" habit.

"You should never say 'I seen him do it.'" she sternly admonished.

"Yeah," piped up a voice from the rear." "'Specially if you ain't sure he done it."

Even though the teacher-student communication may sometimes be lacking, one teacher was given a good chuckle while grading a young student's paper. The small boy wrote about what he had learned about the human body:

"Our body is divided into three parts, the branium, the borax, and the abominable cavity. The branium contains the brain, if any. The borax contains the lungs, lights, and heart. The abominable cavity contains five bowels—a,e,i,o, and u."

Reminds me of my own teaching days of college freshman. At an 8 A.M. class, first day of a new semester, I faced a room full of blurry-eyed students still drowsy. Enthusiasm was below sea level. One boy had his arms folded, no books, pencil or paper, and his hair looked like an explosion in a mattress. With all the excitement I could muster in my voice, I looked him in the eye and asked, "What do you expect to get out of this Agriculture course?"

He kept his head down, lifting only his eyes, and mumbled, "Me? I'm just killing time in this course until I get accepted in medical school."

BUMPY STEAKS, RC COLA, AND MOON PIE

You can always tell when a man starts losing his mind. He'll get that far away look in his eye, put on a slight grin and start talking about "the good old days." Kent Hill and I were swapping lies recently and I was gaining ground until he changed tactics and started to play dirty by telling the truth . . . about the good old days.

"I used to make a meal out of bumpy steaks, RC colas and a Moon Pie," he mumbled as his eyes glassed over.

I soon learned that a "bumpy steak" was a local term for a round, semi-flat piece of reddish hard candy in which peanuts had been added. It resembles the end of a gallon bucket in size and is just about as hard.

When Hill was very young, before he took the oath of poverty and entered the insurance business, he and a couple of buddies went camping down under a railroad bridge on the creek. They were all sixth graders so they took along survival gear, a tent, a big, mean, black dog, the kind that snarled in his sleep, a case each of moon pies and RC colas, and lots of bumpy steaks.

"We'll be safe as can be with 'Killer' standing guard outside," bragged one of the kids.

Well, it took most of the daylight hours to follow instructions and erect the tent. By then, it was growing dark. "We oughta go catch some fish to eat," cried one. "Yuck, I'd rather eat a snake," yelled another.

"Snake, where?"

Working up a good case of nerves, the boys were on the alert for danger. Old Killer was outside barking a challenge into the thick wilderness, frothing at the mouth, a hundred pounds of savage fury ready to unleash his flashing fangs in defense of his masters inside.

Then they heard it. Some say it was a panther's scream, others described it as satanic. Whatever it was, it growled its high pitched, mournful sound uncomfortably close to the boy's headquarters. Just then the tent flap that covered the opening exploded and through it came a hundred pounds of savage beast. It was old Killer with his tail between his legs, whimpering like a pup.

In the midst of this dangerous scenario, some older boys came along and were quickly invited in to dine. "They ate every bumpy steak we had but we didn't care. We broke camp and followed them back to town."

"Ever find out what the wild critter was?"

"Yeh, it was Delbert Smith. He used to come out there and sit on the railroad bridge and try to play his father's old army bugle."

DISCIPLINE IN MODERATION

The administrators for the school system of Oklahoma were once schoolteachers before they quit working for a living and got paid to think. Now they manage things, but they still look back on how it used to be.

An old seasoned veteran got that glassy look in his eye when he started his story about the "good old days." I've seen that same stare on a foundered heifer who has just been given a dose of kerosene.

"My first job was in a little town in Arkansas. The place was so small that the light company was a Sears Die-Hard. I was hired by the board to teach in a one room schoolhouse, all grades. They told me that nobody had ever finished the school year for them, so I knew it must be a discipline problem. I got down there early the next morning and wrote the rules on the blackboard:

"No talking."

"No chewing gum."

"No backtalk."

"No sleeping."

"No strange noises."

"Homework will be completed on time."

"Punishment for breaking these rules will be swift and severe."

"The first student to enter was almost seven feet tall. He had a three day beard, an old black hat, mud all over his shoes, a squirrel in one hand, and a shotgun in the other. He laid the gun under his desk, bumped his knees under the inkwell, and bit off a chew of tobacco.

"The second student was about 13, married, pregnant, barefoot, hair that looked like the Wicked Witch of the east, and dipped snuff.

"Before the rest of the class got there to swell the total enrollment to six, I quietly erased the board and put up three rules that have served me well in every situation to date:

"Spit only through a crack in the floor."

"Check your weapons at the door."

"Never clean your game in the middle of the trail."

Then he gave us a grin that looked like a sun crack in a pie melon, developed that glassy stare, and compared his philosophy to Socrates, Plato, and Pliny the Elder.

BIRTH AND OTHER FABLES

California has a sex expert who says that parents should not tell children "birds and bees" stories to explain where they came from. I agree. In this modern age, it's time for space age fables to hide the mysteries of life from eager young minds that would turn this knowledge into evil deeds of daring-do.

So, I thought up some new parables just in case I was approached by one of the cunning little devils out on the prowl to pry information from the rock of wisdom. My stock answers to the question "Where did I come from?" include the following:

"We sent off to NASA for a milligram of moonlight, a quart of rocket fuel and a ton of patience. After nine months the computer exploded and there you were. The computer had you, your brother, and a nervous breakdown."

"We were too poor to have children so you were made in Japan at an air force base. The details are top secret and will be shown to you in a film upon entering military service."

"The planet Taurus orbited the planet Virgo, with great gusto. The halos turned to jello and you were delivered by Dr. No No in a Christian ceremony sponsored by Blue Cross."

"A laser beam from outer space accidentally burned a hole into heaven and this little angel slid down on a ray of sunshine right into our hearts. You've given us heartburn ever since."

Things have sure changed. When I was a kid, if you asked an adult to tell you about the birds and bees the answer was a rap in the mouth, a ruler across the knuckles, and a paddle across the rear. That's the reason people used to get married so late in life. Who wants to go through all that just to get your honey and a nest egg through the birds and bees? Besides, just when you are looking forward to paying back the next generation for asking those questions, the answers change.

SCHOOL OF HIGHER LEARNING

Ah, yes. Graduation Day. I remember it well. We celebrated ours by going out to the local drive-in cafe (popular in the good old days) and splurged by ordering a round of root beer for everybody in the truck. There were a lot of others "on" the truck, but they had to buy their own.

Then we'd whistle and act obnoxious when the car hops would come out, wearing their shorts, to hang a tray on the door. Hank Williams was singing "Your Cheatin' Heart" over the loudspeakers, the night was sultry and dry, the stars were brilliant in the sky, a faint haze of burned hamburger grease hung over the parking lot.

Off in the distance, someone could be heard spinning the tires of his father's car on loose gravel. "Herbie," remarked one of our class. "Rich kids get all the breaks," said another. They were talking about Herbie. His father was in oil and gas. He owned a filling station.

"The world is an oyster," said Bill, our class philosopher. We never understood Bill but we all nodded and acted pensive. We had learned to do that. Bill was a genius. He took a test in school somewhere once and carried a card in his billfold that proved he was a genius.

That was over 30 years ago. Today, Bill has a Ph.D. and teaches at a major university in England. Every day he gets to wear a black robe and mutter strange words like "Lasers are the undergarments of the universe." Herbie, poor dumb slob, is president of an oil company. He xeroxed Bill's card and now has his own credentials of genius.

You never know what will happen after graduation. Like this red-headed, long haired kid who graduated the other night at the top of his class. Someone asked his father if he was impressed. He replied, "I sure am. I never would have thought it possible to get an Afro inside that little cap."

LIKE IT WAS

One day not long ago it dawned on me. Summer is finally over. The great school recess has ended and only the callous of heart does not recall with tender fondness the experience of romance and adventure—like poison ivy, broken bones, teeth knocked out, blistered feet, sunburn, snakebite, and saddle sores. Now it's just a memory but like Brigadoon it magically reappears in the foggy mist of an August imagination.

We went to school in another time: twilight. Our county consisted of 87 percent Mexican-Americans. However, we never had any integration problems because the Mexicans were big enough to let us go to school with them from the very start. And bussing was never a problem for a simple reason—No bus.

Things were a lot more simple in those days. The school cafeteria had a special gourmet table filled with such exotic treats as peanut butter and Velvetta cheese. All our silverware came from government surplus, stamped with USN on the heavy handles. We were told that USN was a special unisex monogram. Instead of HIS and HERS, we had US'N. Everytime our English teacher, Miss Prentice Prude, overheard the tale she would roll her eyes upward, purse her lips and mutter, "Crude."

Now the schools even have their own nurse who can do little minor surgery chores, like heart transplants, etc. Our nurse was the principal. If we cut our foot, for instance, he just made us soak it in kerosene and told us not to smoke for a few days.

Things sure have changed. A friend of mine said he was offered a job with a school system that would allow him adventure, excitement, and challenge. But he turned it down. He said he just didn't want to head up a SWAT team at recess.

If teachers and administrators show mercy and justice walking arm in arm with discipline, students learn quickly from a course that cannot be taught. It must be lived: Law and Order. Students must respect the system and those who supervise it. Some bad eggs are on both sides.

You can't point an accusing finger at someone without having three fingers pointing back at yourself. Maybe we all need to think about it at recess.

SCHOOL FOR THE BORED

As each summer period draws to a close school boards brace themselves for another season.

While a guest of the Pennsylvania School Board Assoc., I was privileged to see the first school board association in the nation (1895) spring into action.

Nick Goble, their public relations man, says the main problem stems from the fact that the typical student has changed. For example, the boys are now 6 feet 4 inches, 220 pounds, sleep 10 hours a night, get up five minutes before time to leave the house, polish off a box of Wheaties and a quart of milk, stretch, yawn and report, "I'm tired."

However, the youngsters are bright. There's no denying that. Nick's son asked what he did at the office. Nick said, "Nothin'." The son asked, "How do you know when you're done?"

The boy brought a note home from a teacher that read, "All this student thinks about is girls."

Mrs. Goble wrote back, "I have the same trouble with his father."

Problems, of course, are not confined to the student. The administration and teachers are constantly changing. Old superintendents never die, they just change their principals; old principals never die, they just lose their faculties; and do you know what it takes to be a counselor in this atomic age? It takes years and years and years of education and three losing seasons as a football coach.

Education is like the radical who tried to blow up a school bus but gave it up because he burned his lips on the tail pipe. It's a hot issue and the school board members catch a lot of flack whatever they do. But even though they are non-paid workers, they do a great job. When, and if, they give it up we become like the nun who was seen buying flight insurance at the airport: no faith in local control.

Pennsylvania started the whole thing, and now dedicated school board members across the nation are asking themselves the same penetrating question, "How long is it until next summer?"

DEPTHS OF HIGHER LEARNING

Lots of young people are going through the agony of selecting a college to attend in order to stave off going to work. It's a tough time for everybody concerned. The kids want to be free and independent. They expect only minor support from home . . . like tuition, books, lodging, meals, and an unlimited amount of spending money.

One disgruntled parent remarked, "He goes around bragging 'I did it my way'." Then he added, "How can that be? He doesn't even have a way." The mother replies, "Well, at least he went away."

All this causes a tremendous strain on the family budget. Inflation has become so rampant on the college campuses nowadays that this fairy tale really should start out "twice upon a time."

"We've been able to cope with the situation fairly well though," remarked one friend of mine. "In spite of all the conflicts we've had in the family over sending our boy to college, we've never once had what the police called a real fight."

"We'll sure miss him though," remarks the mother. "It's going to seem strange to have instant hot water again. Just the other day he came in, took a two-hour hot shower and when I asked him where he was going, he said swimming." Things like that really tug at your heart.

Maybe an education will do the kids, as well as the parents, a lot of good. For instance, one college freshman I know about was taking an entrance exam. In the Knowledge of World Events section, he was asked to define Yasser Arafat. His answer: "That's the sound made when my daddy takes off off his pants." I know his daddy and the kid makes sense to me.

On the other hand, the parents are not as smart as you might expect. An acquaintance of mine said he bought his son a new suit and tie and personally took him to the local university to look over the facilities there. A sign on the student union building was posted at the door: "No shorts allowed inside." He said, "I didn't want our son to start off on the wrong foot with the university officials, so I had the boy to step over behind the bushes and take his off."

Yes, an education is wonderful . . . ain't it?

EDUCATION—IN A WORD

In Louisville I made the acquaintance of a college student at a dinner theater. He was waiting on tables and I was waiting on service. "I'm sorry, sir," he apologized, "but I'm not cut out to be a waiter. I'm a college student and I've just had to change my major. You see, I was studying to be a priest but I flunked advanced bingo and off track betting." He told me he was getting into international communications. That led to some interesting discoveries for me.

Did you know that 386 million people speak English, 863 million speak Chinese, but 305 million speak Urdu? And Lord knows how many talk Tagalong, Turkish, or Trash.

Translations are important. Remember when the President had his speech translated from "desires of the Polish people" to "lusts . . . ?"

A large computer company lost millions when it had to reprint the instruction manuals for "software" translation errors. The manual called for the operator to insert his underwear in the computer.

The Chevrolet Nova failed miserably in Latin America because in Spanish "no va" means "it doesn't go."

The Arabian oilfield workers were terribly confused by instructions about "wet sheep." Turned out to be "hydraulic rams." A swank French hotel advertised "tea in a bag just like mother" and their beef broth became "the finest brothel of cows in Paris."

Makes sense that international communication would be complicated. We don't even understand all of our own words. I think that's mostly because we borrowed them from some other language. I know folks who think "canape" is the awning over the front of a cafe, a crouton is one ton of crou, and Creole is an old Cre.

Just imagine a foreigner who's told he's going to be fed catfish stew. He visualized one cat, one fish . . . and then is offered some hush puppies . . . and he's wearing a pair.

Even our own people have these difficulties. I went to a swank party with a local friend and we munched on the customary goodies at the cocktail hour. "Never had such tiny food in my life. What was it?" he asked. "Hors d'oeuvres," I replied.

"How do you spell that?" he asked. I told him.

After a long silence, he said, "What a dumb name for little bitty sandwiches."

RULES OF THUMB

In 1872 a list of rules for teachers was printed and posted in the faculty lounge for all to note. It basically said that teachers were expected to open up, sweep out, and clean up the building along with the kids' minds. They were allowed one evening per week for courting and expected to read the Bible for the remainder.

A woman teacher who married or engaged in unseemly conduct was to be dismissed. Any teacher caught drinking, smoking, or getting a shave in a barber shop had "given good reason to suspect his worth, integrity, and honesty." Each teacher was expected to save for his own retirement so as not to be a burden on society, and after five years service without fault could expect a 25 cent per week increase in pay, providing the board of education approved.

Since I haven't seen a modern or old list of rules for ranchers I decided to take care of this overlooked segment of society and compare them to teachers, which is almost like using a human comparison.

RULES FOR RANCHERS

1. Ranchers will start each day by getting up, even when they haven't been to bed.

2. Only beans may be consumed by ranchers. Beef and lamb are reserved for coyotes and the government, neither of whom have ever known beans.

3. Men are allowed one evening per week for courting purposes, depending on which court and the seriousness of the charge.

4. Any rancher caught drinking, smoking, or playing pool will probably be caught by a neighbor who had the same idea.

5. The "Good Book" shall be studied regularly to open both eyes. The check book shall be scanned with only one eye. Prayer shall fill the void of switching from one to the other.

6. A Cadillac pickup will be considered in poor taste during times of drouth even though a gun rack and leopard dog are permanent fixtures.

7. The rancher is expected to set aside a goodly sum of his income for retirement purposes in the unlikely event that he lives past 40.

8. After five years of faithful service without fault, the rancher may expect the same increase in salary afforded teachers, 25 cents per week.

9. Above all, ranchers will abide by the golden rule, "Those who have the gold make the rules."

That's the gospel according to Matthew, Mark, Luke, and Fort Knox.

VALUE SYSTEMS VARY

Most students are so smart that they don't need to go but attend classes anyway, just to give their elders a challenge.

One of the more popular T-shirts around some of the school systems reads "I can't read . . . what are you gonna do about it?"

English teachers love those kinds of messages. One English teacher I know had a sense of humor about that message. She said it wasn't necessary for everyone to read or be understanding. Somebody has to be in the administration.

Administrators and teachers form a fine team. Teamwork has always been important in education. Think of the great teams of the past. Teams like Abbott and Costello, Martin and Lewis, coaches and assistants . . . , and other great clowns.

When I was a kid, we had a principal that we nicknamed "The Cat." This guy could sneak up on you quicker than a balloon note on a home mortgage.

The thing about it was that he never seemed to be around until we decided to do something that we shouldn't. We never heard his footsteps, but "The Cat" was always there at the precise moment that we broke the rules. He was so good at his job that rumor had it that his annual checkup was done by a veterinarian.

"The Cat" always punished us with a stern lecture. Every so often during this lecture, he would throw in a "fear word" that would get our attention. His favorite "fear words" were things like "hardened criminal," "guillotine," and "firing squad."

When you drifted off from his lecture, those "fear words" had a way of bringing you back quickly.

The standard joke among us students was that there was a new doll on the market called "the principal doll." You turn it on and its brain runs down in three minutes. And it can never be replaced.

Education has sure changed. We have so many modern devices now that the old "teamwork tactics" of administrators and teachers no longer works. A teacher assigned some of her students to watch an eclipse of the moon last year and the standard question about the assignment was "What channel is it on?"

The kids going to school today, however, are exposed to lots of new ideas. Some of them may even listen if it is first run through a computer. As one kid explained, "Economics is the study of handling money. It's like money is my allowance and one of the things I want is Pac-Man."

You have to admit though that our young folks today are full of energy. Nearly every morning you'll find young people up at 5 A.M. opening wide their bedroom windows . . . , and crawling in.

Don't sell them short, though. It may not seem like they are paying attention, but just try discussing the facts of life with your teenager. You'll probably learn some things you didn't know.

It seems that the generations just judge things differently. The teamwork of teachers, parents, and students can be a meaningful one. And sometimes the hard core cases turn out surprisingly well. For instance, the valedictorian of my high school class could spell anything in seven different languages, diagram a sentence to the last dangling participle, write like Shakespeare, and speak like William Jennings Bryan. He married the salutatorian and they had three kids that were dumb as a box of rocks.

It just goes to show that there is equal opportunity in this country. We can be just as dumb as we make up our minds to be.

The generations just have a different value system when it comes to education. For instance, grown-ups judge the value of music by the tone, intricacy of the movements, and the mood it creates. Teenagers judge the value of a musical recording by how many neighbors call the police. At any rate, it's back to school and we're just gonna have to dance to the music. If you think that's easy, you ought to try some of the new steps.

REUNION TALES

My old friend David Bade dropped by the other day and reminded me of the adage, "Reunions are a way of getting people together to see who is falling apart."

David says full-scale family reunions are especially interesting because of the conversations you overhear:

"Haven't you lost a lot of weight?"

"Yes, I did it on the highway patrol plan. They made me buy a bicycle."

"So your daughter is getting married. Is he a nice boy?"

"He's okay, but I still get the feeling that it's like handing over a $250,000 Stradivarius to a gorilla."

"Gosh, there are a lot of people here. I never knew we had so many relatives. Have we met? Oh, I didn't recognize you because of the barbeque sauce, Mother."

"Did you hear that Fred died?"

"How could you tell?"

"Why did you get fired from your job?"

"The boss was always early when I was late and late when I was early."

"You look great, Frieda. When did you start watching your figure?"

"The moment I realized men had stopped watching it."

"Are you interested in researching our family tree, old timer?"

"Listen, sonny. There are two ways of learning about the family tree. You can climb all over it or you can sit on an acorn, watch and wait."

"How did you and the family come down? Did you fly?"

"No, we drove. Henry says if God had really meant for man to fly, He would have made it a lot easier to get to the airport."

"Why didn't Charlie come to the reunion?"

"He wanted to but he started cleaning out the attic before we left and you know Charlie. This was his last chance and he loves to read."

A fellow can also pick up a lot of philosophy at the family reunion. Probably the best advice came from a sage who was asked for the secret of his considerable financial success. He said, "Get all you can. Can it. Then, sit on the cans."

MIRTHS AND MYTHS

High school reunions should be guarded against like the measles. When you get the fever, better have your face examined . . . and your head. Especially the 30 year reunions. All those beautiful myths are better left in the twilight zone.

The little five foot nine inch, 120 pound athlete who broke the school record for the 100 yard dash weighs in at 250 and is still five foot nine—lying down or standing up.

What ever happened to the valedictorian? She runs a combination bait camp and wrecker service and has a paper route on the side. She sure looks odd in an evening dress and tennis shoes. But then the prom is to be held on the floor of the high school gym. That's our valedictorian all right, always thinking.

The Homecoming Queen of 30 years past now has a body that's in such bad shape she has to wear corrective body stockings, but that scrawny girl that specialized in spelling bees and debate because boys shunned her like the plague is a Grandmother that looks like Marlene Dietrich.

The class dunce has shaped up—like the Goodyear blimp. However, he's the only millionaire because he was so dumb. He bought 40 acres of worthless salt marsh land which is now Miami Beach. He's big in real estate and everything else, including swim trunks. He's so big they put sun tan lotion on him with a mop.

Time changes everything, but some things are best left as beautiful memories unless you can grow gradually with the changes. It's like one disappointed fellow said at the 30 year reunion, "I never saw so many old faces and new teeth."

HOME SHOTS 5

My brother was an only child.

FAMILY

Alex Haley wrote a famous book called *Roots*. He traced his ancestry back several hundred years to Africa. I've been thinking about writing the Blakely family history and publishing a book. It would be called *Weeds*. It would trace our family history all the way back to last Tuesday. That's about as far as we would want to go if we have to publish the facts.

Milton Blakely, my great, great grandfather was a medical doctor who came to this country from Scotland in the early 1800's. My great, great grandfather was also an old Indian fighter. My great, great grandmother was an old Indian.

In my bloodlines, there are traces of not only my Scottish foundation heritage, but also German, English, Irish, French, and several infusions of Choctaw Indian. History records that many of my ancestors with the Blakely name and the Indian blood were driven out of Alabama on the "Trail of Tears" to what was then called Indian Territory. That territory later became the State of Oklahoma and that's the reason I was born in Rush Springs, Oklahoma. Well, that's not actually the reason why I was born there. I was very young at the time and wanted to be close to my mother.

Apparently as soon as my parents found out where they were, they moved to Texas. I was less than a year old when this relocation took place. The family joke is that all of us left Oklahoma in a covered wagon. And when you look at some of the family photographs from that period, you understand why the wagon was covered.

Growing up in Duval County, Texas, was a unique experience for any family. Ours was no exception. The country is semi-arid, filled with mesquite, prickly pear, thorns, grass burrs, catclaw, rattlesnakes, and rednecks. The saying was that there was nothing there that wouldn't kick, bite, or stick you. But enough about my family.

After marrying my childhood sweetheart, Pat, we settled down to have our own family, which in itself is a novel approach in today's society. We decided the ideal number of children would be three. First came son Perry, two years later, Mike. Then I read that every third child born in the world is Chinese so we stopped at two. I rationalized like the old line, "Somewhere in China, there is a woman giving birth to a child every three minutes. What we've got to do is find her and stop her."

She must be exhausted.

It's really interesting how family traits seem to be handed down generation after generation. For instance, when I was drafted into the U.S. Army, they gave me a battery of tests to determine what I was ideally suited for in the military. I became a helicopter mechanic. Twenty years later, son Mike entered the U.S. Air Force, took a battery of tests and was told that he was ideally suited to become a helicopter mechanic. My father, now in his 80's, said it was obviously an inherited characteristic because he used to work on windmills.

Hopefully, the family situations that follow will bring back some happy memories of your own. As my Grandma Adams used to say, "Blood is thicker than water, but don't ever push your luck by calling me collect."

Now, I have grandkids of my own, Eric and Torie, first cousins. It is my duty to instill within them the fun of being family. So we do lots of exciting things together. Recently, when Torie was ten, just the two of us went to the Houston Livestock Show and Rodeo. We saw every exhibit, every head of livestock, two complete rodeo performances in one day, and capped off the evening with about $50 worth of rides on the midway. We were flung around, spun upside down, slid down scary things, went through the horror house, screamed, and generally had a wonderful time. You know how it is when you can take a kid along so you can have an excuse to become one yourself. It was past midnight and we were on our way to the car, eating cotton candy. She reached up and took my hand. She said, "I really had a great time, PaPa. I'm glad you are my grandfather. Of course, I'll grow older and grow up." She paused a moment and then added, "You'll grow older, too . . . but you'll never grow up."

In the background, the music from the carnival was blaring out the tune "We are Family." That song may also ring out a familiar tune as you read about the family experiences in this chapter.

MID-LIFE "CRAZIES"

If you haven't experienced the mid-life "crazies", you should feel fortunate according to a recent report I read which was written by a prominent 25-year-old psychiatrist.

It seems that we are all supposed to go nuts somewhere past 40. They call it "the change of life" for women and "mid-life crisis" for men. In common language, some men and women get sick of each other about the same time.

For example, my brother-in-law and I were visiting at his lakehouse when he suddenly grabbed an ice chest and put it up and out of the way. "My wife hates for anyone to sit on this . . . and I was the one just sitting on it."

Because of this kind of conflict, more marriage counselors are being used. I have this story on good authority as being true. This insensitive male chauvinist pig married this sweet, charming, young thing of radiant beauty. Everything went well until the "crazies" set in about 20 years later.

The counselor heard their story and saw right through to the heart of their problem. He told this slob that his wife was starved for attention. With startling speed, the counselor grabbed the now overweight matron, pulled her close, kissed her passionately, and whispered in her ear.

"Now," said the shrink, "that's the problem. She needs attention like that at least three times per week. Do you get what I mean?"

With a wink of his eye, the husband replied, "I'll go along with anything you say, Doc. I can bring her in on Monday and Wednesday, but on Friday, she'll have to ride the bus 'cause I play golf."

MOM, DAD, SISTER, AND OH BROTHER

The family is an interesting organization. Most of them start out by someone being born of a mother and father. That is all there is to it. If that happened to you, then you've got one. If that didn't happen to you, then let me know because we need to write a book.

The average family in America consists of a mother, father, and 1.9 children. For purposes of illustration, I'll round that off to two children, and to make it a realistic situation with creative family strife and stress, I'll make the children one boy, one girl, and both teenagers.

Now for the typical family day. Alarm goes off and mother gets up to start breakfast. Father staggers to bathroom. Son's alarm goes off . . . and off . . . and dies of metal fatigue.

Daughter locks self in other bathroom. Mother complains that breakfast is getting cold. Breakfast is cold cereal. Family conversation consists of mother talking to children, children talking to ceiling, and father talking to self, arguing with self . . . and losing argument.

Father goes to work, children go to school, and mother goes to her knees to give thanks that they are gone. As she gets ready also to go to work, discovers that daughter has on her only good pair of panty hose. Wears formal evening dress to receptionist job.

Family comes home for an evening of togetherness, children at 4:00, mother at 6:00, father at 7:00. Boy leaves note that he left at 4:05 and will be home by 6:00. Girl has locked herself in bathroom with telephone. Boy calls at 11:00 to say that he will be a little late. Phone busy.

Family waits up for boy. Conference at midnight. Boy's total defense was a constant response of "I couldn't help it." Girl comes out of bathroom periodically to inject, "I told you so." Mother cries, "I try so hard."

Father takes over as head of family, wisely and patiently yells, "Go to . . . bed." Another evening of fun and merriment ends with lights out promptly at 1:00 A.M.

Yes, FAMILY. Characterized by father who leaps tall buildings with a single bound. Mother who must get running start to leap over tall buildings, son who crashes into tall buildings while attempting to leap over them, and daughter who doesn't recognize buildings at all . . . unless they are shaped like a telephone.

AND NOW THIS

Just before the ball game came on TV recently, I saw so many commercials aimed at adults, kids, newlyweds, older people, health, and a zillion other things, that the following notations were made:

We're all ashamed of our tattletale gray and the rings around our collars, but that's what comes from doing the laundry in the backyard with a water hose.

Just think, if you follow the advice of the health experts and put on a clean pair of socks each morning, by the end of a week, you won't be able to get your shoes on.

I know a guy who retired from civil service after 40 years. As a kind of surprise, the government gave him a retirement banquet and told him what his job had been.

Everything's so informal now. We just received a young couple's wedding invitation. It was stuck under our windshield wiper at the shopping center.

Love is a three-ring circus: Engagement ring, wedding ring, and suffering.

How about that new order called "Marriage Anonymous." When a member feels like getting married, they send over a woman with no makeup and her hair in curlers.

This fellow told a girl that if she didn't marry him, he'd die. Sure enough, 67 years later, he died.

"There must be something to reincarnation," the man said to his wife. "I can't believe I could get this far behind in only one life."

You can't win. My neighbor explained the facts of life to his son with the old birds and bees story. Now the kid thinks he's in love with a woodpecker.

One kindergarten teacher told a five-year-old that he had his shoes on the wrong feet. The boy explained, "But, they are the only feet I have."

The thing a parent doesn't want to hear: "Hey, Mom, did you know it's almost impossible to flush a grapefruit down the toilet?"

Two fathers of teenagers were out walking. One pointed to the other's house and jokingly asked, "I wonder who lives there?" "Nobody," said the other glumly. "They just come and go."

After all the commercials were over, I heard two kids arguing over the words of the National Anthem. One kid got my vote when he ended with "Land of the free and home of the Braves. Play ball!"

THE FAMILY DICTION

Once in a while I come across a word in the English language that I have never heard of and don't understand, so I go to the trusty dictionary to look it up. The dictionary would make very interesting reading except that it changes the subject too often and the plot is absolutely terrible.

The first substantial word is Aardvark (a funny looking animal with a long snout) and the last word is Zymurgy (applied chemistry dealing with fermentation processes, as in brewing). No wonder they have never made a movie from this best selling book; even Walt Disney wouldn't touch a story about a drunken Aardvark.

However, what brought this scholarly presentation to print was a word that ain't in my dictionary: lexicographer.

A man who claims to be one of those says that the 10 most beautiful words in our language are: dawn, hush, lullaby, murmuring, tranquil, mist, luminous, chimes, golden, and melody.

The man who is the expert on beautiful words goes by the name of Wilfred J. Funk. That sounds as unlikely as a pornography expert named Lily White, but Wilfred claims it's true because he is a poet and a lexicographer. Since I can't find out what a lexicographer is I must assume he really is one since it would be more difficult to prove than a politician's real intentions. But, Wilfred, your choice of beautiful words theory is about as appropriate as ugly on a duck around the farm.

There is nothing beautiful about those words when used as answers to questions that come up in rural areas, such as:

"What time do I have to get up this Saturday, Dad?"

"Dawn."

"Elmer, what do you think of women's liberation on the farm?"

"Hush."

"What's your favorite part of your grandkids' visit?"

"Lullaby."

(One grandkid to another), "What's Grandpa doing on the front porch?"

"Murmuring."

Yes, the rural melody from golden chimes shines luminous through the tranquil mist of each hushed dawn as each farmkid murmurs ever so softly the same lullaby:

"Pftttttttttt."

That's not a beautiful word but is expressive, international and doesn't have to be looked up in any dictionary.

THE SCIENCE OF CLUTTER

Some smart aleck is always noticing things around your house, barn, or garage. Some of them even drop little hints to voice their disapproval of your slovenly ways, like "Why don't you apply for disaster aid?"

Now if you happen to like things the way they are, it is important that you be able to explain the advantages of your system to less knowledgeable know-it-alls. In other words, look on the positive side of poor white trash, or whatever color your trash happens to be.

If someone complains that your garage is cluttered tell them that you are training your children to balance on one foot. It will give them confidence to face greater obstacles in later life, like adjusting to marriage.

If the gravel in your driveway has been reduced to pot holes that would swallow a Sherman tank, tell your friends that you are a conservationist. Try to sell them stock in your strip mining operation and assure them that the land will be returned to its original condition (it was a munitions dump before the lightning struck).

If they mention the dirtdobber nests around the eaves of the house just say, "Oh, you mean the kid's science project." Be sure and mention the theory that dirtdobbers prey on the culex mosquito, improving the health of the entire community. They also may be linked with filling in holes in the driveway, which supports your other project.

Peeling paint is the new camouflage experiment that is your patriotic contribution to national defense. Casually mention that enemy agents have likely already marked the traditional homesteads for destruction as a protest against capitalists. The old radios and TV sets in the attic will serve to supply spare parts to the nation's communication network in a national emergency of that nature.

When the kids write things on the side of your dirty automobile, you don't have to explain. Just say, "Free expression is disregarded by all but the intellectual."

However, if the woman of the family just has to keep up appearances, my friend Mary McBride has a solution. Mary says, "Just keep an extra set of drapes, and every two weeks hang them out on the line."

SMELLS SELL

It's amazing how many things are sold around the world by a fragrance.

Lovers are attracted by different scents according to their culture. Rancid butter drives the boys wild when smeared in the hair of an Australian aborigine girl. Many a tribal member has tried to butter up his butter cup to add some aromatic flavor to his romance. The problem is that if you catch one of those girls you can't hold on to her. The girls just hang around upwind from the boys, praying for a sandstorm to improve their chances. That's probably the reason pajama parties never developed in that culture. The girls tried it but they kept sliding out of bed.

American girls try to smell like flowers mostly. We even have girls, named Heather, Rose, Lily, Daisy, etc., that conjure up images of sweet smelling flowers. Perfumes are made from delicate blossoms to sell that image. You seldom hear of products that project the fragrance of ragweed, poison ivy or whale blubber.

How about furniture polish? It has to be lemon scented to signify cleanliness, or have ammonia added to burn your nostrils, indicating strength. You never hear of Prune Pledge with jalepeno juice additives because the only market for it would be retired Spanish teachers.

Few people realize that politics has capitalized on this new nasal science. George Wallace smelled like magnolia blossoms, LBJ like Johnson grass, and Rockefeller like very old money.

No wonder the cattle business is down. You have to smell it to sell it and we should spend more time advertising the fragrant aroma of a prime, aged, juicy, charbroiled steak instead of Corral No. 5.

SPRINGTIME FANCIFUL REFRAIN

About springtime each year a young man's fancy turns to love and his brains to mush. You can see that far away look in his eye as Valentine's Day approaches. I've seen them at the counter stool in the livestock auction cafe, staring into a bowl of grits, when their eyes go out of focus and a grin sweeps across their face like a slow sunrise on a spring day. They have had their eye on a five pound box of heart shaped candy down at the drugstore for the last several days. Since it was left over from last year it is on special and considered a bargain at $1.98 even if the chocolate has begun to crack and flake.

Now if a suitable card can be included. But wait, why not write an original expression of the age old question, "Won't you be my valentine?" Zeno Pfault claims that he won his wife, Lovey, with this lovely piece which he gave me permission to reprint:

My Own Dear Lovey:

I can't refrain from writing you this eulogy no longer. Every time I think of you my heart flops up and down like a churn dasher and chill bumps run over my spine like a young goat over a shingle roof on a woodshed. My heart thrills through and through like pine needles through double knit trousers.

My brain whirls like a bumble bee under a fruit jar. When I see you my eyes stand open like a cellar door, my tongue refuses to wag and it would take a pound of penicillin to cure me of my mad desire. When I look into your eyes I see legions of little cupids like a swarm of fire ants in an old army crocker. When the glance of those eyes first struck me it penetrated my brain like a load of birdshot through a rotten apple.

Away from you, I am as melancholy as a gut shot goose and can hear the june bugs of despondency buzzing in my ears or feel the cold lizard of despair crawling up and down my neck. Uncouth fears like a thousand minnows nibble at my very Soul until I return to your side to gaze into your blue eye and then the brown one. My love for you is stronger than the smell of stale coffee and ripe bananas. So do I long for thee, thee, thee.

If I could win your affection I would be as happy as a possum in a tree of ripe persimmons. If you do not accept my attentions and this expression of undying admiration then I only ask, when you are happy in another love, to come, just once, to look on the last resting place of . . .

Your Own True Love, Zeno.

Zeno said this won Lovey over and they were married. He admits he was too young to marry but, "When you're 59 and in love, what can you do?"

INSTITUTIONAL BEHAVIOR

Love is blind. Marriage is an institution. Therefore, marriage is an institution for the blind. Some might argue that it is an institution for the dumb. It probably wouldn't hurt if we all turned a bit deaf on occasions as well.

A man returning home unusually late was tiptoeing into his bedroom when his wife woke up. "Is that you, John?" she asked sleepily.

"Well," he answered, "it better be."

Then there were the two women who were talking about their husbands. Said one, "I'm more and more convinced that mine married me for my money."

Replied the other, "Then you have the satisfaction of knowing that he's not as stupid as he looks."

You often hear about the husband who is always good to his wife. One woman sighed. "That's my Fred. He never comes home."

The honeymoon is really over when he phones that he'll be late for dinner and she's already left a note that it's in the refrigerator.

You can always tell when you've become an old married couple. That's the day you finally clean out the garage because you lost the lawn mower.

Every couple dreams of owning a home. Quite often the first step is the purchase of a mobile home. The chief advantage of that is that you have a place to live while you're looking for a place to park.

In order to save for that permanent home, you start socking something away for a rainy day. Then something like inflation comes along and the sock shrinks.

One couple I know said they didn't want their standard of living to improve any more. They say they can't afford the standard they have now.

Other couples are forced to put all their money in precious metals . . . braces for the kids.

Couples nowadays skip meals and work two jobs so they can make enough to go out for supper. On an off night, the wife asked her husband, "How do you like the potato salad?"

He said, "Delicious. It tastes like you bought it yourself."

Yes, love is blind. Perhaps a lack of foresight is fortunate because if we all had our lives to live over again, we couldn't afford it.

The one thing young lovers usually don't give much thought to when they marry is children. Of course, kids are great, but you can get an overdose on most anything and nothing makes a man or woman think more seriously of birth control than driving a school bus.

But that's another institution . . . for the study of nervous breakdowns.

FOR BETTER OR WORSE

Marriage is a 50-50 proposition. A fellow from Coleman, Texas, who was taking the guided tour of Brownwood night-life, told me so. His wife told him when they married that if he would make the living for the first 50 years that she would take the next 50. He says he has 90 days to go. She says he only made a half good living and owes her 25 more years before she should start.

"Did you ever argue?" I asked.

"No, he always handled the major decisions and I took the minor ones," she replied.

"Yes," he said, "so far all our decisions have been minor."

He added that his foolish, young head was turned by dazzling beauty early in life, but by then the wedding invitations had already gone out and he decided to save money and marry the one already lined up.

She countered with the statement, "I didn't want to marry him for his money, but it was the only way I could get it. Both dollars."

A marriage proposal can make a guy as nervous as a chicken playing leap frog with a porcupine. Once the move is made your chances are 50-50 of getting stuck with it. That 50-50 proposition has made many a player "chicken out."

EARTH SHATTERING ROMANCE

A friend of mine, who loves to talk, was planning his daughter's wedding. He made the whole group a nervous wreck. During practice the preacher would ask, "Who gives this bride to be married?" Instead of saying, "Her Mother and I do," he would launch into something like, "Well, her Mother and I have been talking about this . . ." They didn't even dare mention the part about "Speak now or forever hold your peace."

So, to try to get the newlyweds off to some peace and quiet, a honeymoon was arranged in Guatemala. They had an earthquake on their wedding night. Although damage was light it was the topic of conversation the next morning. The newlyweds were bragging that they were the first ones out in the hall when the quake hit.

"No you weren't," said an older fellow, "I was next door to you and I was the first one out."

"Oh, no!" blushed the young couple as they excused themselves from the conversation.

The electricity was knocked out, so the bride bought candles and placed them around in the most romantic places. It depressed the groom. He said it made him feel like he was going to bed in a cathedral.

When they returned home to settle down to normal routines they had thrilling stories to tell of an earth shattering romance.

It brings to mind the thought that many a new bride has had on her wedding night: "I'm a little nervous but I'm awfully glad to be here."

A GIFT OF COMPASSION

Christmas is that time of year when people go shopping for things they can't afford to give to people who don't deserve them so they can get something in return that they won't appreciate in order to show that their own heart is full of love.

It's amazing how this spirit of Christian compassion changes the attitudes of so many people that you begin to wonder about their birth records. They can't remember, either, if they were born in a hospital or a manger:

"I'd like to buy a present for the sweetest woman in the world." Translation: "I just spotted a big box under the tree that looks like those duck decoys I threw a fit over not getting last year."

"My husband is such an angel I wanted to buy him something special." Translation: "But one more crack about my mother and he's going to be an angel."

"I'm looking for a present for the man I love." Translation: "I hope my husband doesn't find out about this."

"Can you help me with a gift selection for that special someone in my life?" Translation: "Lucky for me that the boys at the pool hall reminded me that this was Christmas eve."

"That does seem a bit high, but I guess he's worth it." Translation: "Not bad for a purple suit, even if it is used."

"We always open our presents on Christmas eve because the children are so excited." Translation: "We used to open them the next morning until the little devils caught Henry in a bear trap and mugged him in his Santa Claus suit."

Yes, it gives you a warm feeling in the cockles of your heart and warm cockles are very soothing. I have it on good authority, Zeno Pfault, who married a widow with two preschool children, sat up last Christmas eve putting toys together until the wee hours, while his new bride read directions to him. When he had finished he pulled her close to him and said, "Now tell me those three little words that will set my soul on fire."

She gently whispered in his ear, "Batteries not included."

FOR EVERY PLUS THERE IS A MINUS

Opposites attract. That explains why you are so perfect and your spouse is such a louse.

A man who is tall enough to hunt geese with a tennis racket marries a woman who in high heels can't reach past 3 on the elevator buttons.

Remember that sloppy dresser that won't shave, is overweight, and never puts the lids on anything? Don't be chicken, the best policy is to be straight forward and have a heart to heart talk with her.

Make sure it is a nice talk. Be kind. Be gentle. And wear your old army dog tags so they won't have to waste precious time searching for your blood type.

The real source of conflict in the home is the desire by one type of human to live in a neat, orderly environment devoid of bacteria, unless they are stored in containers and filed alphabetically. The counterpart of this type is most happy when living in the immediate aftermath of a boiler explosion.

If you want to find out who has the "Felix Complex" among your friends, sneak a peak at the His and Hers towels in the bathroom. Then comment that disease is transmitted through towel racks. Watch for anyone entering the bathroom wearing a surgical mask.

A friend of mine keeps everything in the original box, stored and labeled. His wife keeps everything in a box too, but it's never the box in which the thing came, never the right size and always labeled wrong. What drives him crazy is she knows exactly where to find all her stuff.

Take the case of where to squeeze the toothpaste. She squeezes the tube neatly from one end rolling it up as it is used. He treats it like the guys on the commercial for Lite beer.

She has her shoes polished and placed in a line that would pass military inspection. He uses fishing cord for shoe laces.

Her clothes are hung on specially formed hangers. His are hung too, usually on a nail . . . on the way back from the garage.

Her motto is "A place for everything and everything in its place." He agrees and thinks the place is on the floor.

So why do opposites attract? Why does one partner have the "Felix Complex" and the other is a walking pig pen?

I was going to tell you, but my wife just told me to stop what I was doing and clean off my desk.

I wanted to, but I couldn't find a rake.

THE GRAYING OF AMERICA

I read an interesting statistic the other day. By the year 2000, more than 50 percent of the population will be "senior citizens." Even that may be a conservative estimate, because statistics show that ¾ of all women are secretive about their age. The other fourth lie about it.

I don't know what it takes to be considered a senior citizen, but I do know what it takes to start feeling like one. It's okay to think like a young person, but try acting like one and you get old in a hurry.

Everytime I go to Hot Springs, Ark., I see a lot of people hobbling around, walking with a cane, drinking hot water out of a bottle the size of a milk churn, and wonder what's wrong with their digestive system. Watching them slosh off down the street reminds me of a machine. The Maytag.

In the grand old Arlington Hotel, I overheard a lady shuffling down the hall in bathrobe, slippers, and mudpack, discussing her "treatment" with her masseur. The consultant said, "Why, a few weeks of that and you'll be 10 years younger."

She wailed, "Oh, dear, it won't affect my pension, will it?"

There was this elderly widower getting a pep talk from the sales staff. He was told, "This will ease your aches and pains, make a man out of you, and women will find you irresistible. I defy you to improve on a situation like that."

The old gent muttered, "I don't want to improve on it. I just want to get in on it."

All this physical fitness and youth oriented activity might be dangerous to your health, but fortunately some of the senior citizens are using their heads. A friend of mine told me, "Times are sure gettin' hard. Pinto beans are 90 cents a pound, the government has stopped giving away cheese, and the fish won't bite. If things get any worse, I'm gonna have to line up a few more lawns for my wife to mow."

I said, "Oh, stop joking around. You heard that old saying that life begins at 40, haven't you?"

He said, "Begins to whut?"

He's got a point, which reminds me of another saying. "Young people sow oats and old people grow sage."

My Uncle Fred says he doesn't know about women, but he insists that men and whiskey improve with age. "The older I get the more I like it," he says.

A friend of mine was telling me of an incident that happened recently when she and her husband were flying to California. She was looking down over the Sierra Nevada Range and thinking about how tough it would have been during the Gold Rush days.

She said, "John, I'm glad we didn't live during those times. I know you. When you heard there was gold in California, you would have packed us up in a wagon and headed for the gold fields. We would have encountered Indian attacks, drouth, and famine. I would have had to bury all those babies, like they did in the Old West, nurse your wounds, and fight off Indians and starvation all at the same time. I don't think I could have done it."

He replied, "Honey, after raising kids and grandkids with you, I know you pretty well, too. You would have buried those babies, you would have buried me, you would have beat hell out of the Indians, eaten the horse, and pushed the wagon to California."

All this just goes to prove that there's no fool like an old fool. If you don't believe that, just ask any young fool.

INTELLECTUAL PURSUITS

So here we go again. What goes around comes around . . . the common cold, flu, and college classes.

A young friend of mine enrolled in this large university as a freshman. He phoned home to tell about his first day.

"How was your first class?" asked his father.

"I didn't go, Dad," he replied.

"Why not, Son?"

"I couldn't find the building."

"What was the class you missed?"

"Orientation."

"What are you supposed to learn in orientation?"

"How to find the buildings."

Then he talked to his sister who had graduated from the same college the year before and really knew the ropes. "You didn't let them sell you on those sucker plans, did you?"

"Oh, no," he replied, "I just bought tickets to all the games, a parking sticker, and the 7-day cafeteria meal plan."

"You did what?" screamed his sister. "Never a night out, a weekend off campus, or holiday meals at home? Why would you choose three meals a day for seven days a week?"

There was this long pause and then he replied, "Sis, I have to eat three times a day."

After the phone conversation, his sister remarked to her parents, "Remember the modern art painting we saw on campus with all those strange monsters and creatures in them? Do you know what they are?"

"What?" asked her parents.

"Freshmen."

Ah, yes, I remember those days well. We wore a beanie, got hazed by the upper classmen and were scared stiff of courses like chemistry. Things have changed. One kid I know is doing research to develop a squash that grows in the shape of a puck for vegetarian hockey players.

They spend their summers working on government projects trying to determine why some Canadian elk took a wrong turn at Little Rabbit, Alaska, during migration season.

We played intramural contact sports like wrestling. I gave it up when the girls learned karate.

What do they do now? Marathon leap frog contests. I recently read that Yale University fielded a team that soundly defeated the Absecom nursing home.

Nearly everybody is back in college, but my neighbor's kid had a close call. He was late enrolling due to injuries received in a failed attempt to take over beer stand #3 at a Willie Nelson concert.

FOUR SCORE AND LITTLE MORE

As some philosopher once said, "If I had known I'd live this long I would have taken better care of myself." This fact is demonstrated over and over again every time I attend one of those 40th birthday parties. There are the usual presents wrapped in black, birthday prune cake, and a volunteer fireman poised with fire extinguisher to put out the candles.

Presents include shawls, walking canes, Exlax, Geritol, liniment, hearing aids, magnifying glass, false teeth, vitamin pills, and a subscription to Arizona Highways (special issue on Sun City).

"How do you know you're over the hill?" asks the written question on the outside of a card. On the inside it reads, "When everything is worn out . . . and what isn't worn out, won't work."

Some of the over-40 girls still have appeal, though. Younger fellows would throw their room keys. These people were tossing Polident. Wild applause of appreciation was created by slapping their Social Security cards together. It was the first time I'd ever seen a "crouching ovation."

So what is so bad about getting old? You just have to deal with a few extra problems, that's all. Like tripping over the loose skin under your neck, or philosophers using your face for proof that man descended from roadmaps. So you are living examples that gravity exists. Big deal.

It may open up a new career. If you're a man, you could serve as inspiration for children who can't afford to see the Goodyear Blimp. Those little fellows love a good gas attack. If you're a woman, it all depends on your complexion. You stand a chance for cover girl of either Oil of Olay or Fish and Wildlife.

Take the case of the woman lamenting her passing youth. At her over-40 party she was heard to wish that she had the complexion of a teenager just once again. Next morning she woke up with acne.

GOLDEN OLDIES

Bradenton, Florida, is unique for several reasons. First, it is the ancient home of the Seminoles and the Ringling Circus headquarters. Secondly, the population changes during the winter, from 60,000 to over 120,000. The place was dry as a politician's speech but my cab driver asked if I could see all the wet footprints on the sidewalks.

"Are we on the beach?" I asked.

"Nope," he cackled, "that's caused from all the 'snowbirds' that get off the plane from Baltimore."

They come by the thousands, for the winter, and to retire permanently. The Kiwanis Club here has the unique distinction of being the richest in the world. Years ago the club bought some land, and, as a service to the elderly, rented trailer space. Land was cheap back then and they got a big piece of it. It's now next to the airport and brings in $300,000 annually from the snowbirds who sit in their portable roosts.

In addition to snowbirds, the area has its share of retirees who came to stay year around—sunbirds, funbirds, toughbirds they call themselves.

"The average age around here is 55," said Virginia, a lady about that age. "Do you know what that means?" Before I could admit I didn't, she answered her own question. "That means a bunch of them are on the launching pad now getting ready to go pffft!" as she skipped her hands together and pointed skyward.

Virginia turned out to be a delight. She was a Texas girl who had to move here because her husband was transferred to work in Bradenton.

"We had some of our older friends over for supper last night," she related. "A man and three widows. During the meal, the man got choked and had to go outside. When we got him settled down, we asked what seemed to be the problem. He said 'I heard a terrible noise and it startled me.' It turned out to be next door—a baby's cry. Now that's old!"

Virginia says it's fun to deal with the older generation. "Everyday they grow less noticeable. Strange how young the retirees are these days." She left a teaching job in a well known university and doesn't miss it. "My Lord, they were all majoring in hat making, parachute jumping, opium smoking . . . I'll take Old Power any day."

She plays golf with Clara, in her eighties, who can only see about three feet, but Virginia points her in the right direction, rattles the flag in the cup for "sound" putts and regularly gets beat.

Clara also has arthritis so bad that she has to slide off the bed and crawl for a while before she goes for her morning jog. When Virginia expressed empathy for her condition, Clara remarked, "Prop me against a tree and rattle the flag, Virginia. This getting old ain't for sissies!"

RELATIVELY MEMORABLE REUNION

Years ago there was a sign in one of the parks around Corpus Christi, Texas, a large naval base, that read "No dogs or sailors." No, it didn't last very long because the decent folks down there were incensed by this inhuman affront to good manners and hospitality. Besides, they were kind people and loved dogs. They loved sailors too as long as they stayed in their place . . . with the dogs.

Now I know how they feel (the sailors, not the dogs), because I just returned from a family reunion on Lake Corpus Christi. What made this a memorable trip was the fact that I had to come in later than everybody else because of a speaking date the morning of the big arrival, making my appearance on the scene in late afternoon. There is no telephone at the lakehouse, and I'm flying my Cherokee. So I send word with my wife to have the "family" do a Chinese fire drill when they hear me fly over, form a human arrow, and point to one of two airports nearby so I'll know where to land and they'll know where to pick me up.

The only problem was that I didn't know exactly where they were on the lake, having never been there even on the ground. So I flew to the approximate position.

The next challenge was that the area had built up so that there were houses, boats, and people everywhere but no human arrows that I could see. After a half hour of cruising up and down the lake shore,

I spot a flash of light from a mirror, a white bedsheet waving frantically, a smudge pot pouring black smoke, and 30 people imitating a crazed fire ant colony.

They were doing all this on an open piece of ground between other people's lake retreats, and most of the people were sitting in the shade of their porch. I made a pass low enough to let my folks know I had seen them, and people everywhere started running, jumping in the lake, in the canal, under the porch.

Then the family lined up along a garden hose so they could make a recognizable arrow; I waved my wings to signal and landed. Upon arrival at the reunion, I noticed a rather cool reception from neighbors who were booing from their foxholes.

Family members also complained because they had gotten sunburned, started a grass fire with the smudge pot, and were reported to the sheriff's office as a riot in progress.

One brother-in-law had a mobile phone in his car and kept phoning around while I was in the air.

"You can't call an airplane," they told him.

"Who's trying to call an airplane?" he snorted, "I'm calling the National Guard to see if we can get a ground to air missile and shoot him down."

I'm told there is a new sign up on the lake now. "No Dogs, Sailors, or Family Reunions."

VANITY - VANITY

A few days ago I picked up the daily newspaper to see what terrible calamity had befallen this country during the night while I slept. It was refreshing to find a different article, one that I could relate to. It was about the actor (Ed Asner) who played the part of Lou Grant on television, editor of a newspaper. Everybody knows that editors are mean, nasty, ill-tempered misfits (except for the gifted, talented genius who guides this publication). So much for the humor—on with the facts.

This TV character was described in the article as an emerging hero on the American scene. His rating in the polls was attributed to his realistic, non-fictional assets. He is balding, middle-aged, overweight, beady-eyed and shrewd. But this guy has won the hearts of viewers as a wise, often sentimental sage PLUS one unexpected attribute. He has the distinction of being a new type of sex symbol.

Well, I got on the airplane standing a little shorter, broader, dumpier, thinner on top and wearing a rakish, slanty-eyed expression. Maybe,

I thought, my people are about to come into terminal puberty. Strange how a positive attitude can cheer you up. I expected any moment to be discovered by Cosmopolitan scouts. The stewardesses seemed to hover over me, making excuses to gaze at my baby blue eyes.

As I deplaned at my destination, stewardesses grabbed me by each arm and escorted me off the aircraft.

"Is anyone here to meet you?" one cooed.

"Surely," sighed the other, "he is already taken."

I made an attempt to straighten my tie and then realized I wasn't wearing one. Just as I was clearing my throat to explain that they would have to learn self control and discipline, I was approached by two attractive young women, waiting in the lobby, one blonde, one redhead. Closer, closer they came. Suddenly two toddlers running ahead of them grabbed me by each leg and yelled, "Pa Pa, Pa Pa."

The stewardesses signaled to a special airline attendant who shoved me into an electric cart and off I went with two daughters-in-law and two grandkids.

"Smart-mouthed kids," I muttered "have no respect for an aging sex symbol."

The airline girls were met by two young fellows who looked like they had been taking hormone shots to grow hair. I heard one ask: "That the old fellow you had to help off the plane?"

Well, win a few, lose a few, who knows, it could be worse. I might even someday become an editor.

POT SHOTS 6

Uncle Fred went on a liquid diet. He lost 80
pounds and his drivers license.

DOCTORS, HEALTH, AND DIET

Physical fitness has become a religion in this country. An overweight fellow took up jogging, ran three blocks to his local church, yelled, "Oh, God," and collapsed in a heap. Lucky thing for him that his two high school sons were weight lifters. They bench pressed their father and brought him home in a wheel barrow. He learned that he had to ease into physical fitness. Besides, he was in a weakened condition. He had also started on a diet and had cut down to only four meals per day.

"I just lost 120 pounds," bragged a fellow. "I just sent the wife home to her mother."

It seems that everyone wants to be young, vigorous, healthy, and strong. Most authorities agree that one way to keep those qualities as long as possible is through regular check-ups by your doctor or a specialized fitness center, exercise, dieting, and a regular visit to your clergyman. Pray that you live through what it takes to become healthy.

One of the most diabolical schemes ever concocted by the mind of man (surely no woman would have thought of this) is the treadmill. This is a continuous belt on a couple of speed controlled rollers that allows you to walk or run without getting anywhere. It's sort of like having an argument with your spouse. The treadmill can be elevated to simulate going up a hill thus putting more and more stress on muscles, joints, and heart. A physician or nurse monitors the condition of your heart and lungs through wires and tubes that run to

110

devices designed to measure the exact moment at which one or all the organs are about to explode. Then they pull you off, tell you how long you lasted, and give you a rating. Average, athletic, super athletic are just a few of the categories. I saw what the nurse wrote on my record. I don't like to brag, but as far as I know, I'm the only one who was ever listed in the category of "Couch Potato."

Being in top shape is a necessity for professional speakers. I had a talk once in Bakersfield, California, and had to catch a flight to Los Angeles for a close connection back for another engagement in Dallas. The airport was fogged in in Bakersfield. Immediately, I used my physical fitness to jog over to the rent car counter, about twelve feet away, and to my dismay, had been edged out of the race by a competitor. He only beat me by about ten feet. He was a long-legged, skinny sort who rented the only car available. I asked where he was going. "Los Angeles," he replied. "I've got to catch a plane to Dallas." I explained to him that I needed to catch the very same flight and wondered if we might share the car and the expenses. He readily agreed. "You carry the luggage," he suggested. "I'll run get the car." He was gone like a gazelle to the distant lot. I met him at the baggage exit, huffing and puffing, loaded down like a pack mule. "Better get in shape," he remarked. "You drive while I do my isometric exercises." I gave him something to tense up his muscles about when I accidentally threw the car in reverse and backed over his luggage.

On the way to Los Angeles, we introduced ourselves. He was Dr. Kenneth Cooper of the famed Cooper Clinic in Dallas, the author of the first and probably the most famous book on aerobics. It was a mad dash even after we got to the airport in Los Angeles. It really made me realize how important it is to be in shape. It's like comparing day and night or a soda straw to a bowling ball.

Once on the plane, Dr. Cooper told me the story of a mutual friend of ours, Dr. Jim Tunney, the NFL referee who has been seen for many years on national television on Monday Night Football and Super Bowl games. At age 55, Jim was still in superb shape as one might expect he would have to be to run up and down the field with players who were not only richer, but much younger. At the time of this telling, Roger Staubach, famed quarterback of the Dallas Cowboys, held the Cooper Clinic record for endurance on the treadmill.

Dr. Cooper was telling me that Jim Tunney had, just the past week, broken Roger Staubach's record. He thought it was extraordinary that anyone that age could be in such superb condition. Since he knew that Jim Tunney and Roger Staubach knew each other well, disagreed frequently on the football field, but were nevertheless close friends, Dr. Cooper said he immediately picked up the telephone and luckily caught Staubach in his office. "Roger," he said, "you will find this hard to believe. Your record on the treadmill has just been broken. Not only has it been broken, it has been shattered. Not only that, but it was broken by a 55-year-old man. Not only that, but it was broken by someone you know very well . . . NFL referee Dr. Jim Tunney."

Without a moment's hesitation, Roger shot back, "I never questioned his health. It was his eyesight. . . ."

For anyone who has ever even thought about shaping up, feast your eyes on this chapter. Even if you have to adjust your bifocals, it will jog your memory.

A HINDU HOT FOOT

Doctors in India are studying the feet of Hindu devotees who walk on fire. They need to study their heads for telling their feet to do that. Nevertheless, the study goes on, since the government is footing the bill and the research is billing the foot. The main expense for materials are for brickettes, lighter fluid, and Mennen's Foot Powder.

The Hindus say their religious faith protects them, allowing them to walk on fire. Some walk in measured steps, others dance and leap frenziedly as though possessed by spirits (maybe an ember popped in their overalls).

One guy took two quick steps forward, about 200 quicker ones straight up as he lifted off the launching pad, cleared the fire pit, did a backflip off the local temple, landed on a block of ice and burned two size 8½ D footprints clear through.

He then asked directions to the nearest Christian mission and when last heard from was doing research on how to walk on water, studying the writings of Evinrude.

The medical men doing the study came to the conclusion that successful walking on fire depended on two things—how long they stayed on the fire and how quick they got off. Twenty-five percent of most firewalkers, they found, are doing it for the first time, which could mean that 75 percent are doing it for the last time.

Why can't those fellows test their faith like we do, by walking barefoot through a bull nettle, grass burr, or briar patch while chanting incantations approved and tested by the U.S. Navy?

HEALTHY AS A HORSE

The jet setters love to brag about having their own doctor who travels with them. I know a fellow who travels with his own personal veterinarian. Inflation has taken its toll even on the rich.

Having a veterinarian for a doctor might not be all bad. Even if you couldn't talk he should still be able to find out what is the matter with you. Pawing the ground at the first sign of discomfort or kicking at him for more severe pains are something they expect. Try that with an M.D. and see what happens. They'll call the police.

Not so with the D.V.M. They'll put your head in a squeeze chute, shoot you with a tranquilizer gun or put a twitch on your upper lip. Then just to show you who's boss, they may shove a tube down your throat, deworm you on the spot, and put a tag in your ear. You see, D.V.M. stands for Devious and Very Mean.

Medical doctors always make a big show of coming into the examining room and washing their hands. It always makes me wonder what they've been doing to have to wash that often. The veterinarian hasn't got time for all this nonsense. He's not treating his hands. He disinfects the whole patient by either turning the water hose on him or running him through a dipping vat.

But, what the heck, I thought, maybe the jet setters had a point so I asked my veterinarian to have a look at my health. A nurse led me to a nice clean stall, brushed my hair and patted me on the neck. Kind of nice. Never got this type of treatment at the people clinic.

My veterinarian was just like the people doctors, though. He said I was in great shape for a 60-year-old. "I'm 47," I replied. "I know," he said. The upshot of it was that I had to get more exercise and go on a high roughage diet. I don't mind eating oats for breakfast, but that three miles a day is tough to gallop.

MEDICAL WONDERS

Medical science is wonderful, but not always an exact science. A doctor's reputation often rests on his bedside manner.

"I've heard he's gentle and sincere," says one person.

"Yes," replies another, "but it could happen to anyone. Besides, he usually gets over it by the time he starts the examination."

After a recent physical, I asked my doctor, "How do I stand?"

"That's what puzzles me," he replied.

Who would think a heart attack would be funny? Strangely enough, it's a subject for joking. After triple bypass surgery, Henry Kissinger remarked, "Contrary to popular opinion, the operation has definitely confirmed that I do have a heart." Hank continued to quip during convalescence, "Doctors tell me that I am now in excellent physical condition and will be stronger than ever, terrifying news to my staff."

Back surgery is no laughing matter, either, until it's over; then it feels so much better that the former patients can't resist joking about it.

One good-natured guy had a ready answer for "How's your back?" He always replied,"How's your front?" The ladies loved it.

"My doctor told me to give up coffee, smoking, and shoveling snow," said a chance acquaintance from Michigan in an airport.

"Is that Sanka you're drinking?" I asked.

"Folgers."

"What's that you're holding?"

"A cigar."

"So, you gave up shoveling snow, right?"

"A reasonable man doesn't mind a compromise. I'm moving to Arizona."

A patient complained once that his doctor should be publicly reprimanded for inhumane humiliation of naked people. The local newspaper sent a reporter out and asked him to define inhumane humiliation. He replied, "It's like pornography. I can't define it, but I know it when I see it."

But if you think our doctors have it tough, pity the poor Russians. They can't even blame their problems on an act of God.

10 WAYS TO CATCH THE FLU

Hopefully, the flu season will pass and you won't.

There is nothing more irritating than to have all those rotten germs flowing through your system and not be able to give them to somebody you dislike.

Did you ever wonder how you got the flu in the first place? I've made a study of the situation and found some very logical ways of coming down with the flu:

1. Being rude to the waiter in a Mexican restaurant. He sneezes into your guacamole.

2. Kissing a person whose nose just set fire to a Kleenex.

3. Standing too close to a person pronouncing the city "Pocatello."

4. Drinking from the same glass as a nonalcoholic.

5. Shaking hands with anyone except Willie Nelson who speaks through his nose.

6. Gasping at the hospital bill while walking through the respiratory disease section.

7. Licking the hand of a nurse.

8. Being introduced to an oriental named Ah Choo.

9. Smelling a swine's snout.

10. Streaking through cold storage at a meat packing plant.

Also I have found in this research that if you lead a wicked, rotten, immoral life, it is almost a 100 percent certain probability that the flu bug wouldn't touch you.

I suspect an angel of the devil paints a little spot over the doorsill so the flu bug can attack only the righteous. It's God's way of saying, "That will teach you not to say 'things couldn't be worse.'"

A lady, I know, named Sue was coming down with the flu, but like everybody else, she refused to admit it. She and her husband Bill went out to eat with two other couples. She should have known something was wrong because she had this strange craving for aloe vera ice cream.

She told Bill she wasn't feeling well, so he quickly volunteered to dash outside and have valet parking send the car around. Everyone followed Sue to the covered entrance where several fellows were waiting for their cars. Sue spotted Bill's familiar figure from the back, walked around in front of him, laid her head on his shoulder, and silently began stroking his chest. After 30 seconds or so, Sue looked up and saw a stranger's head instead of her familiar Bill's. Startled, she pushed back and said, "You're not Bill."

He said, "No, ma'am."

"Oh, I'm terribly sorry. I haven't been feeling well."

"Oh, yes you have," replied the stranger, "I'll bet I've got the smoothest chest in town."

She said, "Why didn't you say something?"

He replied, "Honey, with those green eyes, you can do anything you like."

Guys like that never catch the flu and they just grin and bear it if they come down with a chest cold.

UNTIMELY QUESTIONS

A guy went to see a psychiatrist. "What seems to be your problem?"

"I can't seem to make any friends . . . you big, fat slob."

There are probably lots of questions like that to which we get answers and wished we hadn't brought up the subject. I can think of several questions to which there is only one acceptable answer and not even silence will keep you out of trouble. Questions like, "Will you marry me?", "Do you think I'm too fat?", and "You're not pregnant again are you?"

Usually these are asked in that order, separated by several years and several cases of beer and/or diapers.

"What did you ever see in her/him (your old flame)?" is not a wise question for friendly discussion. Neither is "What's wrong with my side of the family?" It ranks right along side of "Who do you think you're talking to?" and "You call this dinner?"

We usually resort to questions when we are frustrated. Although we know the answer, we still ask the question. Take the case of the thief who suffered from anxiety. He wanted to impress his date. Walking down the street late at night, she saw a fur coat in a window. "Wish I had that," she cooed. He threw a brick through the window and got it for her. Passing a garment shop, she sighed, "What a beautiful dress." Another brick. Passing a jewelry store, she asked, "Can I have that diamond ring?"

Already a nervous wreck, he blurted out, "What do you think I'm made of . . . bricks?"

The question went unanswered but both are still thinking about it. They were given time to ponder the answer . . . about 20 years.

THE DIET JIGSAW

More people are watching their diets than ever before. Men and women with the natural configuration of the Goodyear Blimp fancy themselves as Donny and Marie, having about as much shape as a hoe handle with a glandular condition.

What other reason could there be for lettuce selling for more than beefsteak? The lower middle class dieters can't afford lettuce so they have switched to cabbage. The lower class can't afford cabbage so they have changed to mustard greens.

The poor and underprivileged have had to settle for steak and potatoes—and fat.

What would happen if everybody took the same attitude? We'd all soon look alike, we'd have a terrible shortage of lettuce and we'd be up to our ears in lard. Fat people do a great service to humanity by eating all that greasy stuff and storing it inside their bodies. Otherwise, it could be a summer road hazard comparable to the slickest streets of winter.

And don't ever fall for that sympathy story that crops up on TV so often. You know, the line about "Seventeen million Americans go to bed hungry in the U. S. every night."

Of course they do, but it's their own fault. About ten million of those are on Metracal and the rest are on fast-food hamburgers.

Years ago it was not popular to be slim and suntanned because that was associated with people who worked hard, stayed outdoors, ate all they wanted, and had parasites.

Then the rich, affluent, aristocrats adopted the look. Now it's hard to tell whether a guy is rich, affluent, and aristocratic or just a suntanned fellow with worms.

On the other hand, moderation appears to be in order for any great variation in weight from the acceptable norm. My fat Uncle Clyde was finally frightened into dieting by six little words from his doctor— "Have you ever seen skin explode?"

YOU ARE WHAT YOU EAT

Medical science is finding more and more that you are what you eat. I've learned, for instance, that if you eat garlic, you are apt to be very lonely.

If you are a kid, nearly everything you eat turns to hair.

We also know that some kids become hyperactive when they eat sugar, so behavior may be a function of diet. It's not as simple as feeding hyperactive people snails to slow 'em down or putting grandpa on a diet of gazelle meat, but I did hear of a fellow who wanted to try the theory on his wife and inquired about the eating habits of Bo Derek.

A missionary doctor in South America recently reported an unusual case. There was a woman in a remote village who had a drastic personality change. Traditionally subservient to her husband, she gradually became wild-eyed, strange acting, mean, and unmanageable. Everyone in the village said she had gone "loco."

The missionary doctor had read of the effect of Lithium and other elements on mental health and wanted to prescribe something to help her but no such elements were available in his remote practice. So, he studied the nutrition books and discovered that tuna fish had high levels of the element he had in mind.

After only a few weeks on tuna fish, her behavior turned back to normal. He left her a year's supplementary supply of the canned tuna and complimented himself.

Three weeks later, word was sent to the medic that the woman was "off her rocker" again.

Upon visiting the village, he found the woman worse than ever. It greatly puzzled him.

Then he got to checking and solved the riddle. Her husband had eaten all her tuna fish.

It gives new meaning to the theory that some husband's simply "drive their wives crazy."

Rumor has it that the fellow finally got what was coming to him when he took a siesta under a tree and was licked to death by leopards.

COFFEE CHAOS

As Americans, we can take bad news as well as anyone. The threat of economic collapse, nuclear holocaust, or the rumor that Dolly Parton wears false . . . hair is something we can cope with. The war in El Salvador, threat of invasion everywhere, Russian interference, and warning labels on everything from asparagus to hard rock adds to our frustrations. But they've gone too far now.

Coffee can cause cancer of the pancreas: the most ridiculous idea ever dreamed up by the mind of man. It's a communist plot, trying to get us used to doing without El Salvador so they can take over Guatemala, Costa Rica, and San Francisco, not to mention 20 million cafes in this country.

The Marxists couldn't hang it on saccharin and they won't get away with this scheme either, although they did succeed in reducing most of the cream in the U. S. to a non-dairy poisoned powder.

Imagine getting up in the morning with no coffee. Just think, ladies, your spouse could be like that all day long. Think of the damage that could be done to the kids having to look at a face like that continually during their formative years.

Let's face it: if coffee goes, the nation would be in chaos. Coffee shops closed, waitresses out of work, the percolator industry ruined, Joe DiMaggio forced out of retirement, office breaks eliminated, and the burro of Juan Valdez converted to Superglue.

Even though all patriots should see through this pinko plan, a few misguided souls take it seriously as a threat to their well being. I saw two fellows in a cafe recently, at breakfast, gagging on a cup of tea.

"We've got to think of our health," said one.

"You bet," nodded the other.

Then they would take turns choking, coughing, and spewing tea all over the formica table top.

"How do those Englishmen stand this torture?"

"I guess they realize they're saving their pancreas."

"Smart devils . . . cough, cough . . . though, ain't they?"

"Yeah, that bag was quite an invention . . . cough . . . cough."

"The tag and string are even more clever."

"Yeah, and the string is just the right length."

"True, but if it wasn't for that tag, catching in your teeth, we would have long ago swallowed the bag."

"Well how's your pancreas?"

"Never felt healthier. Gimme a cigarette."

YANKEE GO HOME

Eating in a Japanese restaurant is sure different. No wonder those people are so skinny. I think the Creator must have left, unsnipped, an elastic attachment from the inside of the belly button to the base of the chin. They can only hold their head up for so long, then down it goes. They say that bowing is very polite, but they could just be checking to see if their belly button has ruptured yet.

The doorman greets everybody with the name of one of our states. Apparently he's on the payroll of the Chamber of Commerce because he says, "Ohio" to everybody. I tried to teach him to say Texas, Kansas, or North Dakota. He'd just smile, squint at me, and repeat "Ohio." One thing you have to admire about the guy, when he gets bought, he stays bought.

Next you have to take your shoes off because the Japanese make a big thing out of being clean. The Texans always complain about this part because it takes a Sumurai warrior to help pull off their boots. Then they usually don't have on the same color matching socks.

Japanese restaurants are supposed to be expensive, high class. So how come you have to sit on the floor? After you get the bill, you find out. You can't fall out of your chair if you're not sitting in one. And you have to pay up because they're holding your shoes for ransom.

The food is all synthetic, probably made from polyester or scrap iron. Not a single thing did I recognize as coming from a plant or animal. And communication . . . forget it. They listen to English but only speak gibberish. It was all delicious until I spotted a Philipino businessman who spoke English, I didn't know that I had dined on squid, octopus, herbs and seaweed. Ever since, I've had the strangest desire to sleep in the bathtub.

As we were leaving, I had one last question about some large, square, cream-colored substance that looked like a cross between a jellyfish and cardboard.

"What was it?" I asked a pretty kimono-draped waitress.
"Curd," she replied.
"Who shot it?"
"Ohio."
I might have known that somehow this money-making scheme involved some Yankees.

A JUICY MIXTURE

Florida is crazy about orange juice. They drink it straight, on the rocks, under the rocks, down on the beach, everybody's up on orange juice. It's making money for Florida so it's good as gold, good for colds they say, lots of vitamin C. Some people mix it with Vodka and look forward to the flu. The coke machines have a companion now, the orange juice machine. Take a big drink of that citrus elixir and you can almost see Anita Bryant on a stepladder, little birds fluttering through the groves, hear that tune about sunshine and natural C.

The tourists haul those oranges out in little sacks that look like they were made from old fish nets. After you eat the oranges the sack makes a dandy hair net which could catch on with dumb streakers who want to cover their identity, or part of it, behind a veil of citrus secrecy. "Don't look, Ethel. There he goes streaking through the grove."

Too late, he peeled off right in front of her. "Ethel, drink your orange juice . . . Ethel, you hear me?"

SHAPING UP ON WATER

At the ripe old age of 25, nature lets you down. The pounds start to lose their shape and the barrel chest takes pot luck. Dr. Irwin M. Stillman and his water diet became famous. Whether you like it or don't, the idea can build up bladder or blood pressure. Some people can drink Canada dry (Lake Ontario) and gain like it was Apple Pie. Others can eat Detroit, burp and starve to death before your very eyes.

Some people like to drink, but not water. Dr. Stillman (remember him?) had a new idea for those folks, he even allows alcohol in moderation. Too much is not good because nobody likes a skinny drunk. You can't eat mayonnaise, oils, bread, macaroni, or anything that could make life worthwhile. Oh well, a piece of cardboard, a handful of non-salted marbles, and a martini sounds like an interesting diet. If the subject is unduly affected by alcohol then everyone knows to immediately force feed black coffee. That way you get a wide awake drunk on your hands. I like my diet better: all you can eat of everything you don't like.

Of course, the water diet is still used by some. It's like Roosevelt said, "Speak softly, carry a big stick, and drink lots of water." That was Roosevelt Garcia. He said it just after losing 20 pounds. His bladder fell out.

A REAL DUMBBELL

Everybody else is doing it so I got some weights and have gone into training. I should have gone into hiding. I couldn't pick them up down at the freight office. This young, smart kid had to show off and throw them in the back of the pickup for me. I hate people like her.

It's embarrassing to have the whole family stand around and watch you roll all the pieces into the house.

The instructions said to rip open the first box and assemble the parts as shown in the diagram. I took a deep breath and ripped open the box and my index finger. I bled all over the instructions. Step two read, "Wipe blood from diagram."

After assembling the bench and other parts, I had what appeared to be the superstructure of an Apollo launch pad. But all this thing did was sit there in reverse thrust.

The instruction booklet said to start off slow, which I readily agreed to consider. The beginners' exercises consisted of squats, thrusts, and lifts. I figured one out of three wouldn't be bad, so I did a squat and had the wonderful opportunity of examining the floor until help arrived.

Consulting the manual again, it said one should always train with a partner, preferably one who has memorized the routine and the ambulance phone number.

I wondered if Arnold Schwartzennegger was available, but decided not to call because I wasn't sure how to spell Arnold.

Remembering how Charles Atlas used to be so weak that bullies kicked sand in his face at the beach, I became motivated once again and worked up a good sweat. Then I picked the weights up high over my head and learned a good lesson. Never lean backwards near a couch.

In that flash of a moment, amidst the crash of furniture, clanking of iron, and cracking of bones, I had a vision of how to prevent bullies from kicking sand in your face at the beach. Always lay on a big, flat rock.

After all, the old saying "Strong as an ox" is not without wisdom. Did you ever see an ox lift weights?

Next time I want to improve my physique, I'm just gonna take a deep breath and swell up.

Now I know the true meaning of a weight training word, Dumbbell.

MIND-OVER-MATTER STUFF

They say attitude is the key to good health. If you think you will not catch a cold you won't catch it. Of course, you may get hepatitis.

While you are concentrating on a cold germ, a virus can sneak in and give you something worth worrying about . . . like being dead for a good while.

I believe in this mind-over-matter stuff, but if your mind doesn't work, or, in some cases you don't have one, it may not matter.

It's like this fellow told me: "Just thinking positive thoughts won't do it. Believe me, I know because I have seven kids."

I said, "Did they think good thoughts and catch something anyway?"

He replied, "No, my wife caught something. I thought I was going to be a bachelor."

Sally was a healthy young lady I watched grow up. She was an unusual Korean war baby. Her mother was a sailor. Her father was a successful Kamikazi pilot.

Sally was an independent child with a mind of her own. No brains, just a mind of her own. She married in her late teens. It was a turbulent marriage from the start—normal.

It appeared to me that she had married for all the wrong spiritual reasons. Her husband owned a honky tonk.

Soon the marriage was on the rocks, straight up, frozen, and distilled history.

She resolved next time to be very careful. She married a safety engineer. He died in an accident.

Husbands three and four were not an improvement in her lifestyle. They ran off with each other.

What does this have to do with Sally's health? Well, she became depressed, unhappy, and ill with each failure. Her body had changed from that of a healthy, young female to that of a middle-aged, out-of-shape woman. Of course, it took a while—about 50 years.

And why did this happen? Old age, that's why. That and negative thinking. Just as we can think ourselves out of catching a cold, we can think ourselves out of getting old. We can be young and healthy all our lives. And if it doesn't work out that way, we can do the next best thing. That's what my Uncle Fred just did. He felt poorly for a long time, so he has decided to donate his body to medical science. Until they need it, he's preserving it in alcohol.

THERE OUGHT TO BE A LAW

Our county just approved an ordinance regulating the massage parlor business. The ordinance doesn't say that there can't be some, but it does require a permit, along with the complete disclosure of names of the owners, partners, and stockholders. That sure lets a lot of our local investors out of the picture. The banks and savings institutions were getting a little nervous for a while. But cooler heads prevailed and regulated sin clean out of the county.

The ordinance prohibits co-ed massage for pay, which surprises me because most fellows would be willing to massage a co-ed for free. It also establishes rules for dress. Apparently designer jeans are okay, but it seems to me if you're going to get massaged, you wouldn't wear jeans or a dress either. You have to strip down at least to your underwear, otherwise you could get a terrible fabric burn from a three-piece suit.

Ordinance regulations prohibit alcoholic beverages on the premises which, mark my words, is going to lead to a lot of trouble. If a guy is stripped down, sweaty, and decides to run out to the car to get a drink— well, I think you get the picture. Besides, he wouldn't have a place to keep his car keys anyway, so the regulations make sense. Violation of this law is a class B misdemeanor punishable by publishing your name and picture in the Ecumenical Council's newsletter.

However, like most ordinances, there are loopholes. Exempt from all these regulations are physical therapists, chiropractors, cosmetologists, and barbers performing functions authorized by their licenses. The law is quite clear on this point. A barber can cut hair in his underwear and there's not a thing we can do about it. In fact, I think some of that has been going on outside the county anyway. That's the reason so many people wear their hair so long.

Soon the word will get around though and decent folks will find out what's really going on behind those sinister signs that so innocently proclaim BARBER SHOP. If you should walk inside one and see your barber standing barefoot in a pile of hair, clad only in sweaty underwear, call the sheriff, it's another clip joint not covered by the ordinance.

HALF SHOTS 7

You've had too much to drink when people say
things like, "That was a wonderful girl you
married last night."

ALCOHOL

There may be some who may feel this chapter is inappropriate. Because of the terrible consequences of alcoholism, death-related incidents involving liquor, and the advent of such organizations as MADD (Mothers Against Drunk Drivers), I fully understand any sensitivity to the consumption of alcohol in a joking manner. Alcohol, like any other drug, can be misused. Doctors generally agree that a couple of drinks per day may actually be beneficial to health. More than that can actually kill brain cells and be detrimental. For some, it will become a demon master; for others, merely a pleasant diversion. I joke about it simply because it exists. Pretending otherwise will not make the associated problems go away.

You've probably heard all the old jokes. "I feel sorry for a man who doesn't drink because when he gets up in the morning, he's gonna feel as good as he's gonna feel all day long."

Then there was the temperance leader who said, "Lips that touch liquor will never touch mine." According to legend, she dies an old maid . . . with very dusty lips.

Yes, there are two sides to every story. Perhaps no story in modern history illustrates the point better than the London Women's Temperance League meeting that invited Sir Winston Churchill to speak. Sir Winston gave an eloquent presentation on the needs of all British citizens to pull together in the reconstruction effort shortly after the

126

end of World War II. During the question-answer session, one of the ladies just had to point out the difference in the Churchill philosophy as opposed to the Women's Temperance League. The meeting took place in one of the huge, palatial ballrooms of London that had mercifully been spared by the bombing.

"Sir Winston," she asked, "is it true that during your lifetime you have drunk enough brandy to fill this ballroom to a level six feet deep?"

The elder statesman lifted his eyes to slowly gaze around the width, depth, and height of the room, obviously measuring the capacity just alluded to, then answered, "Yes, madam, it is true. And as I gaze around this room, it only serves to remind me how very much more work is left to be done."

Like Sir Winston Churchill, in this chapter, I've tried to use the sense of humor to put into perspective the evils of drink as well as the good side. Used in moderation, with good judgment, and a sense of humor, alcohol is just another substance. Moderation and common-sense are integral parts of its use.

Like one fellow asked another, "When you drink too much, does your tongue burn?"

The other guy replied, "I don't know. I've never been dumb enough to set fire to mine."

"Don't drink and drive" is a worthy slogan to plaster far and wide as a reminder of life's hidden pitfalls. There are no pitfalls in the articles that follow . . . only a few pratfalls, but that's what humor is all about.

ONE FOR THE ROAD

CAJUNS ARE HIP DEEP IN ALLIGATORS. That's what a recent headline read in a New Orleans paper, which sounds like the author didn't know much about cajuns or alligators. An alligator that close to a cajun spells danger—to the alligator, because there is a gumbo shortage in Louisiana. Hamburger helper and cajun fear of the large reptiles could lead to a new ground-up dish called gator-aid, a large reptile accidentally beat to death with a broken beer bottle because he sneaked up hip high to a cajun and hissed.

They are getting so numerous that some have entered the sewer system (alligators, not cajuns) and have surfaced in New Orleans. Alcohol fumes in the sewer make it hard to stay down, while Mardi Gras makes it too frightening to wander far from the manhole. So they lay in the gutter where they are bought an occasional drink by tourists from the Midwest who are told they are cajun dogs. One yankee philanthropist bought a big cajun dog a drink and remarked, "It's the only animal I've seen that drinks bourbon, hiccups and hisses while wagging his tail for more. What a trainer he must have had."

A 12 foot, 500 pounder was recently seen headed toward the Governor's mansion escorted by two highway patrol cars—with their steel belt radials chewed off and their windows rolled up. A liquor crazed gator was apparently fed up with leading a dog's life and was going to complain to the Governor. An emergency appeal went out on the police airway asking for instructions on how to handle the situation since gators are protected as an endangered species. An anonymous caller replied, "Point him out to a cajun, tell him the limit is one, the season is closed and they make real good gumbo."

SHORT SNORT

On the corner of Conti and Bourbon, New Orleans, is the Absinthe Bar, a famous Old French Quarter place that has been visited by such prominent people as Andrew Jackson, Mark Twain, Al Jolson, Jack Dempsey, and many others. Jean Lafitte was the first big name to drop in for a grog. Since then many pirates have come, mostly from Washington, D.C. It makes a good place to practice the same old song and dance that we are exposed to in November. Also nobody listens to your campaign speeches, or can remember one having been made.

If I should ever completely lose my mind, I think I'd hang out at the Absinthe and study law prior to entering politics. Lots of people there doing graduate work on their bar exams. Here are two things I learned about this historic landmark:

The term "short snort" started here. During WWII many servicemen came through New Orleans enroute overseas. The GI's would give the bartender an extra dollar or two with their signature on it which was tacked to the wall, for those times when they were short of cash. Since the terminology for a drink in those days was a "snort," a redeemed bill was for a "short snort." Many were shipped out on a moment's notice before they were able to claim their drinks. It became a superstition that as long as the money hung on the wall, the owner would be protected in combat. The wall today has $10,000 tacked on it and has an estimated value well in excess of $900. Inflation has seen to it that no single bill will now buy a drink.

Secondly, in the days when dueling challenges were hurled, it was not the slap in the face with a glove that constituted the acceptance but the exchange of cards. Therefore, on entering the Absinthe Bar, the bartender insisted on being given the gentlemen's card which was then posted on another wall. By giving their card, the gentlemen were also giving their word that they would conduct themselves properly while in the bar. Many cards were forgotten, as evidenced by another wall of cards. That's why to this day it is believed that if two things belonging to you hang on the wall of the Absinthe Bar, you'll have a happy and prosperous life and will return someday to view your possession.

I'm looking forward to a prosperous life because I had a short snort and left two things on the wall—my hat and coat.

SPIRIT OF ADJUSTMENT

It seems that every convention or gathering nowadays is preceded by a cocktail party. Some have even given it cleverly disguised code names like Attitude Adjustment Hour or Personality Persuasion Period. Some guys enter a Saloon Safari with a face looking like a plate full of worms and leave looking like Raquel Welch had just sent them a personal love note. But, others come in with a grin like the grill of a 1948 Buick, and the fumes from a Champagne cork can transform them into Attila the Hun. The mean ones brighten up a party just by leaving.

Some people are very open minded about public spirits. The others sit out in the car and drink. Either way, an excess can create problems. Take the case of the guy who had a nervous hangover. He cut himself shaving and bled so much that his eyes almost cleared up. That doesn't sound like a problem until you discover he was using an electric shaver. He's the kind of guy the Red Cross won't take blood from anymore because they keep finding olives stopping up the tube.

Some quiet guys take a nip and are drawn out of their shell, like the Lovable Lush. Others take on the character of a boa constrictor with halitosis bent on freeing your date from an evening of mediocrity. I overheard a description of one of that type: "He's alright until he starts drinking, but he's the only guy at our cocktail parties that was ever hit right in the mouth by Dale Carnegie."

W. C. Fields once said, "Ah, yes. It was a woman who drove me to drink." Then added, "And I never even wrote and thanked her for it."

Remember fellows that MODERATION is the key to good health. Life is more than wine, women and song. I'm tapering off myself. I've given up singing.

TEXANS TURN OIL INTO WINE

The latest thing on the grape scene is Texas wine. Experiments by the University of Texas have proven intoxicating.

The vineyards are mostly in the arid parts of Texas, established in rocky soil and nurtured by water piped to it by drips . . . and a few flakes.

Varieties of grape vary but the most adaptable are the Cabarnet Y'all and Burgundy Bubba.

Grapes are gathered by hand in the traditional manner and hauled to the vats in the traditional Rolls Royce.

It's a festive time when the crew stomps in unison as musical refrains fill the air. The most enthusiasm is created by the tune Cotton Eyed Joe.

The bottoms of the vats have to be reinforced because of the unbridled energy created. They finally made the fellows get off their horses.

Then there was the problem of the stains on the feet. In a lifetime, you are not likely to see that many purple alligator boots.

Wine tasting panels were set up last year and members of the news media were invited to participate. The credentials were pretty stiff. One had to be a food editor or demonstrate ability to siphon gas out of a truck.

Texans knew they had a new hit product on their hands when Chateau San Jacinto released their product through Neiman-Marcus under the Texadough label.

Naturally, His and Hers specials are available in matching 55-gallon drums.

If you buy a tank truck load, they throw in a convenience store with a self-serve island.

The island is in the Rio Grande . . . on the Mexican side.

That's where the headquarters is located for the Neiman-Marcus wine distribution system. Sort of a Tex-Mex operation, run by Neiman Garcia and Marcus Retail.

Eat your heart out Italy, Paris . . . and all those other wine producing places in east Texas. West Texas has finally found a crop suited to their soil and climate. Only one major problem is left to be solved. How do you prevent the cork from being eaten by the Chablis Jalapeno?

RATION OF GROG

The Rusty Anchor Saloon is in Capitan, New Mexico. With a name like that, it deserves to be there.

It's a mighty friendly place and lots of fun. One of the few old-time saloons where a fellow can stand at the bar if he feels like it. Or if he feels like it, he can sit on the floor. Chairs are scarce.

However, it's usually so crowded that nobody wants to sit, or could. Very tight pants.

Especially on the girls. Both of them.

I asked why they named a place "The Rusty Anchor" that was a thousand miles from the ocean. All I got from the patrons was a blank stare and a long silence. Then one of them asked, "You a Communist?"

"No sir," I replied.

"You a foreigner?" asked another.

"Certainly not," I retaliated.

"Where you from, boy?"

"Texas," I said proudly.

"He's a foreigner," smiled a gray-bearded patron.

"So why do they call a place between Albuquerque and El Paso Rusty Anchor?" I pursued.

"Well," sighed an obviously good natured customer, "I guess we're gonna have to tell him."

"When God decided to destroy the world with the Great Flood, Noah actually lived on this very spot and built the Ark right here between the bar and the shuffleboard."

"Listened to Hank Williams on the jukebox the whole time."

"Forged a great anchor from iron ore in the Capitan Mountains."

"Everybody scoffed."

"Everybody scoffed," echoed a chorus of listeners.

"Then the rains came, the wind blew, the water rose."

"It was during the elections," wailed a buddy.

"Finally, the strain was too great. The Ark lurched at its moorings and snapped the anchor chain like a bull breaks binder twine."

"It rained for 40 days and nights."

"It was on a Tuesday," cried a companion.

"When the water receded, only Noah and his family were safe."

"I read about it in the Wall Street Journal," mumbled a local investor.

"So," I said, "I suppose you guys are going to tell me that you are the decendents of all those who drowned in the flood."

"Noooo," said the teller of tall tales, "the Flood story is not completely accurate. When the flood came, it was a flash flood. We jumped on our horses and raced the wall of water. I myself never felt a drop of rain but my dog, not 10 yards behind me, had to swim all the way.

"Staying ahead of the water was tough, but when it started to go down, we came back to find all the sinful people drowned, homes gone, everything changed. The only way we were able to find our homes was to search out the Capitan Mountains and look for signs. We finally found the rusty anchor of the Ark. We rebuilt this saloon and gave it that name to commemorate that epoch event."

"Is that true?" I asked.

"Do you see the anchor?" he asked.

Looking around, I replied, "Frankly, no, I don't."

"There, you see . . . that proves it. It rusted away."

Then we all drank a toast to the iron-willed people who died in the Great Flood.

Naturally the toast was "May they rust in peace."

DEVIL'S BREW

During the days of prohibition, there was also a depression. What they were prohibiting was probably partially the cause of depression, at least in some people.

Whiskey, white lightnin', peach brandy, pie melon wine, you name it, bootleggers and distillers were trying to get this nation back up on its feet again, so they could stand at a bar and think prosperous thoughts.

This distillery operation consisted of two basic parts—the moonshiners and the bootleggers. Of course, all of it was outlawed by the government until they could figure out how to get in on it. A two-pronged attack was planned. Find the source of supply and the distributors. Seemed simple enough.

So one revenuer took to the woods where he had a tip that a still was operating. He stumbled on to a young boy.

"Is there a still in these parts, sonny?" he asked.

When the boy nodded affirmatively, the government man said, "I'll give you a $5 reward it you'll show me where it is."

The boy replied, "Gimme the $5 and I'll tell you which way to go."

"No, sonny, you tell me and if you're right, I'll give you the $5 when I come back."

"Mister," said the kid, "gimme the $5 now 'cause you ain't comin' back."

The revenuer retreated gracefully and decided to dry up the bootleggers who were handling the stuff. So one night in an undercover role, he made a contact just outside town. "Where do I get the stuff?" he asked his informant.

The squealer replied, "Two blocks down Main, take a left, third house on the right is all you gotta' remember."

"Wait a minute. I know that house. That's the Baptist minister's house. You mean . . . "

"That's right. You can get the stuff at any house but his."

STONE BLIND ON SINKING CREEK

Kingsport, Tenn. is in the heart of sippin' whiskey country. Several of the inhabitants have been known to do their sippin' from a large, economy size jug. It's cheaper that way because it can be bought wholesale. The story was passed along to me that several guys did so much elbow bending down on the banks of a creek that they couldn't tell their wholesale from their retail.

The rolling hills seemed to be especially rolling this night. To complicate matters even more one of the fellows in the party of three had just had his eyeglasses prescription changed. He went down stream a distance to wash his face. It was a beautiful, moonlit night. He knelt down on the edge of the bank, saw his reflection in the water through his new glasses, reached out his hands to cup enough water to wash his face and fell 20 feet to the water below. He lost his glasses, his composure and his body temperature down on Sinking Creek.

When he finally felt his way back to the campfire he whispered through chattering teeth, "Hey fellows, I can't see."

That sobered up the other two because they thought they had broken into a bad batch of squeezins and their buddy had gone stone blind with a case of the chills.

I asked one of these farmer boys if they didn't suspect something like that when the splash in the creek was heard. He said, "Naw, we heard the noise, but it gets so quiet around here that you can hear the sun go down. We thought it was the mortgage falling due on the farm."

MOONSHINE STILLS

Along the ridges and "hollers" of eastern Kentucky live hardy, realistic people that have come to characterize Appalachia. I recently made a tour through the Appalachian Mountains looking for stories or stills. The moonshiners never stopped making white lightnin' even after prohibition was repealed. This is why they call it the Bible Belt. The mountaineers take a little belt just before they grab their Bible and head for church.

A classic mountain story is told of the preacher who admonished his congregation about the evils of falling victim to the devil's brew. For over an hour he lashed out against the poisonous substance that cripples the mind, numbs the senses and robs body and soul of spiritual pride. Then he ended his sermon by saying, "Now if you've just got to drink the infernal stuff, buy it from Brother Ephram. He makes it mighty good."

One old moonshiner who said he "lived so far back in the sticks there ain't any sticks behind me," got to feeling poorly and finally went to see a doctor. The practictioner told him that bad whiskey had finally caught up with him. He was given just a few months to live.

When the family asked what he planned to do he replied, "The first thing Monday morning I'm going to join the government Revenue Service." When they asked why he would do a dang fool thing like that, he said, "Better for one of them to die than one of us."

When he did pass through that big copper tube up in the sky, the preacher asked if anyone wanted to say a few words about the dearly departed. Another mountaineer stepped forward, laid his black hat on the edge of the coffin, shifted his Allen County twist chewing tobacco to the other side, hooked his thumbs in his bib overalls, lifted his eyes skyward and prayed, "Brother Tobias here raised fast horses and he rode 'em, he drawed good cards and he played 'em, he made good whiskey and he drank it . . . such is the kingdom of heaven. Amen."

PRAY FOR RAIN

We think we have had a heat wave in Texas, but I was recently in Florida where they say the weather has been so hot that people have been driven to drink by the weather bureau . . . any old excuse will do in a drought.

One group appears to have gotten into the spirit and the spirits into them because they formed an association called the Board of Realtors Education Workshop (BREW) in Melbourne, Florida and I was invited as the principal speaker. It seems that everybody who retires anywhere moves to Florida and goes into the real estate business.

It appeared that the heat wave had taken its toll, because everybody was having a cool one at BREW.

"Business has been off. What do you suggest?"

"Have a drink."

"Business is great. What do I do for an encore?"

"Have a drink."

"Boy, is it hot!"

"I'll drink to that."

One fellow who didn't drink told me he wished he did because he had been at the workshop for three days, had his apartment thermostat turned down to 50 degrees and the temperature was just reaching 85. He left the refrigerator door open, slept nude. Nothing worked. Now he's starting to worry because he's afraid when he returns home, his wife won't understand his habit of standing naked in front of an open refrigerator.

Everybody wears a lapel button with a special "R" that stands for Realtor. The reason they wear those is so they can tell who is not a customer. Since everybody wore one, the frustration of not being able to practice a sales pitch drove them to the brink of normalcy. Some of them nearly went sane.

That's when things got dangerous because everyone was laughing loudly. Just the serving of the salad set off frenzies of wild applause and merriment. The M.C. couldn't get the crowd to be quiet, so he just motioned to Dr. Dennis Bennett, a Presbyterian minister, and said loudly, "Rabbi, get up here and pray for these sinners."

A slight hush fell over the audience for his invocation, but not for long. The invocation for BREW was intoxicating. "Lord, your good book says that 'where two or three are gathered in My name, there am I also.' THIS IS A TEST. Amen."

Dr. Bennett has already been invited back for next year.

THE DRINK THAT MADE A CITY FAMOUS

Whenever a product gets in trouble or competition gets too keen, the advertisers usually come up with an old campaign using the word "NEW." The new taste of Coke was inspired by gains made by the NEW generation of old bankers.

People are still complaining that they don't like the taste of new Coke. A leading expert was subjected to a blind taste test to see if he could really tell the difference. Without hesitation, he picked his favorite and proudly proclaimed, "It's the real thing." It was the real thing all right, but it was RC Cola.

Obviously this "expert" didn't know "Come here" from "Sic 'em." The Pepsi generation knows. They get a rock star to do the moon walk on a bed of hot coals. That builds real thirst . . . and sales.

Of course, Pepsi hadn't cornered the market yet and that's probably good. Sure would be dull seeing everybody walking backwards to work wearing one glove and a band uniform.

The one glove is for picking up cold stuff. Like hard cash.

I tried one of those taste tests the other day. Some friends lined up a bunch of unmarked samples out on their patio while waiting for the hamburgers to cook. After the first sample, they all tasted alike. I started with the charcoal lighter fluid.

Never spit what you think is new Coke into a fire.

Where do they get all those names anyway? Ever think about that? Coke sounds like a rock falling into the water. Pepsi sounds like an Italian pasta. And 7-Up sounds like a dead spider with a missing leg.

Then there is RC which used to stand for Royal Crown but now is just RC. Soon it will probably be just R. Then nothing.

How about Sprite? I looked it up in the dictionary. It means elflike person. So why didn't they call it elf? Because it's a diet drink. Even though "Elf" would give the impression that drinking it would make you smaller, diet drinks are sold in a lot of dimly lit restaurants. Nobody would say "Elf" without blowing out the candles.

It's all very confusing. I asked a waitress if she had the new Coke in stock and she said she had not heard of it. But she did have a good idea. She said, "How about an Old Milwaukee?"

DREGS AND SOCIETY

Two fellows were constant companions, birds of a feather, Spike and Suds by name. There was nothing Spike wouldn't do for Suds and nothing Suds wouldn't do for Spike. So they went though life doing absolutely nothing for each other. They also kept the economy strong by supporting several breweries and a string of fast fillies—mostly blondes.

Spike was the type of guy who was very considerate of the girls he dated. If she dropped her hanky, he would kick it along until she had a chance to pick it up.

Suds, on the other hand, never gave girls a second thought. The first one covered everything.

The two old buddies celebrated New Year's Eve this year down at the police station where there was laughing, dancing, singing, and playing a game called "try to remain conscious." When both of them lost the game, they decided to make the best of a very sober situation.

"Hey, Sheriff," yelled Suds, "ain't I allowed one phone call?"

A few minutes later Suds is led to the telephone. With shaking hand he stabs a grubby finger at the dial and rings a number he knows by heart. "Hello, Salvation Army? Do you save bad men? You do? Well, I'm relieved to hear that.

"Listen, I've got an even more important question, then I've gotta go cause I have to keep a business appointment with a government official who doesn't like to be kept waiting.

"Do you save bad women? You do? Well, save a couple for me and my buddy. We'll be out of jail next week."

Suds and Spike paid their debt to society and checked in at the

Salvation Hilton who failed to see the humor in their telephone call. They were promptly put to work to earn their keep. They became part of the famous marching band. Late one night Suds and Spike, exhausted, flung themselves on their cots.

"Spike," said Suds, "you've got the biggest navel I've ever seen."

"Yeah," replied Spike, "tomorrow I'll beat the drum and you carry the flag."

BUDDY CAN YOU SPARE A BUCK?

There is always the danger, when one starts looking into the family history, that some unsavory characters could crop up, like a horse thief, counterfeiter, or politician.

It turns out that my great-uncle Harvey was one of those characters who was "wild and woolly and full of fleas; had never been curried below the knees."

Uncle Harvey was a hobo, but he had class. Always claimed he was a boxcar inspector for the railroad. He lived to be 90 and never used glasses. A doctor once told him that if he didn't stop drinking, he'd go blind. "Take your choice—drinking or seeing," said the doctor. Uncle Harvey reckoned he had already seen about everything worth seein'. On his way out of the doctor's office, the nurse asked sympathetically, if there was any hope for his case. Uncle Harvey said a case was too much to hope for, but could she spare the price of a bottle?

My uncle was never one to be discouraged, though. Once he took on a job, he would see it through. As he used to say, "I gotta go get drunk and I sure do dread it."

Believe it or not, there are still some of those characters around today. I saw a fellow on the streets today who looked like he had been raised in a garbage dump and was finally asked to leave because he was giving the place a bad name. This bum was the type who would be banned from water skiing because if he ever fell off he would leave an oil slick.

I really had to admire his independence, though. He was so much the same kind of character as my uncle Harvey. He didn't ask for a government handout, he went straight to the taxpayer himself. "Gimme a dollar for a cup of coffee," he boldly asked as he tried to focus both eyes in my general direction.

"Look," I said, "You've got to be realistic if you're gonna be successful. Coffee doesn't cost a dollar in this town. You should ask for a quarter and you'll get a lot more subscribers to your cause."

"Mister," he said, "Just gimme the money or don't gimme the money, but don't tell me how to run my business."

IRRATIONAL ENCOUNTER

While waiting for a plane at San Francisco airport, I decided to have some lunch. Out of 10,000 people and half a dozen restaurants I select the number one restaurant with the number one drunk. It was the only seat at the counter and it just happened to be next to him. The reason I knew that he had been imbibing was because people kept tripping over his breath.

Also, he proudly announced to me, "Hi, I'm drunk." I like a man who gets right to the point.

"Hi, yourself. I'm sober." I thought I would repay the courtesy.

"You're lucky. They won't let me on a plane until I sober up. They told me to come over here and drink coffee until I did. I've had 16 cups."

"Having any luck?"

"Yeah, now I'm getting drunk off the coffee."

"Where did you get drunk?"

"On the plane. I have learned a great lesson. You can get drunk on a plane but you can't get on a plane drunk. It's like my father always said, 'What's right is what's wrong.' He told me that and made me promise never to forget it."

"What does that mean?"

"I don't know but I never have forgotten it."

Sensing a story I let him ramble on and mentally recorded excerpts from this glassy eyed philosopher.

"My Mother used to tell me, 'Son, you no drinka too much the vino, be proud of Italia, worka hard and see Venice before you die.' And I would say, 'Mama, why do you talk like that? We ain't Italian!'"

"Where did you grow up, or have you finished?"

"Lower side, Manhattan. What a neighborhood. My sister could speak four languages before she was seven."

"That's quite an accomplishment."

"Yeah, unfortunately none of them was a language that the family spoke. We never did understand that kid."

Just then they announced, "Flight 984 is ready for boarding passengers with small children and those who have difficulty in walking."

He muttered, "I qualify for that last part but I think I'll steal a kid just to make sure. Hey Lady, Wanna sell that kid?"

GUN SHOTS 8

Never stalk anything that won't run from you.

HUNTERS AND HUNTING

Hunting has been a great challenge since the cavemen days. At first, man hunted beasts with primitive weapons. Then they got smart and started hunting unarmed beasts.

Dinosaurs with giant tails, flying reptiles with razor-sharp teeth . . . man has not known such terror in modern days except when stumbling on to a game warden.

First, man hunted woman. Once he caught her, she didn't want him to go out hunting again. To this day, when a man mentions hunting, she still says what the first woman said on the subject, "Keep your trap shut."

Of course, when the family started to grow, he had to hunt to support the kids. "We're going out for dinner" usually meant everyone had to go to the site where dad had clubbed a Brontosaurus rex into twelve tons of stew meat.

There was none of this "Eat everything on your plate" bit then. It was "Eat what you can before the herd misses this one."

The hunter often became the hunted. That's all changed now. We have seasons, controls, limits, quotas, licenses, leases, guides, equipment, clothing, vehicles, and everything imaginable to totally annihilate poor, defenseless budgets.

You can no longer use a gun; you have to use a weapon. You can't buy bullets anymore; you have to ask for ammunition. Ammo is specially loaded to within a grain of gun powder to fire a precision-molded lead missile to the exact spot where the animal is not.

"A miss is as good as a mile" means that no matter how much camouflage gear you wear or how magnum your intentions, you still have little advantage over the caveman. Shooting at a moving target in the wild can be intellectually stimulating, however, especially if the target is moving toward you and looks something like, oh, say a mountain lion.

That's usually when you get so shaky and nervous you get what is known as "buck fever," a term meaning you'd give lots of bucks for a big club . . . the kind you can run inside of and order a drink.

Of all the outdoor events, probably the most popular is deer hunting. I think it's because deer are under the big game category but easier to carry out of the woods than a Holstein heifer. And you seldom have to unhook one from a milking machine.

They say that deer never travel more than a mile from where they were born. I thought this was a myth until I started keeping an eye on one down at the zoo.

And in all fairness, I think we would have to rule out the exception of the occasional buck that travels many miles, not because he was afraid of being shot at, but of being hung. Hung on a wall.

Then there are the legendary, crafty old "mossbacks" that have outsmarted man. Only glimpses of them are reported, usually just at dawn or dusk. Just last season, a friend of mine solved the mystery of one "mossback." He had tracked him for weeks before he discovered the old codger had been feeding only at night. During the day, he slept safe and sound, in plain sight at a truck stop lying across the fender of an abandoned car.

If you have ever sat around a campfire and listened to or told legendary stories about the "one that got away" or slightly exaggerated your claim as a great hunter, then you will appreciate the stories in this chapter. If you have ever enjoyed the health-giving properties of the great outdoors by moving your camp stool to sit downwind from the campfire smoke to keep the mosquitoes off you, then you can identify with this chapter. And they thought we were out there just having fun.

One night a group of my friends were hunting in the Rocky Mountains of Colorado. Around the campfire, they were telling stories of narrow escapes from wild animals. Winston won the storytelling contest hands down. In India, he caught a cobra by the tail, whirled it around, and popped its head off like one would crack a whip. He killed a polar bear in Alaska armed only with an icicle. And, in Africa, he had single-handedly downed a charging bull elephant by hitting him between the eyes with a can of Spam. Then Winston got in his camper and went to bed.

The rest of the guys sat around the campfire for awhile and just about the time they were ready to turn in, they heard a blood-chilling scream in the night that they all recognized as that of a panther. "Let's get him before he gets away," said one of the guys and the race was on.

"Get up, Winston. There's a panther out there in the darkness," another yelled.

With guns and flashlights and all the paraphernalia of modern warfare, they charged into the darkness. An hour later, they all returned, empty-handed, to the campsite to discover that Winston had never left the camper.

"Why didn't you come with us, Winston?" yelled one of the guys through the wall of the camper.

"Back trouble," replied Winston.

"What'd'ya mean 'back trouble'?"

"I've got this yellow streak down the middle of it holding me to the mattress."

My old friend and colleague, H. O. Galloway, had a unique hunting style. He is what I would call a sympathy hunter. He's such a nice guy that if he doesn't have a place to hunt, someone invites him. If he doesn't have a gun, someone loans him one. He's the kind of guy that everybody loves and wants to see him get his limit. They all go to great extremes to see that he does. Well, H. O. received an invitation to go deer hunting once and since I just happened to be with him at the time the invitation was offered, the fellow issuing the invitation half-heartedly said, "You can come, too, if you want to, Doc."

We arrived at the hunting lease the night before in pitch darkness. Neither Galloway nor I knew the lay of the land or where we would be hunting the next day. Long before daylight the next morning, they jammed us inside a jeep and we bounced toward our deer blinds. We stopped at Galloway's blind first. Even in the darkness I could tell it was in the midst of a plush oat patch. A miniature house had been built high in the air, carpet on the floor, propane heater, and I suspected a wet bar and sauna bath. As we roared off into the forest, the fellows were saying, "Nothing's too good for Mr. Galloway." "Salt of the earth." "He'll get a big one there."

We arrived at a place that was little more than a cow trail. They said something sympathetic and encouraging to me, too. As I recall, it was "Get out."

I was told to follow the trail and I would find my blind. It was an old pile of brush that had been arranged in a semi-circle and from the looks of it had been unused for many years. The underbrush was so thick that I couldn't see more than 25 yards in any direction. It was miserably cold, rain had turned to sleet, and I had no heat. After an hour of teeth chattering, I decided I was in the worst spot on the lease (surprise, surprise) and had no chance of even seeing a deer, so I proceeded to build a fire with wet leaves and icy twigs. Looking up through smoke-filled eyes, I saw a large buck not fifteen feet away looking straight at me. Hypothermia and smoke inhalation probably has made me hallucinate I thought. Just in case, I reached over to pick up my rifle and the deer ran. I couldn't see where he went, but I could hear him running through the underbrush. There was only one little clearing about the size of a basketball through the trees, roughly 100 yards away. The deer stopped at that spot, turned his head slightly to look back my way, and I fired through that tiny opening. The deer disappeared. I hacked my way through to the spot and found him lying there. I field dressed the deer but couldn't find a bullet hole. Since the only target I had was the head area, I confined my search there and finally found a tiny wound just below the ear which no one would discover unless they knew what I knew. At noon, the jeep appeared to pick me up. What I suspected about my deer blind was obvious when I told the other fellows I had killed a deer. "You've got to be kidding," they all said in unison.

"Well, I killed one, anyway," I said.

"But we didn't hear a shot," said one.

I acted very mysterious and asked them to follow me. "He doesn't have a deer down here. He's just pulling our leg," I heard one of them say.

Although amazed, they helped me retrieve the deer and we returned to camp. Galloway who had been in the midst of an oat patch had seen absolutely nothing and returned empty-handed. I was the only one who made a kill. So naturally, all the guys got to examining the deer to find out where I had shot him. They found no bullet hole and became suspicious.

"He probably brought that deer with him," I heard one say.

Another remarked, "He may have bought it and planted it out there."

H. O. just kept muttering, "Old Lucky."

Around the campfire that night, their curiosity got the best of them. They were all feeling sorry for H. O. because he had not bagged a big one and "Old Lucky" had. What's more, they couldn't figure out how it happened. "Probably talked him to death," was the rumor.

Finally, H. O. said, "Doc, we've been friends a long time. We couldn't find a mark on that deer. I want you to tell me and the other fellows how you did it as a favor to me."

A hush fell over the camp area. I explained, "Well, you're exactly right, H. O., when you called me 'Old Lucky.' Everyone here knows that you guys put me on the worst spot on the lease. I realized I wasn't going to get a deer, so I was trying to build a fire to at least get warm. I had a long stick in my hand with a crook on the end of it that I was about to break up and put in the fire. All of a sudden, I looked up and there was this huge buck staring me in the face not six feet away. I'll have to confess that the reason you didn't find a mark on that deer is because I didn't use my rifle, I killed him with that stick."

"Awww, you couldn't have hit him hard enough to kill him with a stick," said Galloway.

"I didn't hit him," I explained. "I used my head. I knew I didn't have time to pick up my rifle, so with lightening like speed, I put the crook of that stick over one of his horns before he could move. This startled him and he started to run. That's when I jerked the stick so hard that his nose got hung in his ear. This scared him so bad that he snorted and blew his own brains out."

That's the kind of stuff that made men like Jim Bridger, Daniel Boone, and Davy Crockett. It's not easy being a legend in one's own mind.

I encourage you to hunt through the tales in the pages of this chapter . . . they may provide a covey of ideas on the fascination of this sport.

RED MAN SPEAK WITH FORKED TONGUE

Hunting season always brings out the wild instincts in man, to rough it, to get back to nature. The name of the game is survival of the fittest at the primitive level, preferably at a lodge with a sauna and wet bar.

America's wealthy live in $200,000 climate-controlled homes but are willing to pay a guide to teach them how to track an animal in the snow. Don't laugh, I know of a guy who went by himself and tracked an animal all the way back to its dairy barn.

We were sitting around the campfire one night swapping stories, enjoying a wild game supper of Wolf brand chili, soda crackers, and Colorado kool-aid when the yarns started.

One guy said he was attacked by a charging bear. He reached into its open mouth, grabbed a handful of innards, and turned him inside out. The bear kept on charging but he was going in the other direction.

Another said he could have shot a huge buck but didn't have the proper position to shoot him anyplace but what is known as a "Texas heart shot," so he let him go. The deer was standing with his rear toward him.

However, he did make a perfect silhouette shot later at a jumping deer way off in the distance. It cost him $37.50 to have the hole patched on a green tractor.

Our half-Indian guide, Big Bucks Goquickly, entered the contest and won hands down. "I was given an old rusty rifle and one bullet when just a boy," he said. "My grandfather showed me a set of rabbit tracks and told me I could find supper where they ended. He was right.

"The rabbit tried every trick to throw me off his trail, even swimming underwater across a stream. I was following his faint underwater tracks, when in midstream, I saw a flock of geese flying west. I took aim, then saw a flock of ducks flying east.

"Then I saw a big buck to the north, off to my left. Suddenly another appeared slightly to the right of him.

"I had to make the most of my one shot so I took careful aim at a rock between the two deer. When I pulled the trigger, the old gun exploded. Half the barrel flew into the geese, killing seven. The other half knocked down eight ducks.

"The bullet sped true to its mark splitting in half on the rock and dropped both deer.

"The stock flew back, knocking me down in the stream. When I came up, I had a beaver by the tail in each hand and my pockets were so full of mountain trout that the strain on my pants caused a button to pop off with such force it killed the rabbit."

AL AND GATORS

Remember when alligators were an endangered species? Now they are so numerous that in Ville Platte, La., there is a commercial farm raising and selling alligator meat to supermarkets. Soon they'll be in convenience stores. Management is looking for a suitable building site near a busy intersection in the swamp.

Gator meat is really good they say, and comes in grades of prime, choice, and hostile.

You may wonder how they raise gators in confinement. They put them in water filled vats and feed them raw meat. The alligator farmers feed them carefully and avoid acting raw.

Of course, a lot of gators are still hunted wild. Instead of Crocodile Dundee killing crocs with a knife, the most legendary Cajun is Alligator Alfonse who prefers a broken beer bottle.

The processing plant butchers, skins, and handles the by-products. The guys who work there are real alligator wrestlers. They say it's a good job, but they have this constant, strange compulsion to go out and buy a billfold.

Altogether there are 14 alligator farms in Louisiana. There used to be 15, but the gators ate one.

They even have recipes for the meat. They usually start out with "Take a medium size pan and a .357 Magnum. . . ."

No joke, there are dishes called Bean Sprout and Gator Bake (one got caught in the garden), Gator Meatball and Spaghetti (run over by a gondola), and Le Cocoarie, which is French for H-E-L-P!

A Cajun cook told me that alligator meat is weird because if you cook it like red meat, it tastes like red meat, if you cook it like fish, it tastes like fish. I asked, "What if you cook it like water buffalo?" He replied, "Don't do dat or it won't taste nothin' like gator."

At cocktail parties, the latest rage is Alligator hors d'oeuvres. They put some small chunks in a used shotgun shell casing and call it gator on the half-shell.

There is a difference between the pen-raised and wild gator meat. The Cajuns say the difference is you try to eat the tame ones. In the wild, it's the reverse.

Well, tame or wild, gators are making a comeback. A Cajun hunter told me that he recently came face to face with a giant alligator. "My whole life flashed before my eyes."

"Wow!" I said. "Did you kill him?"

"Naw," he said, "I had a good time. It was an X-rated flash."

To complete my research, I asked this fearless hunter if he ever took a step back when facing a gator. "To told you de trute," he said, "dat's de most dangerous ting you could done. You either step in a possum trap or fall out de boat."

SEMI-SPORTSMEN

My friend, a nature enthusiast, Kent Hill, gets the fever every year about this time. Kent and some buddies are semi-sportsmen, which means they'll hunt anything that won't attack them.

A few years ago they started hunting in the Rockies of Colorado. They soon discovered the law of the wild. If you kill a deer in the bottom of the canyon, the law says it'll drive you wild trying to get it up the mountain to the truck.

One of the fellows shot a deer down low and had to call for help. Four weary hunters struggled up rocky slopes, over ice glazed tundra, and dragged their heavy prey to within 18 feet of the top . . . a sheer cliff. Undaunted, the strongest man took off his shoes, dug tooth and toenail into tiny cracks on the cliff, scaled the wall, and lowered a stout length of cotton clothesline rope. Small avalanches were occurring with frightening frequency all around them. In the face of such imminent danger it was decided to save the most important things first—the deer.

The rope was attached to the buck's horns, the three guys on bottom were instructed to push as long as they could, and the strong man on top pulled. Fifteen agonizing minutes later the buck was hauled over the top, followed by three weary hunters who had hung on to the deer. The stout man threatened to whip them all but instead just lay there spread-eagle, melting his form in a snow bank. They say the spot where he cursed the ground has never since grown grass.

They decided to put up a money pot for the widest spread of horns. Three hunters soon got their deer. Everyone but the weight lifter. He had seen deer, but too far away. On the last day he took a drastic step, resighted his weapon on a paper plate to shoot three inches high at 100 yards, figuring to calculate trajectory at 300 yards and over. His three companions, staying in the camp, heard their buddy shoot one time. They went to help him with his kill and found him with his head in one hand, and a single horn in the other.

"Boy, you sure came close," they consoled. "How far away was he?"

"Twenty-seven steps," sobbed the artillery-man.

However, there was a happy ending. The man of iron won the pot. He convinced the others that the spread between his trophy horns had to be at least five miles.

HUNTIN' TEXAS STYLE

Our deer hunting lease in South Texas was officially opened this season by me and some of my partners. What a crew—Bunkie and son Bubba, Moose and sons Beezer and Wiggles, O. D. and sons Bo, Bud, and Bat. "I can't believe the names of these kids," I said to my son "Miquelito."

Everyone else had cowboy boots but me. I'm the sneaky type so I wore my jogging shoes.

"He's got on his Tenny Lamas," smirked one wag in reference to the fine Tony Lama boot. Bunkie joked, "I should have known that Doc was gonna try and beat me to the best pasture when I saw him wearing Tenny Lamas, holding a stopwatch, and starting gun, but it was five miles over there and we took the Jeep. We would have beat him if we hadn't had to stop and open a gate."

Around the campfire, the older hunters gave instructions to the youngsters. "Always look for the fresh deer pellet signs." When questioned how one could tell if it was fresh, the answer was "It's fresh if it's still rollin' and smokin'."

"Can you tell a new track from an old one?" asked one of the kids.

"Sure you can."

"How?"

"Well, sometimes if you look up real fast you'll see a deer still standing in 'em."

One day at noon when we all got back to camp for lunch, Moose threw a mesquite chunk in the camp pond and fired several neat holes into it with his .38 pistol. "Let me try that," said Bunkie. Everytime he fired a shot, Moose would tell him if he shot high to the left, low to the right, etc. Everyone behind Bunkie quietly slipped out of their camp chairs and lay on the ground in the "dead man position."

"Your last shot ricocheted, Bunkie," said Moose, "turn around and see what you've done."

Without a moments hesitation, Bunkie replies, "Looks like it's shootin' low and behind me."

Later that night around the dim glow of campfire coals when most of the others had gone to bed, a lone coyote howled in the distance. With a faraway look in his eye, Bunkie philosophized, "The trouble with huntin' out here in the big country is that nights are too short . . . and the days are too . . . short."

SPINNING YARNS

Recording historical anecdotes is sort of like getting drunk, "Somebody has to do it." While it's a thankless task at times, there is the satisfaction, as Dizzy Dean used to say, that "You seen your duty and you done it."

Recently I was sitting atop an aluminum picnic table during a thunderstorm listening to the colorful tales of George "Brother" Northington. Brother was spinning a yarn when lightning blew the top of a pecan tree into a product resembling low quality toothpick rejects. Since I was seated on a natural lightning rod platform, I got a little anxious. Brother grabbed my arm with his free hand, stuck his walking cane into the river bottom soil and said, "Don't worry, I got you grounded."

There are lots of tales yet to be told along the rain-soaked, sun-baked junction where the rich bottoms give way to the prairies.

Years ago, before they perfected accuracy and economy of powerful "goose gunpowder," the natives used to hunt geese by outwitting them. One old timer recalls soaking corn in whiskey for several days. This "bait" was set out in a rice field and geese allowed time to gorge themselves. They got so drunk that they just sat there in the mud trying to fly backwards. It was rumored that the flavor was also greatly improved.

They used to hunt bear in these bottoms but hunters didn't waste whiskey on that big an animal, preferring to ration it out to snakebite victims.

According to an old report, a hunting party was out in the mid 1800s, using the latest manufactured ammunition. Individual pre-loaded "shells" were not all that common, and very expensive, so they were not wasted.

Well, this hunting party got on the trail of a bear. The dogs finally brought it to bay. The bear fought with the strength of a hundred. He killed or crippled every dog in the pack.

When the owner of a prized hound saw his favorite dog limp as a towel, he went wild with rage. At point blank range he fired a shot between the eyes that stilled the savage monster. Then he carefully reloaded again. And again.

"Didn't you get him with the first shot?" asked his hunting partners.

"Yep," he seethed.

"Then, why did you shoot him twice more?"

"Cause I only had two more shells."

TELL TAIL SIGNS

It was just too hot in south Texas for the deer to be moving like they usually do, and after awhile the hunters started getting a little anxious. "Those deer have such big, beautiful brown eyes. They are so soft and gentle. They never hurt anybody. They're gonna have to do something real blatant before I shoot one of 'em . . . like walkin' across our lease."

"You'll know I've seen a big one if you hear me shoot once . . . real fast."

Not too many shots were fired on our lease and in fact not a single deer was taken . . . or even a married one. Not that we didn't have plenty of chances. We saw lots of does, but I'm proud to say that all of our hunters were too much of a sport to shoot a doe. Besides these does were about a mile down the road, across the fence, on somebody else's lease.

However, I feel lucky about my season because I heard about one guy who decided to take the plunge and go for the big mule deer up in Colorado. He didn't have a gun, so he went out and bought one. He also bought a tent, a 4-wheel drive vehicle, 30 days of grub, and headed for the high country. When he got there, he found his uncle had gotten in the day before, killed three deer and used up everybody else's tags. Being the generous sort, his uncle gave him a hindquarter of one of the deer, which he promptly threw in the back of his 4-wheel drive vehicle and made the return trip home. It's hard to explain to a wife how venison is worth over $1000 per pound.

Action was so slow on our lease that me and my hunting partner passed a coyote that someone had shot beside the road. My partner asked me, "Doc, did you shoot that coyote?"

I replied, "Nope."

Quick as a flash, he shot back with "Well, would you like to?"

Perhaps the best tale came from another buddy who claims he saw a buck following very closely behind a doe. He had to hurry his shot as the deer immediately disappeared in the brush. When he got to the spot, he found a buck holding a doe's tail in his mouth. He said he started to shoot again and ask questions later, but curiosity got to him. On closer examination, it was indeed a buck holding only the stub of another deer's tail in its mouth.

"Didn't have the heart to shoot him," he said, "this buck was blind. I accidentally shot off the tail of the doe that was leading him and he didn't know which way to turn."

SKY HUNTERS

It's duck hunting season but I doubt that our feathered friends are in any danger of extinction. "Sky hunters" in our area fire magnum cannons with birdshot patterns the size of a canned ham without ever ruffling a feather. Sure, it's expensive but as the old saying goes "Spending money without getting any joy out of it is known as economy."

Duck hunting is seldom economical but always joyous. You have to keep convincing yourself that it's fun to get up at 3 A.M., lay in a cold, wet place, and make strange sounds. A plumber does the same thing under a house and gets paid for it.

Making those duck sounds is a real art. I've seen guys who could make such realistic mating calls that they had to shoot drakes in self defense to keep them off.

My imitations have been described as accurate duck calls, too— Daffy. I guess I'm just too busy worrying about the finer points, like if ducks eat a big meal and then go in the water, will they get the cramps?

About the only improvement in my hunting score would be a surface-to-air . . . make that surface-to-duck missile. I've had the surface-to-air kind all along.

That's why I was impressed with the story of the guy who was seen soundlessly knocking ducks out of the air. A curious sky hunter, so far unsuccessful, approached the fellow and asked about his source of power and deadly aim.

"I ugly 'em down" was the reply.

"How do you do that?"

"Watch this." A duck flew over, the guy twisted his face into a horrible contortion, his eyes met the ducks and suddenly the air was filled with feathered cartwheels as the duck fell at his feet.

"Wow," exclaimed the intruder. "Why don't you bring your wife out here with you and get double your limit?"

"Unh, uhh," muttered the old pro, "She's too good at it, and can make magnum ugly. She tears 'em up too bad."

I Q OF HIQ

Lots of dog stories have made the rounds for years, usually about the intellect of our four footed friend. Next time you get to feeling superior to your mutt, remember who he has supporting him. It just goes to show how smart they are. Like the fellow who raised a dog that was so smart that while he was being paper trained, he learned to read.

I remember one of my old college profs bragging about his squirrel dog "Kodak" who had a photographic memory. Kodak never forgot where a nest was or which tree the critter ran up. He was a little impatient, however, with my old prof for being too slow to get to the scene of action once he had "treed" a squirrel. For a while he went along with the traditional method of getting the scent, running while barking, baying so his master could tell when to come to the kill. After the squirrel was shot and fell from the tree, the dog picked him up and laid him at the feet of his master. A few quick pants, a wag of his tail, a pat on the head, and he was off again.

After a while Kodak got impatient with the whole procedure. If the prof didn't show up real quick, old Kodak just picked up a stick with his teeth and leaned it up against the tree to mark it, then took off on the next scent.

But the most remarkable story is of a pup out of Kodak and the paper trained dog that learned to read. "HiQ" was his name and his feats became legendary. Once while competing in the county championship, HiQ was shown to the judges in a conformation class.

"Classic," remarked one judge.

"Marvelous," said another.

Then they set him loose. Quickly he caught the scent and began to sing his canine song.

"What tone!" cried a judge.

"What clarity," remarked another.

"Never heard sweeter," commented the owner.

"But is he smart?" quizzed the chief of the panel of experts.

"Smart as they come," boasted the owner.

Just then HiQ abruptly stopped barking and there was complete silence in the distance.

"Too bad," remarked the judge, "lost the trail."

"Nope," the owner confidently replied, "too smart for that. He always does that when running across posted land."

GONE FISHING

A top banking executive, a friend of mine, is always telling me about his hunting and fishing trips. He goes to the most exotic places, always hinting that he was in the company of some famous politician or personality.

I used to think he was personally wealthy but have since found out how the game is played. It seems that he is financial and spiritual advisor to a very wealthy client who owns yachts, airplanes and people. He has islands in the Caribbean, hunting preserves in the Rockies and recently tried to purchase some salt water fishing property—the Pacific Ocean. The man has so much money that he can go into a restaurant and order only by looking at the left side of the menu.

However, the tycoon has a health problem. He has lived three lives in double time and his heart is giving him trouble.

"How much is a new one?" he shouts.

My banker friend advises him that the technology does not exist for new installations, but perhaps the old one can be repaired.

"I want the best," screams the old moneybags, "get me Bernhard."

"Dr. Bernhard may not be the best," says my banker friend, "but he thinks he is. He's very busy, but I've got to get him."

So there I was, not intending to eavesdrop but enchanted with this skillful manipulation.

The banker picks up the phone, "Get me Dr. Bernhard." After a lengthy wait the sales job began: "Bernie, I know you're busy, doing lots of bypasses . . . you're booked solid for a year? Yes, well how would you like to take a break, fly down to a resort island, deep sea fish, take your wife, dine on a fabulous luxury yacht, stay in a plush condominium, get a tan on a gorgeous private beach, all expenses paid, for as long as you like, in addition to your fee? You think you might be able to work that in by clever rescheduling? Good. All you have to do to enjoy these plush facilities is save the life of the old codger who owns all of it."

The operation was the next day. A sign in the bank president's office read: "Gone Fishing."

GORILLA WARFARE

My friend "Bunkie" Hill has had an interesting life because in his youth he ran around with some dangerous desperados. All of them lived in the woods practicing an art form known as gorilla warfare. The gorillas maintained their fragile supply lines with the pride of a General Patton. Supplies consisted mainly of 410 gauge shotgun shells, Vienna sausages, and army surplus stuff.

Bunkie and the others learned that in order to bring down an enemy aircraft (like a crow or chicken hawk), they had to shoot in front of the target. A miss always brought forth the cry "You didn't lead him enough, stupid." Another precious shell expended from the gorilla supply line while the enemy grows stronger.

One night Bunkie and two of his gorilla commandos, Slats McGonnelgal and Chicken Winkel, were on night maneuvers in the big thicket. Chicken had one of those army surplus flashlights that had a 90 degree turn at the end, used for "seeing around corners." However, if you held your mouth just right and concentrated hard, you could make the light shine any which way, even straight. This night, the trio had a small campfire going with an old H&H coffee can full of branch water just starting to bubble softly. The water would be later poured through a surplus mosquito net to strain out the sticks, leaves, and impurities.

Slats was supposedly out on a mission to gather some intelligence on a nearby watermelon patch. But secretly he had secured a surplus battery-operated phonograph and a wild animal recording of a panther's scream.

After about the third scream, Bunkie looked over at Chicken. Without a word, Chicken unhooked his army flashlight from his belt, took one foot and turned the coffee water over into the fire, then ran in full battle retreat. Bunkie followed in hot pursuit, a feat made possible on this dark night only because that gooseneck flashlight was shining down or backwards most of the time. Suddenly the flashlight flew straight up in a somersaulting motion. A loud cracking of wood and the unmistakable twang of taut barb wire was heard. Chicken had torn a wooden gate clean off its hinges.

That's when Slats caught up with the boys and explained about his test of courage under fire. In the eerie glow of a gooseneck flashlight half buried in the sand, Slats with howling laughter, explained how "You guys ran right past me. I should have jumped out and grabbed you."

With his hand over his bib overalls where his heart used to be Chicken replied, "If you had, you would have had to lead me by about 10 yards."

SHORT HOP HUNTERS

My friend, Bill Coplin, is a professional actor and speaker who has invented a character called R. J. Saxet, which is "J. R." and Texas spelled backwards. With his $150 hat and $500 eel skin boots, he portrays a character who is in oil and cattle, owns his own Lear jet and is worth "about 35 million." What follows is one of R. J.'s typical stories.

"Me and my son Bubba were visitin' with Robert Redford, Roger Starbuck, and a few friends at a Dallas party the other day when the subject came up of huntin'. Me and Bubba got so excited that we just jumped in the Lear jet and flew to Alaska.

"We hired one of them fancy guides to take us in a float plane and landed on one of them little bitty lakes. Me and Bubba shot a moose, record class of course. We drug it back to the edge of the lake and told the guide to strap it on one of the pontoons and get airborne.

"The pilot said we couldn't do that, that it would make the plane too heavy and we couldn't take off. Well, that's when I told him a thing or two. I told him that me and Bubba seen a pilot just last year who was good enough to take off from this very lake with a moose that was almost identical in size to this one. Well, that pilot got all inspired and decided that he wasn't going to let some other pilot outfly him. Sure enough, it was just like I told him. We finally got airborne at the very last moment and got off the lake. The problem was that we skimmed the tops of some little ol' saplin's and crashed in a great cloud of dust, tangled metal, and moose horns.

"Everybody was unconscious there for a spell. When I came to, I looked over at Bubba and said, 'My gosh, Bubba, where are we?'

"He said, 'Well, Daddy, as near as I can figure, we're about 500 yards further than we were last year.'"

BIG D SAFARI

It was a great day for pheasant hunting. The sun was shining, the wind was calm, the game warden was in the next county.

Pat Johnson, El Campo, Texas, is a young game guide who specializes in geese, ducks and pheasants. Son Mike and I went on this pheasant hunt with friends P. J. Moose, Sue, Patches, Dallas, Eddie and Sam. Sue, Patches and Dallas are dogs. Moose is their handler. The others are jokingly called hunters. Laughter was a very important weapon in our arsenal. Someone was always saying, "You call yourself a hunter. Ha!"

Sue and Patches, Brittany Spaniels, set off along a rice canal sniffing through the thick weeds and grass. I was first on the scene when Sue assumed the point. I couldn't see a bird where she was pointing but Moose yelled, "Kick the grass and flush him out." I did and the grass exploded with a pheasant rocketing skyward. It sounded like World War III. Sue and I hit the dirt.

You don't see many dogs that point with one paw over each ear.

After I got the hang of it, I began to enjoy the thrill of the hunt except that I couldn't get my safety off and my shotgun up quick enough. Patches felt so sorry for me once that he tried to help by catching a bird. I was too much of a sport for that. I was not about to be humiliated by shooting at a bird being held down by a dog. What if I missed?

When Moose put Dallas—a big bird dog—to work, business really picked up. Dallas had an unusual point. What you might call Cavalier. He would point laying down, on his back, over the shoulder, and several other variations probably caused from watching NFL games at Moose's feet. I've never before seen a retriever spike a pheasant.

Those dogs are hard to fool. At one point, all three pointed at a pool of water. We fired into the water. Blew out an old . . . Three Feathers whiskey bottle.

It was an afternoon to remember, a shooting score to forget.

We all got our limit even though the pheasant population was never in danger of extinction because of our marksmanship. Still you have this image of yourself as Rambo, First Blood, Part II. Never mind that. I looked like Bimbo, First Grade, Part Time.

I'm practicing my marksmanship and expect to be ready for the next migratory bird season. Moose has already stimulated my hunter's instincts. He's promised me a chance to hunt again with Dallas so I'll stand a chance to see him slam dunk a duck.

HEAVY ADVICE

With the heavy hunting season over, it's time to look back at some of the heavy tales that will be told around next year's campfires. It's amazing how many men will get up at 4 A.M. to lie in a wet rice field to shoot up $20 worth of shells at geese that are too far away so they can swagger into a cafe wearing camouflage clothes and brag that they got their limit. What they got their limit of was cold, wetness, and lack of sense.

Still it's worth it just to be able to tell the stories. I've got a couple to relate myself. They both involve a local landowner who leases out his property and seems to know the whereabouts of every animal that comes through his place.

This was the first year I had hunted on Alton's place. I had the use of a cabin complete with hot and cold running water. It was hot in the summer, cold in the winter, and you had to run outside to get it. It was deer season and I arrived at the cabin a few hours before dark on unfamiliar land, but I had a map of the place so I started scouting for signs, tracks, and clues. I had covered the whole place when minutes before dark, close to the road, under a tree, I spotted a doe, then two, finally a shadowy figure whose head I couldn't see. In pitch darkness, I worked my way through a barbed wire fence onto the caliche road. Suddenly, the headlights from a pickup switch on. It's Alton.

"C'mon, boy. I'll give you a ride. See anything?" Before I could answer he continues, "There's a buck and doe that hang out under a tree right where you were. Big buck, sneaky devil, keeps his head low. Always in the late afternoon. Yep, that's where the deer are . . . in the afternoon that is . . . yes sir, if I were hunting deer, that's where I'd be in the afternoon. By gosh in the afternoon that's where the deer will be."

Thoroughly impressed I thought I could avail myself of some expert advise, "Alton," I casually asked, "where will they be in the morning?"

"Same place," he replied.

He later gave me advice on duck hunting. "Hundreds of 'em, east of the creek. Get my limit every time I go."

"When do you go, Alton?" I asked.

"Day after the season closes."

WILD SHOTS 9

You can lead a mule to water, but you've really
got something if you can make him float
on his back.

ANIMALS

My friend Mickey bought this big dog that turned out to be about half mean. The other half must have been groundhog because he dug up everything in the yard. Since he chased every cat, squirrel, and bird in the neighborhood, they named him simply, "Animal," and chained him to the oak tree near but just short of the rabbit hutch.

Mickey was gone a couple of days and when he came home, the wife and kids were downtown. He went out back to check on Animal and found an open door on the hutch. Obviously, the beautiful white rabbit that the kids had enjoyed for the last two years had escaped. Permanently. Animal had him in his mouth and he was deader than a door nail.

Animal hadn't chewed him up, but the rabbit was very dirty, a real mess. Mickey washed the rabbit off, shampooed the fur, did a job with a hair dryer that a veterinarian would have charged for, and placed the rabbit back in the cage in a natural position. The kids would find him, think he died of a heart attack, and all would be well with him and Animal.

Watching through the window, he saw the wife and kids drive up. They went straight to the rabbit hutch clutching a shoebox between them. In the shoebox was a baby rabbit.

Much commotion went on in the backyard. Kids were jumping up and down, happy as could be. The wife seemed less happy. She stormed into

158

the house and confronted Mickey. "Are you and Animal responsible for this?" she screamed.

"Something wrong, Sweetheart?" he innocently asked.

"Yes, something is very wrong. While you were gone, "Bugs" died of a heart attack and we buried him under the oak tree. You go out and explain to the kids about rabbit resurrection."

Mickey and Animal both spent the night in the doghouse.

Wives and animals just seem to have some kind of repelling aura between them. It even creeps into their dreams. My wife had this dream recently. She was trapped in an elevator in a tall building. She pushed 19 and the elevator went up, but the door wouldn't open. She pushed 1 and it went down, but still wouldn't open. She pushed PH (for Penthouse). This time it opened, but a huge, full-maned, African lion jumped in with her as the doors closed. The lion was right in her face, fangs showing, growling, "Ah-h-h-h-h, Ah-h-h-h-h, Ah-h-h-h-h."

Terrified, she awoke and learned the source of her dream. It was me snoring.

When I woke up, she was screaming, "Animal, Animal!" All I could think of was that under cover of darkness Mickey's dog must have dug his way into our bedroom.

Pets are adored around the world. Whether your favorite pet was a horse, dog, cat, parrot, parakeet, guinea pig, duck, or something as exotic as an Easter chicken that grew up to take over the family garage, perhaps you can relate to these stories. Animals can be funny, outrageous and crude, but most of what they do is totally innocent and comes from instinct. As Mark Twain once wrote "Man is the only animal on the face of the earth who blushes . . . or has need to."

MONKEY BUSINESS

Eugene, an Illinois school superintendent vacationing in Acapulco, was a double casualty of hotel overbooking. While entering a taxi to take him to the other facility, he was attacked by a monkey being transported in a bag by a woman. Apparently enraged by the woman's treatment, the monkey broke out, jumped through the open cab window and declared war on the first human it saw—Eugene. Although bitten 47 times, Eugene choked the monkey unconscious and threw it back out the window where the bellboys beat it senseless with a set of nearby golf clubs.

Afraid that the chimp may have been rabid, a school board official called the Acapulco hospital room where the injured man was being treated.

"Eugene, we just heard you were attacked by a crazed chimpanzee but that can't be right. There are no monkeys in Acapulco."

"Believe me," replied Eugene, "all it takes is ONE."

"Was he mad?"

"The last time I saw him, he wasn't too happy with the bellhops. It could be fatal not to tip those fellows."

"Was it the yellow cab driver that rescued you?"

"No, but he did turn a little pale. He says he'll never drink another banana daiquiri and is looking for a can of mace that smells like lion's breath."

"But aren't monkeys supposed to do cute little things like swing on vines?"

"I think this one had been smoking 'em."

"How many times did he bite you?"

"I don't know for sure but, when I stand in the wind, my body whistles . . . and when I drink, it leaks."

"Do you have to take rabies shots?"

"No, the chimp tested negative."

"So there's no side effects from the bites?"

"Well, I do have this unnatural craving for coconut . . ."

Eugene spent a week in the hospital and fully recovered from this bizarre incident. However, he has two new phobias—riding in cabs and the expression "The monkey's on your back."

To quote Eugene on his return from Acapulco, "It's a jungle out there."

BEARLY ABLE

In Alaska at an airbase recently some fellows noticed a little brown bear that appeared every day about dark to raid the trash cans. The cans were dumped nightly into a large container that was picked up every morning by a civilian contractor. So, they baited the little brown bear into the container and slammed the lid. After a long night with a short temper that little bear had a big urge to get out . . . and get even.

Can you imagine what it would be like to a sleepy eyed garbage contractor to open that lid?

Bloodshot, red eyes, white fangs glistening in the morning sun as an apparent hydrophobic bear explodes from a mountain of tin cans and potato peelings, ear splitting growls, hot breath that smells of chipped beef and chopped liver, covered with gravy and bread crumbs, celery stalks sticking out his ears, a small scale war just looking for a place to happen.

The first peak of daylight brought the contractor who opened the lid as the little bear sang out, "Let my people go." The contractor did the only sensible thing under the circumstances—he fainted. He looked so peaceful laying there in his white Hefty uniform with bear tracks alternating in ketchup, mustard, mayonnaise, and chicken fat.

When he came to, he replied from his prone position to the crowd gathered around him, "What happened? The last thing I remember I was having this terrible dream about my mother-in-law."

The moral to that story is that you don't have to have references to borrow trouble, but keeping his sense of humor enabled Davy Crockett to "grin down" many a bear. So, a good thumb rule is, "If you open the lid on a mad bear and he tries to get away . . . let him."

THE OLD COW

Back when cattle were even cheaper than they are now, I bought a ragged, smooth-mouthed, old cow because she had raised a huge calf. This old sister was so skinny she had to stand twice in the same place to cast a shadow but I reasoned that if she could produce a big calf just one more year she would pay for herself. She was already older than dirt but she had five more big calves at 10 month intervals. That's quite a record. And not belonging to the union, she worked without threat of a slow down.

Then one day it happened. She got bogged down in a mudhole. Being of advanced age she soon expended her energy and gave up trying to get out. With ropes and a horse we finally pulled her out but she never offered to get up again. She had gone on strike.

I called our stockyard specialist to see if they would salvage "downed cattle" for dog food. He said regulations forbid that now but asked, "Have you tried whiskey?"

That seemed a bit personal, even unnecessary, so I responded with a quick witted remark like, "Huh?"

"I mean for the cow. Whiskey has a lot of easily burned energy and we use it on occasions to get weak cattle on their feet. It would be worth a try. Just get a pint of the cheapest whiskey you can get," he advised.

So I entered our local liquor store and asked for the cheapest fifth on hand. A hush fell over the store as every eye shifted from a bottle label to my blushing cheeks. The clerk, trying for a better sale asked what kind of party was being planned and what else would be needed.

"It's not for me," I laughed nervously. You see, I have this down cow . . ."

"Hey, man. That ought to make her high," crackled a bearded longhair.

Meanwhile, back at the ranch, I poured a fifth down the old gal, resulting in a far away look in her eye and breath that could dent a fender at 40 yards. She had long horns and in thrashing around had managed to rip my pants, bust my lip and soak my shirt with whiskey. Thinking that I might not have poured enough down her, I returned to the liquor store for another bottle. The fumes from my shirt smelled so strong they warned other customers not to smoke. I told them about my sick cow again but the only comment was from a little old lady who offered to drive me home.

The old cow was waiting for me. She didn't spill a drop this time. I think she finally grinned herself to death. I never did get the smile off her face. And at the cremation that fire would not go out.

HIGH STRUNG CATS

"Cats are full of music," wrote Mark Twain, "and when they die it is taken from them by the fiddle makers." I think most fiddle players are using strings made of something else now, which probably accounts for the decline in catgut and an increase in that smug look on feline faces. Cats are independent cusses. Maybe they still harbor some suspicions that the fiddle makers will revert to their old ways. No need to get strung up tight by just being friendly.

A cat is actually a snob. You can whistle at him all day and he won't come to you. He won't get your pipe, slippers or paper even if you soaked them in fish oil. They don't even bark when strangers come around the house. Did you ever hear of a watchcat? If you got one to attack someone, how would you command it? Nobody ever says "sic 'em" to a cat.

They are obnoxious devils, filled with evil thoughts. A dog will wag his tail and bust his bones to try to please you. Anytime a cat wags his tail he's trying to charm the family canary into a minor starring role of "Jaws." I've seen them sit for hours behind a water trough waiting for a sparrow to try to get a drink. There are probably as many sparrows with high blood pressure caused from drinking water as there are humans with high blood pressure caused from cussing cats.

Throw a clod of dirt at one when he is crouched in position ready to spring on a poor unsuspecting bird and watch him uncoil like an old clock mainspring, rocket up the side of a tree, blast down the other side and then calmly walk away with a look that would cause any jury to vote for acquittal. "Who me? I just happened to be passing by. I tarried for just a moment in eventide to secretly watch a little bird quench his parched throat in the coolness of lengthening shadows when I was attacked by Clod Kamikazie. Unprovoked, unwarranted and unnecessary, Ladies and Gentlemen. I throw myself on the mercy of the court."

Think of the evil things associated with cats. Cat burglars, catty remarks, cat-of-nine tails; nobody ever wrote a song about their faithful cat companion who ran a coon up a tree or gave his life trying to rescue his drowning master from a raging river.

That's probably what drove the early musicians to get it out of them the best way they could. But pure economics caused the decline of catgut. Nine lives for only one string just ain't practical.

Cats no longer make any contribution to anything but the furniture business where they spend three lives sharpening their claws on the sofa, three lives converting your carpet to a shag rug and three lives swishing their tail under the runners of a rocking chair. Watch out for a dedicated cat with a crooked tail. He could be the cause of nine heart attacks.

FLYING TIGERS

There is an old controversy about which is the best pet—a dog or a cat. Opinion polls vary about 50-50. Fifty dogs out of 50 dogs hated cats.

This intense dislike of cats is shared by my Uncle Fred. On a tour of the zoo one windy day, his hat was eaten by a leopard.

A dog wouldn't do that. A cat will scratch or bite just to hurt you. A dog will slip up behind you with a cold nose and make you hurt yourself.

A friend of mine was telling me about an incident that happened out on his farm. He had a bunch of chickens in a hen house that was being raided by something big, and from the looks of the tracks it was a big cat. One cold night he heard a commotion in the hen house just as he was going to bed. He had stripped down to his boxer shorts but he jumped in some old house shoes, threw on a coat, got his double-barrel shotgun and a flashlight, and sneaked into the hen house.

Tensely, he took the safety off his gun, quietly opened the door to the hen house, shined the light inside, and stood shivering in a crouched combat position ready for anything.

"About that time," he told me, "I saw a pair of bright eyes shining in the darkness."

"Was it a cat?" I asked.

"I dunno," he said. "About the same time, Ol' Blue stuck his cold nose in my groin and we've been patching roof ever since."

That was one case in which dog was definitely not man's best friend. Next time you think you have influence, try ordering somebody else's dog around.

I'm surprised, with the new developments in genetic engineering, somebody hasn't come up with a cross between a cat and a dog.

That would be ideal. It would be called a dat or a cog. It would make sense to see an animal like that chase its own tail.

Think of it, what a retriever! It could run, swim, and climb trees. These animals would be very neat, smart too. They would bury bones as well as waste material and speak two languages.

Cross a lion with a St. Bernard, teach him to practice these habits in the right spot, and you'll be the envy of the Spring Garden Club.

It sure would make life interesting for the people who enforced the laws against loose animals in cities. Can't you just hear an officer calling for reinforcements to capture this "thing" on top of a telephone pole?

"What is it, Harry?"

"Oh, it's just one of those new three-way crosses. That breed is called a Siamese Shepardkeet. Quick, get the tranquilizer gun before it flies away!"

DOGGONE GRANDMA

We used to have an old dog that just came to our place. Her teeth were worn and she was already gray about the mouth so we called her "Grandma." She was one of those characters that everyone loved and inquired about. Strangers or folks who didn't know her used to cut their eyes from side to side when they heard the following conversation.

"How's Grandma. She still alive?"

"Yeah, but her teeth are worn so bad that about all we let her have is chopped liver and corn bread."

"I'll bet if you gave her a raw egg and wormed her, the old gal would perk up. That's a good remedy for anybody's Grandma."

"We tried that once but she ran up under the house and we had to turn the hose on her to get her out. When Pa grabbed her by the leg she nearly gummed his thumb off. She scaled that picket fence around the house and spent the rest of the day limping like she was hurt, looking for sympathy."

One day this do-gooder who just couldn't stand it any longer suggested that the elderly should get more respect even if we were just kidding about our Grandma. To which we would reply, "We ain't kiddin'. We love Grandma. That's the main reason we came to town today, to let her ride in the truck. She always likes to hang her head out the door and slobber in the wind.

"Grandma used to hide in the grass by the side of the road for hours and when an old, slow, rattletrap came chugging by she would attack.

For about ten yards she could make that driver think a crazed Banshee was about to deliver him from among the living. The rest of the day she would just lay up next to the water trough and grin."

To top off our day the Widow Perkins passed by and sweetly said, "Hello, boys. How's Grandma? Do bring her over for a visit. I just love the way she lays on her back and lets me scratch her belly."

That's when the do-gooders start looking behind them and backing out the door.

Lots of people are just waiting in the wings to jump to conclusions without the burden of facts. Never believe anything you hear and only half of what you see.

FIVE'LL GET YOU SIX

This story is so sensitive that the names of the jerks involved have been changed to protect the guilty. Any resemblance to the characters in this plot to any person living or dead is purely intentional.

Hiram Plenty, mayor of a dry, strict city, had just called his select group of city councilmen to order. "I'll have a hamburger" chuckled one. "Make mine pizza" cried another. The important business of the day taken care of, the court took up the next item of business—a citizen complaint.

"Dogs are running loose in the streets, cats are in every garbage can, Willie Smellitz is even feeding mash from his still to a hog in his back yard. All this inside the city limits. We need an animal warden," complained Edna Clampett.

The court was sympathetic. The mayor whispered to a councilman who swiftly left only to return with a prisoner from the drunk tank, Robert (Five) Measley, a name he acquired, long before the movie "10," which referred to his beer limit. Since he always ordered an illegal six pack, he let his lease expire on the alley back of the Ritz Theatre and became a strong supporter of law enforcement by living in the city jail.

"Five," says Hiram, "some men seek greatness, some find greatness and some men have greatness thrust upon them."

"I ain't gonna do it, Mayor. Last time you gave me that speech, I was used as bait to catch a renegade alligator down on the river."

Later as Five Measley, dressed in his new animal warden's uniform, approached Willie's hog pen operation with a warrant for his arrest, Willie got the drop on Measley.

"He took away my only weapon, a five cell flashlight, and threatened to feed me to his hog," said Five. "Then he poured beer all over my clothing and sent me back to you guys with the message that unless you left him alone, he was going to publish details of an illegal booze scandal that one of you might find very embarrassing."

Now it just so happened that Willie was feeding this hog in an old two-wheel trailer put up on concrete blocks. With news of an impending scandal about to break, council courageously sprang into unanimous action.

"Case closed," cried Mayor Plenty. "It has been determined that the hog in question was in transit."

Robert Measley then retired from public life to take up part time employment as a door stop behind the Ritz Theatre. His constant plea: "Gimme a ten Mister and Five'll get you six."

SICK AS A DOG

The couch was crowded with victims coughing, wheezing, scratching. Phones were ringing; other patients were anxious to get in to see the doctor. Finally one patient, overcome with the agony of waiting, jumped off the couch, his tongue hanging loosely out of his mouth, fell on his side and began to howl like a dog. Which is not unusual because he is a dog. Veterinarians have those seasons too when all their patients seem to catch the same thing at the same time.

Animal doctors have to be smarter than people doctors because their patients can't tell them what's wrong with them. And they ought to charge more because they have to put up with the owners too.

"What seems to be the problem with your dog, Mrs. Vandersnoot?"

"Please, Doctor. Fife doesn't know she's a d-o-g. All we've ever told her is that she is adopted."

"I see little resemblance. You should have gotten a horse."

"What was that?"

"I said, These icy little spells could have gotten her hoarse."

"Well, she hasn't been feeling well. This morning she didn't even bark at the postperson."

"Probably been indoctrinated by the ERA movement. There, I've completed my diagnosis. She's got the swine flu."

"Why, that's disgusting. I know my Fife and I know she would never catch such a revolting disease. I want a second opinion."

"O.K. She's also got worms."

After some discussion, the lady asked if the veterinarian could correct the difficulties.

"Yes, Mrs. Vandersnoot, but it will take about $50."

"Will it involve a dangerous operation?"

"Don't be ridiculous, madam. You can't buy a dangerous operation for $50. That would cost at least $500."

So shots were given, pills prescribed and the next case admitted.

Meanwhile, out back, the partner of the small animal practitioner rushed in for a quick conference.

"You know that prize bull that our banker sent over for a check up? Well, I gave him a shot and just as we were loading him back in the trailer, he dropped dead in the gate. How do we explain this?"

"Don't panic," said his partner, "First thing you do is turn him around so it looks like he died coming in."

FREDDY'S FROG FRENZIE

An ad in the Wall Street Journal said a meat market in New Orleans was buying froglegs and will "contract up to a million."

The recent rains caused a Friona, Texas entrepreneur to lose interest in ranching and speculate on the bullfrog market:

"This is it, Mabel. Our chance to hit the bigtime. Since the rains, the frog population has exploded. Listen to 'em out there, must be at least a million. If we can just get 'em before it dries up, at a dollar each we're sitting on a gold mine or, better yet, a frog mine."

"Do you know where you'll get warts if you sit on a frog mine, Fred?"

"It'll just make me ride taller in the saddle. I'll bet Hopalong Cassidy got that name from frog hunting. That's it, Mabel, fame, fortune, then the movies."

"Yeah, I can see your stage name in lights now. 'Freddy Friona starring in From Ferdinand To Frogs,' with a cast of thousands."

A call was made to New Orleans confirming the need for froglegs. Fred promptly got a jumpstart on his tongue, contracted for the whole million, put the icehouse on emergency standby, had a 747 on call, and hired so many school kids that pool halls failed for forty miles around.

As darkness fell, the drenched West Texas desert came alive with the sounds that had driven Freddy Friona to a frog frenzy.

Six sections of dead grass and rocks were completely surrounded by kids wearing carbide headlights and wielding frog gigs as the circle tightened.

Refrigerated trucks stood by the center of the circle with a butchering crew.

All through the night the circle decreased until all hunters were a few yards apart.

Then, just before dawn, one big-mouthed frog leaped from the grass and let out a million dollar croak. Gigs filled the air like raindrops in a thunderstorm. They hit everything but the frog. Every truck had a flat tire and the sideboards looked like a porcupine with gland trouble; the casualty list was enormous and Freddy Friona got a gig where he feared he would get warts.

One loudmouth frog leaped back to his temporary pond to teach those tadpoles a lesson. What sounds like a million may not be worth a dime and our dreams may get punctured in the end. Even so, we may still find reason to ride tall in the saddle.

PLAIN HORSE SENSE

Horses are wonderful animals. They are just dumb enough to stay in a pasture with one wire around it and just smart enough to keep you from catching them in anything but a squeeze chute. I put a bridle on one the other day and he tried to get my sympathy by acting like he had a sore tongue. It's the first time I ever saw a horse spit and go, "Phooey."

Put a saddle on one and they take a deep breath and swell up like a blimp taking on a load of helium. All the time they have that far away stare in their eye and try to act like they had no intention of doing that on purpose—just happened to need a little air at that particular moment. If you should forget to really tighten the cinch when he ain't looking you can really impress your neighbors as you gallop across the plains . . . underneath your horse. If you live in cactus country you only let that happen once. That mistake is called "Brush Country Acupuncture."

The Arabs might just be smarter than we are in other ways besides oil. Their horses are funny looking things called camels that have built-in saddles, don't have to stop for a drink of water at every mud puddle and even lie down so you can get on.

It's about time some researcher developed a horse with one hump or two so a saddle wouldn't be needed. Maybe a stepladder could be bred into the rib cage, and a Zebco factor in the genetic makeup should be studied so you could reel him in from the pasture when you wanted to ride.

Whoever gave the name "Hayburner" to a horse never had one of the later models because oats cost money and that ain't hay. A horse eats all the time. When he's not eating he's thinking about eating. The only reason few people train horses to go out and fetch the morning paper is because they would eat it. Besides, they are too nervous to curl up in your lap next to a winter fire. They would eat the firewood. I saw one chew a gate into toothpicks. All that wood almost did him in, though. He came down with a terrible case of Dutch Elm Disease.

But, in spite of all these flaws in his animal character, the horse is revered by man as being bright. We talk about "horse sense" as a high form of intellect. I'll bet Einstein never chewed down a fence. On the other hand, I never heard of Flicka betting on the people races. I'll have to discuss that point with my old mare. If I can catch her.

PARROT PAL

The jet set loves to have you ask "Where have you been lately?" They always give some exotic answer like "Crete, Malta, and Zaire." I usually hear these conversations on my way back from Sears, Eckerds, and McDonalds.

That's why I was so excited to get invited to speak in Grenada. When the word got out, all my jet set friends were jealous until they found out it was Grenada, Mississippi.

Grenada is between Jackson and Memphis and resembles the Caribbean Islands with the same name only at night. Even then, the similarity consists of both places getting dark.

Some local residents claim that the city was named for Grenada, Spain, but others insist an immigrant Italian, a shell-shocked war hero did the honors when an immigrant Irishman threw him a potato. He ran from the council meeting that convened to select a name, yelling, "Gren-ade-a, Gren-ade-a!"

To this day, people have gathered to swap potatoes, produced from the rich delta, and stories. As a Texan, I felt obligated to uphold the honor of the state, but speaking at a Boy Scout fund-raiser really cramped my style. All that talk about honesty and loyalty dulls your enthusiasm for imaginative lying.

Fortunately, an old Scout who had outlived his youthful oats told me this story:

This Southern gentleman called on a beautiful belle who had a very protective father. A few hours later, he staggered into the country club with his clothes ripped to shreds, cut and bleeding all over.

"What happened?" his friend asked as they fed him a double mint julep.

"Parrot," he moaned as he lapsed into periodic unconsciousness.

"A parrot did this to you?"

He nodded affirmatively.

"How?"

"Well," he gasped, "Miss Scarlet's father told me to wait in the parlor with this dumb parrot and a trained Doberman.

"I had waited over an hour with this parrot saying, 'Polly wants a cracker' over and over. The Doberman alternated looking at the parrot and then looking at me."

"Finally, I couldn't take it anymore. I yelled, 'Can't you say anything else, you stupid bird?' That's when the parrot did it."

"He attacked you?" asked a listener.

"No, he said, 'Sic 'em.'"

THE ALBINO SQUIRREL

Olney, Illinois is the home of the white squirrel. I didn't realize the significance of that until I spoke to their chamber of commerce and met a few of their old gray, "squirrely characters." They said they just had two seasons this last year—July and Winter. They knew it was going to be a tough winter because all those white squirrels were storing nuts in antifreeze.

The white nut chompers are unique in Olney, the only place in America where true albino squirrels (white fur, pink eyes) exist in large numbers. They breed true, can be seen all over town and are protected by Illinois law. There is a rumor out that legislation has been introduced to seek federal funds for bussing of the dark squirrels into white neighborhoods but so far that hasn't been necessary. All the squirrels seem to be nuts about each other. Besides, every year there are quite a number of white young born to dark adults. They don't seem a bit confused or concerned. The only thing that upsets them is when the utility companies trim their trees back from the power poles. And you think inflation is eating away at your property.

I have it on good authority from Dr. Wise R. Albinus—the squirrel scientist stationed in Olney—that these small creatures have a family system like us. They communicate, raise their kids, grow old, just like we do. Dr. Albinus claims that he was listening with his stethoscope and heard this conversation through the bark of a hickory tree:

"Well, Ethel, here we are, nearing the end of our years. It's been a wonderful life, full of ups and downs, watching out for dogs and BB guns, wearing out tooth and toenail. Now it's time to relax and enjoy our retirement. Ethel, Ethel! Why are you crying?"

"Oh, Herman. I can't bear to make you unhappy."

"There, there my dear. You've been a wonderful wife. You've given me six wonderful children, four of them albinos, who have gone into show business, all of them successful, educated, out on their own. With those children you've made me the happiest husband in the world as I near the September of my life."

"Oh, Herman. I'm so glad you feel that way because I'm going to make you even happier. We're going to have another baby."

Now I know what turns them white in Olney.

ALL THINGS CONSIDERED

A British veterinarian wrote a best-selling book, "All Things Great and Small," followed by "All Things Bright and Beautiful," and possibly some others that I don't know about. As a writer, I decided I should do a little research in this area to see what all the fuss was about. I started hanging around a veterinary clinic, taking notes. Here they are.

7 A.M. Waiting in truck outside clinic. Farmer arrives with sick sow in back of Toyota pickup, front wheels barely touch pavement.

7:30 A.M. Rancher arrives with trailer load of goats. Parks upwind.

7:31 A.M. I move truck to other side of goats.

8:00 A.M. Lady in Lincoln Continental arrives wearing strange fur around neck.

8:05 A.M. Fur crawls off ladies neck. Turns out to be a monkey.

8:30 A.M. Parking lot full. Waiting for veterinarian. Includes young man on bicycle with boa constrictor, father and child with turtle, mother and child with parrot, boy holding goose by neck, cat with allergies to people, German Shepherd with cowardice problem, Doberman with constant show of fangs holding dead chicken in mouth. Line of cars extends over horizon. Includes two Rolls Royces, five Mercedes, and one Porsche convertible with a banker leading a bull alongside.

8:31 A.M. Veterinarian appears from dirt road in cloud of dust over horizon. Slides sideways into side entrance of clinic. Aerial antennae bangs side of clinic. Assistants rush out from behind barricaded doors, applaud wildly, give boss appointment schedule and whip. Veterinarian complains of ear pain. Assistant removes mobile phone from ear.

8:32 A.M. Doors of clinic unlocked. Sow given Swine Di-gel.

8:33 A.M. Goats unloaded for treatment. Diagnosis is: "Phew."

8:45 A.M. Monkey given vitamin pills.

9:00 A.M. Doberman given whiff of ammonia, releases chicken. A Col. Sanders called inquiring about disposition of chicken.

9:15 A.M. Boa constrictor checked for pregnancy. Crawls into dipping vat. Goose disappears. Assistant dispatched to find both.

9:30 A.M. German Shepherd given pep talk and lie detector test.

10:00 A.M. Turtle escapes to dipping vat. Parrot disappears in same vicinity. Assistant dispatched to find both.

10:30 A.M. Pills prescribed for bull to increase pep. Banker asks for glass of water.

11:00 A.M. Assistants report all animals accounted for except boa.

11:15 A.M. Boa found in dog grooming area making advances at garden hose.

11:30 A.M. Assembly line surgery to neuter five cats, three dogs, and a lizard.

12:00 noon Veterinarian leaves for Rotary Club luncheon where he is awarded Man-of-the-Year in Agriculture award.

From 1:00 P.M. on, things really got interesting, but I don't want to tip my hand on this wonderful material. It'll be in my new book, "All Things by Gosh and by Golly."

QUICK SHOTS 10

Never play golf for money with a guy who has a
suntan and carries a one iron.

SPORTS

Most authorities agree that the basic foundation for all sports started in Greece. As a matter of fact, aging athletes still rely on the Grecian formula.

Supposedly, Mercury, the god of speed, initiated the whole idea and passed it along to mankind. Personally, I never put much faith in a mythical character who had wings on his feet, wore a loin cloth, and a crash helmet.

His accomplishments in sports could be summed up the same as mine . . . in a word, clumsy.

But there are gifted athletes in football, basketball, baseball, track and field events, tennis, golf, and every conceivable form of sport that should be recognized. Naturally, some of you sports fans are going to be disappointed because I didn't cover such thrilling games as cricket, water polo, or Jai-Ali. So if I miss your favorite game, please just assume the position of "The Thinker" and be a good sport about it. I think the guy who posed for that statue was actually in the locker room pouting over a loss anyway.

Representative of the many macho sports is football. At the end of the year, college football selects an outstanding back who receives the Heisman Trophy. The real macho guys, who do all the work up front, have an outstanding lineman who is honored with the Lombardi Award. A formal banquet for these giants is sponsored each year by the Houston, Texas, Rotary Club. Huge linemen are invited into a fancy hotel and told to make themselves feel at home. That's dangerous because they feel at home knocking people down.

Invited to appear on the program with sportscaster Dick Enberg I felt like a pygmy at a Watusi convention.

This huge fellow came by and stopped very close to me. After a few minutes, I just had to ask him some questions.

"Are you a Lombardi finalist?" I asked.

"No," he answered.

"Are you a football player?"

"Nope."

"Are you a coach?"

"No."

I said, "Then get off my foot!"

Tony Degrate (pronounced just like it looks) won the Lombardi Award the year I was a part of the program. His coach, Fred Akers, University of Texas, recalled the first time he ever heard from this Snyder, Texas, lineman.

"The phone rang in my office," recalled Akers and he interpreted the voice as saying, "Hi, Coach. I'm Tony De-great!"

Fred replied, "Oh, yeah? Well, I'm Atilla the Hun."

It's obvious that players, coaches, and spectators all have to have a sense of humor about sports. The ancient Greeks knew that the games were a way of letting off a little steam. They just never dreamed it would get as out of hand as it has in modern times. After the Lombardi Award, I overheard two of the coaches talking.

"My wife says she has had it with this season. She told me if I didn't quit talking about football, football, football, that she was going to lose her temper. Well, I forgot myself the other night, came home, started talking football, and she hit the ceiling."

"Really?" replied the other coach. "What was her hang time?"

Well I'm not going to be a Monday morning quarterback, run your interference and open holes in the line so you can score a few points to tie-up the conversation in your household. That could lead to sudden death. Let's call time out and study the following lines from our play book.

SPORT'S THREE STEP PROGRAM

Without the Super Bowl to talk about, maybe we can discuss other sports, like bowling. That's just one guy in an alley trying to get a lucky strike. In the old days, that also described a bum who had just spotted an unused cigarette.

A fellow said he'd rather bowl than eat. When I asked if he had his wife's blessing for this sport, he said, "Sure, she'd rather play bridge than cook."

A local macho jock took up bowling but soon gave up the sport . . . said the ball was too hard to dribble.

Not many football players make it in bowling either. Jim McMahon, for instance, tried it and failed miserably. You don't see many overhand deliveries.

Fishing is another sport that doesn't have enough coverage on television. It's hard to get tarpon to show up in the Orange Bowl under their own power. Although occasionally I have seen in the parking lot a two-door stingray.

One good thing about fishing, as opposed to hunting, you seldom ever hear of anybody mistakenly being shot for a fish. Of course you have to use your head. It would not be a good idea during the off season for the Refrigerator to go scuba diving near a whaling vessel.

A fellow asked another how many fish he'd caught. With intense concentration, the guy answered, "If I can catch the one I'm after here and two more, I'll have three."

Being a sportsman is enough to turn a mother's hair grey. A lady I know tried to get her husband to take their two year-old daughter "bank fishing" with him. When he came back without any fish, she asked why. He said, "She ate all my bait."

Basketball is still in the news. Did you ever notice how many people who tell us to eat right, stay fit, and manage our money drop dead and die broke? Then some kid from the ghetto raised on junk food grows to be seven feet tall and makes five million per year.

A kid from my hometown bragged he didn't need an agent and negotiated a $500,000 contract for himself. The fine print says he gets $500 per year for a thousand years.

Sports is a tough business. The coach of the Houston Oilers lost his job due to illness and fatigue. The owner was sick and tired of him.

But regardless of the time of year, some sport will be in the news. Those lucky athletes, regardless of the sport, who can keep their health always hope to progress to the ultimate level of achievement. It's a three-step program. Rookie of the Year, Sports Hall of Fame, and finally Lite Beer commercials.

BATTLE OF THE SEXES

Girls have now won the legal battle to be allowed to play Little League baseball, but a Chicago specialist who holds the Ph.D. degree in physical education (he majored in throwing his weight around) says the girls should not be allowed to play for three good reasons. He has lots of other reasons, but these are just the good ones:

1. Girls have bones that break easier.
2. Reaction time is slower.
3. His son was recently beaten up by a fast girl who broke his arm.

A woman athlete, spokesperson (that always sounds like they ain't sure of the sex) for the other side, claims she is an authority because she is married to an orthopedic surgeon and says the theory is a lie. Her doctor-husband says, "Yes, Dear" to back her position.

Anyway the girls have won the legal battle, but there are some problems cropping up with the two sexes competing against each other. It's difficult for the pitcher to do his best fast ball when a female batter is throwing him kisses and mouthing the words, "I love you" from the batter's box. The entire infield could fall down in uncontrollable giggles, allowing a home run on a cross handed bunt.

The catchers may have difficulty keeping their minds on business while downwind from Chanel No. 5, and it sure could be embarrassing to try to steal second base and be run down by a shortstop who skips instead of runs.

Besides, whoever heard of a girl athlete, a few teeth missing, chewing tobacco, batting 300, named Shirley Dimaggio? And if a girl makes it to first base in the business and the coach yells "Go on home," she may get offended, go sit in the car and have a good cry . . . and break somebody's heart . . . or arm.

So turn the other cheek, fellows. Some day you'll learn to love your enemy.

BEER BASEBALL?

Get ready, sports fans. This news could start a national trend. Everybody knows about baseball and beer, but have you heard about beer baseball?

A California friend of mine invented the game and has all the lawsuits to prove it. Here's the way it works: Two sober teams meet on an abandoned cow pasture. The game is played according to traditional rules except the pitcher has to have a four-ounce shot of beer before he throws each ball. If the batter hits the ball, he has to drink a similar shot before he advances to first base. If the fielder catches or chases down the ball, he has to drink a shot before throwing the ball to wherever he's supposed to throw it. Get the picture?

The game is especially tough on pitchers. Talk about losing control, an active pitcher can lose his arm, sense of balance and direction to the bench. One such superstar shook off so many signals from the catcher that the catcher crawled out to the mound to see what was the problem. The pitcher said he couldn't make out the signals and needed to revise the system. "So what additional signal do you need?" asked the catcher. "Like which way is up . . . and forward," replied the fastballer.

The first and only time this game was played, it set several records: The most pitchers ever used in a game, including pitchers of beer and pitchers of baseball; the first unassisted triple play because three players could not find their respective bases; and, the only daytime game ever called on account of darkness. The actual outcome of the game will forever be disputed because nobody remembers the score. In fact, a few can't recall 1989.

And there were many lawsuits filed, so all should be forewarned, but as might be expected, eyewitness accounts are rather sketchy. My friend says he persuaded everybody to spend the night at whatever position they were playing.

The remedy for the worst cases of bloodshot eyes was to throw the guy in a bale of hay until they cleared up. This may sound strange, but for California it's rather normal. Going into the next state, there is a rumor that a sign reads "Leaving California, Resume Normal Behavior."

FAVORITE PASTIME

The World Series is a strange name given to two teams from the same country playing a kid's game, wearing tight pants and one glove. Who do they think they are, Michael Jackson?

The catcher wears his hat backwards and probably his underwear, too. That's understandable when a fellow spends that many afternoons on grass.

The pitcher sometimes leans forward and squints in the general direction of the catcher, scratches, spits, and throws to first base. A nearsighted fellow with that many problems can't be expected to throw a strike every time but that's 90 degrees off.

For his troubles, the batter may get a ball, a walk, a home run, or a hernia.

They have fellows on first, second, third, and a shortstop. They have more base security than NATO but still have some of them stolen.

The outfielders are supposed to be such great athletes. It's a strange ritual. They stand around in a pasture, chase flies, and run into walls.

The managers are rather calm people except when faced with some difficult, ugly situation . . . like an umpire.

But baseball is one of America's favorite pastimes because of the colorful characters who play the game. How can you not enjoy guys with names like Whitey, Lefty, and Yogi? As Satchel Paige used to advise, "Go light on vices such as carryin' on in society."

Maybe they don't mean to be funny, but they sure are. A player from St. Louis had an audience with the Pope, who politely asked the occupation of the unknown subject. "Your holiness," he said, "I'm a Cardinal."

Maybe playing in front of all those people, accepting both boos and cheers, teaches poise. The World Series title for that has to go to Dizzy Dean. As a radio announcer, the colorful ex-pitcher worked with a polished partner. One night Dizzy announced, "Folks, there's a fat lady down behind home plate surrounded by fellows with walkie-talkies. Ah don't know what's goin' on but she's creatin' quite a stir."

"Diz," interrupts his partner, "it's the Queen of the Netherlands."

"The Netherlands, where's that?"

"Holland, Diz."

"It's okay, folks," announces Diz. "The fat lady is the Queen of Holland."

BATTER UP

Baseball is a sport made up of people who chew tobacco, scratch and yell obscenities at the umpires. But enough about the fans. . .

The players are all great athletic specimens who make a living with eye-hand coordination, and this system sends three messages to the brain . . . swing, don't swing, and DUCK.

I had a course in baseball once when I was about 8 years old. It was a short course that ended my career. The opposing pitcher was a tough kid with a fast ball you could hardly see. I got to examine one up real close.

When I came to a few seconds later, some of my rowdy friends taunted me to rush the mound and beat up the pitcher. I didn't do it for the same reason they didn't. I was afraid of her.

Ever since then, I approach the plate with a bat in my hand for one reason: protection.

Some people choose a Louisville Slugger or a Spalding Special. Not me, I want a suit of armor and a broad canoe paddle.

Throw a fast ball my way and you'll get the same reaction the army got out of me when the First Sergeant yelled "GRENADE!"

I was one of the few kids who was never intentionally walked and I never had any reason to run.

Seemed like a dumb game to me but I gave it my best. They had me playing several positions including chaser. With others, they called it catcher.

That wasn't too bad, but they wouldn't let me bat wearing the mask, shin guards, and chest protector so I switched to right field. I figured that was the safest position, as far away from the ball as possible. I had a technique that is still talked about today. I developed eye-hand coordination that was 100 percent accurate. I watched the ball closely and picked it out of mid-air as soon as it stopped rolling.

I could have made a fortune if I had gone into pro baseball. I'm sure the endorsers would have paid millions for me not to use their products.

It has haunted me to this day. I'm just not the athletic type. I was in the locker room recently after working out with the weights. I thought I was making progress when I overheard a couple of friends talking about me.

"Do you think he's taking steroids?" one asked.

"No," said the other, "he wouldn't do that, but we did have a portable TV that came up missing."

Then he added, "But he wouldn't take your steroids. He can only hear out of one ear anyway."

I'm a walking example of why they need to wear those hard baseball helmets with an ear flap on one side. Mine didn't work. As a chaser, I forgot and put my helmet on backwards.

DUMB, DUMBER, DUMBEST

A basketball and a football coach were discussing the intellect of their respective players. The roundballer said, "Talk about dumb, I've got the dumbest center in all the world of athletics." The football coach replied, "Nope, I've got a tackle that would be crowned 'King of the Dunces' in the world of athletics."

So the two made a wager and set out to prove it.

The basketball coach yelled into the intercom: "Send Stretch Jones up to my office." Moments later Stretch appears, out of breath. "Ouch," Stretch said as he bumped his head on the doorsill, "you want me, Coach?"

The hardfloor man turns to his colleague and whispered, "Watch this." Then flipping the young man a quarter he ordered, "Stretch, run downtown and buy me a Rolls Royce."

"Right, Coach," says Stretch as he headed for the door. "Ouch," he exclaimed as he bumped his head.

The pigskin specialist grinned an evil grin and confidently bellowed into the intercom, "Send up Tank Sherman." Tank made three attempts to get through the open door. Finally, turning sideways, he squeezed through and with a grunt uttered, "You want me, Coach?"

"Tank," said the coach, "run downstairs and see if I'm in my office, on the double."

"Right, Coach," replied Tank as he thundered off, creating a man-shaped opening where the door used to be.

As the elevator doors opened, the two athletes hustled inside.

"Move over," said Tank.

"Ouch," said Stretch from his crouched position, "Boy, the dumb things I have to do for my coach. He gave me a quarter and told me to go downtown and buy him a Rolls Royce."

"You think that's dumb," grunted Tank, "my coach told me to go downstairs and see if he was in his office."

"What's so dumb about that?"

"He had a phone right there on the desk. He could've called and found out for himself."

CAUSE OF A STROKE

Every Sunday, thousands of heads are bowed in meditation. Concentration is needed for a good putt.

For some fellows, the three most important ingredients in playing golf are the three "V's"—velocity, vocabulary, and Valium.

How can a little white ball bring out the larceny in people? Easy, that's how. I've seen fellows record their score, glance over both shoulders then wipe their fingerprints off the pencil.

It has to be one of the most frustrating games ever invented by the mind of man, assuming it was a man and assuming he had a mind. I doubt that a woman invented golf. They are too smart to take credit for such a dumb game anyway. They invented the country club so they would have three essential luxuries in addition to golf: a restaurant, a bar, and a place to have weddings.

I like to hang around the country club and watch the action. I saw a bride recently who had something old, something new, something borrowed, and something blue. The something blue was her father's face because her mother had to choke him off the course.

You don't see many fathers give away the bride and follow through with a back swing.

Afterwards, the reception featured his and her cakes decorated with tiny golf carts, authentic down to the low fat Coors.

Then everybody hit the golf course. They hit the trees, the ground, the sand pits. It was too much for the father of the bride. He had not only gained a son-in-law, but too many penalty strokes. In a fit of anger he raised over his head his entire set of clubs in an expensive leather bag. With one mighty scream of frustration, he charged the nearest deep-water hazard and threw the whole set a full 12 feet into the lake. As he yelled obscenities all the way back to the club, grass began to die everywhere he cursed.

The dumbfounded fellows watched this amazing scene. "Do you think he'll leave the clubs there?" asked one.

"No, he'll be back when he cools off," replied the other. "Let's just keep an eye on the lake."

Sure enough, 10 minutes later the irate golfer returned and marched calmly, fully clothed into the lake. Chest deep in water, he fished around until he located the bag. Then without moving from the spot, the old golfer raised the bag slightly above the water level, unzipped a compartment, removed his car keys, released his grip on the waterlogged bag, letting it slip back to the bottom and sloshed off—never to return.

I don't blame the guy. There is something wrong with a game where the guy who gets to hit the ball most is the loser.

SUDDEN DEATH

The scene is any average American home, blue collar, medium income, middle aged. The television is set on a special edition of Monday Night Football. Nobody questions the fact that it is Thursday night and this is the third special of the week in addition to the regular Monday Night feature which went into a sudden death playoff lasting until Tuesday morning.

She, hungering for companionship, has tried to become interested in sports.

"Boy, this is thrilling ain't it Ethyl? If the Cowboys win this one and Tampa Bay defeats New England, provided Denver ties Seattle, it could throw our division into a five way tie. What a race!"

"Yes, it is exciting Fred but I don't understand why those grown men cut off their trousers like that. I love it when the referee gets so excited and blows his little whistle. It's so nice of the coach to let them participate even if they're not big enough to make the team."

In between the halftime highlights of 47 games played last week and a spotlight report on 17 of America's greatest quarterbacks, she finds time to converse with him, in depth, during a beer commercial.

"Fred, if I died would you remarry?"

"Hmmm. Yeah, I imagine so."

"Would you still live in this same house?"

"Hmmm. Guess so, this is the best part of town for TV reception."

"Would you let your next wife use my silverware?"

"Hmmm. Don't see why not. The plastic forks go well with the aluminum trays and TV dinners."

"Fred?"

"Huh?"

"If I died and you remarried, is there anything of mine you wouldn't let your next wife use?"

"Hmmm. I wouldn't let her use your golfclubs."

"Oh, Fred. That's so sweet. Why not?"

"Cause she's left handed."

Another episode of modern America is played out with organized violence on the tube and light comedy in the home.

"Just kidding, Ethyl. You're not mad are you?"

"Of course not, Fred."

"Why do you keep smiling that funny way?"

"I just bought a bow and arrow and it occurs to me that you have to sleep sometime."

NORMAL FRUSTRATIONS

At the Camelback Golf Course in Phoenix, there are miniature, foot-high concrete camels marking the tee box. When I arrived, there was some kind of disturbance going on at the tee box on hole number three. We later viewed the disaster and learned that a fellow had made a wild swing, knocking the head off a camel.

The ball ricocheted off one of the $300,000 homes lining the fairway, bounced across the street, and cold-cocked a Springer Spaniel. Ironically, his clubs were made by Ping.

Needless to say, several people were hostile toward this golfer. His friends later presented him, at the company awards ceremony, with a mock bill from the country club for $823 worth of wounded camel repairs, a neighborhood petition branding him a terrorist, and an information packet from the Humane Society on endangered species. The latter said that if he didn't want to become one he had better take up another sport.

They didn't suggest what the sport might be, but did urge him to consider something that required no movement of his body.

The proclamation further cancelled his subscription to Golfing Magazine and banned him from the entire state of Arizona.

Some other guys were playing a game called "Fort Worth" which I had never heard of, but certainly had some entertaining aspects. The guy who made the longest shot in a party of four had to make his next shot with his pants waistband exactly at his knees. "You have no idea how hard it is to hit a golf ball with your pants around your knees, but even in February you sure don't worry about catching a head cold," a participant told me.

Few people say, "Wow, what form!" either. The funny stances golfers take are further exaggerated by bony knees and the most unusual assortment of underwear. Somehow you loose all fear of an opponent standing there with that intense concentration enhanced by boxer shorts in a Mickey Mouse print.

One guy's game and confidence was so destroyed, he lost 7 balls, 3 of them in a ball washer.

Another said he got so flustered, he lost one of his brown and white golf shoes. I told him I'd keep an eye out for it. He said, "Okay, it's the brown one."

What a bunch of characters. As my group got ready to tee off, I asked a "Fort Worth" player if I should get some extra balls. "Do they lose many in the lakes?" I asked.

He replied, "Only if you knock them in the water."

COMMON GOLF COURTESY

It happened at the famous Doral Country Club in Miami Beach. Two conventions were meeting there at the same time. One was a small, all-male group. The other was very large, 75 percent female. The males conducted themselves as true professionals. The only things that gave them away were the numerous reports of eyestrain and hyperventilation.

It is also rare to have that many cases of sunburn to the tongue.

A fellow brought his video camera to record all the other guys' golf swings. He never left the pool area. "These are my kind of guys," he said.

There was this one beautiful girl who struck up an acquaintance with the video man, mainly because he convinced her he was a scout from Hollywood. He had the credentials to prove it, an old Tenderfoot badge from Hollywood, Florida.

He invited her to play a few rounds on the golf course. She accepted but stubbornly insisted on playing the course in the daylight.

She had never played golf before and, because of her build, really wasn't suited for it. When she put the ball where she could hit it, she couldn't see it. When she put it where she could see it, she couldn't reach it.

He convinced her that golf was mostly instinct anyway, put his arms around her, and patiently instructed her on developing a smooth, swinging motion . . . somewhat akin to his hormone production.

She was beginning to take a liking to this young fellow but she didn't want to be too obvious in encouraging him. So she buttoned even the top button on her string bikini.

He was a gentleman though and just wanted to treat her like a lady, no strings attached.

On a par 3 hole, she took 37 strokes to get within a foot of the pin. He picked up her ball. "Hey," she asked, "what's the big idea?" He explained that when the ball is that close it is assumed that the player can make the shot, counts one more stroke and is called a "Gimme."

"It's common golf courtesy," he explained, "extended to your playing partner."

Being a pretty good golfer, he issued a challenge to his lovely friend. On the next hole, he asked if she would like to wager a kiss on the 26-foot putt he was facing. By now, understanding the complexities of the game, she called the bet. The ball fell as if he had hired a heat-seeking gopher.

Termination of the kiss broke the sound barrier, charged the batteries in the cart, and set fire to his 3-wood.

She surprised him on the next hole by teasingly wagering a bet of her own. "If I make this putt, we'll go to a quiet place for dinner, in the corner, in the dark, and maybe later a moonlight swim."

It was a 35-foot putt attempt, downhill, with a two-level slope breaking in different directions.

Casually he strolled over, looked at the shot, picked up the ball, and said, "That's a gimme."

I never saw them again. Neither did anyone else.

THE BREAKERS

The Breakers Hotel in West Palm Beach, Florida, is one of the world's most elegant hotels. In an international survey, it was ranked number six. I quickly lost interest in the five hotels ranked above it after I paid my bill.

The driveway was lined with Rolls Royce automobiles. I've seen that before, but these were all owned by the maids.

You don't see many maids who have a chauffeur.

The chauffeurs claimed they were at the bottom of the economic ladder. Some of them even had to sell some of their polo ponies.

I was there as a guest of the Tennessee Realtors Association, invited to speak one night to the ex-presidents at the Polo Club and the next night to the general membership at The Breakers. We all got on a bus and went to the Polo Club. Guess what? Wrong Polo Club. We went to two more before we found the right one. Is this a wonderful country or what?

At the Polo Club, I was told that this was the one recently visited by Prince Charles. "Thought you'd like to see a place visited by the rich and famous," said my host, "instead of the dumb and lost."

Next morning, I had a bucket of oats and galloped over to the golf course to play 18 holes with the Thoroughbred set. I felt more like a Shetland pony.

Shetlands are accustomed to grazing in the rough.

Most golfers are aware that the customary irons used in golfing are numbered 2 to 9. Lee Trevino described the difficulty of hitting the 1-iron by carrying one around holding it in the air during a thunderstorm. When he was warned about a lightning strike, he grinned and replied, "Not even God can hit a 1-iron."

So I rented some clubs. To show you what kind of golfer they thought I was, my irons started with number 3.

I'm not easily intimidated though so I played with this foursome. "Let's bet five," said one of the guys. I was going to risk it until I learned they were talking thousands.

The tall dark stranger with whom I was paired up in the golf cart calmly said he'd take the bet. He played like a machine, won the bet and gave me a generous tip for driving the cart. I would have felt a little special myself except he kept calling me "Boy."

When the other two guys paid off and the stranger had gone, I heard one say to the other, "I should have remembered the advice of my golf coach: "Never bet with a man who has a suntan and carries a one iron."

Now, I know why they named the hotel The Breakers.

TOUGH COURSE

In primitive societies men still yell and beat the ground with clubs. Civilized man does that too but we've dignified the ceremony by calling it "golf." The game was invented by a Scotsman because it was then a cheap form of entertainment. Civilization has fouled that up too. Country clubs have become so exclusive that most applicants don't want to join one unless the club won't have them as a member.

Such was the case at the legendary Royal Peppercorn Duck Club of Boola Boola, formed by an elite group of fighting Scots serving Her Majesty the Queen in the wilds of India, a fortnight's hard ride out of Calcutta. The club was a bastion of refinement, a retreat from the rigors of constant skirmishes with the insurrectionists of the fierce Bwala Lampur Tribe. The fairways were planted to grasses brought in by overland caravan from Kensington Close; the greens were manicured by servant boys from Bombay skilled in the art of vegetative reincarnation. A thousand Bimbaubwi bearers worked two 12-hour shifts daily bringing buckets of life sustaining water from the Jaipur river a thousand meters down the slopes from the fort.

One day a new British officer arrived and went straight to the immaculate lounge area where he was barred from entering by a Gurkha guard resplendent in bare feet, beard and turban, his nickel plated bolo knife flashing tiny stars of reflected sunlight in response to his swift movements.

"Whom do I confront," he asked, "to be allowed a round of golf?"

Silently the Gurkha motioned him toward the officer of the day, seated in a huge rattan chair, holding a snifter of brandy in one hand, an ivory carved swagger stick in the other. Dressed in kilts and regalia of the famed Heather Highland Commandos of the Royal Marine Division, he spoke softly, "Ye know, Laddie, we have certain standards 'ear. I'll be after askin' a few questions. Name?"

"Stanley Higginbotham," replied the hopeful candidate.

"Titles?"

"Lord of Sussex, Earl of Lincolnshire, Viscount of Nottingham, Duke of Dover."

"Education?"

"Cambridge, Middleyork, Oxford."

"Campaigns?"

"97 missions throughout the empire, the last 42 consecutive days during the bloody siege of Khatmandu, sole survivor on either side."

"Decorations?"

"Legion of Merit, Victoria Cross, Queen's Order of Valor, Medal of Honor by order of Parliament. Modesty prevents me from going farther."

With that the old Scot wrinkled his brow, squinted his eyes and yelled to the Gurkha, "Ghandi, give the wee lad a set o 'clubs, place 'im on probation an' let 'im have nine holes today."

JOGGERS AND JOGETTES

Jogging is supposed to be an inexpensive sport that adds years to your life. It really doesn't, it just seems like it. Statistics show that runners increase their heart rate, muscle tone, cardio-vascular system and chances of being eaten by a dog.

The old law of physics is that for every action there is an opposite reaction, and that pertains to jogging. Building something up while tearing something down has caught on big among runners. Fallen arches, turned ankles, bad backs, floating kidneys, and trick knees are all part of the red badge of courage for these speed merchants. Mercury, the ancient Greek god of speed had wings on his feet and wore a crash helmet, but not our modern daredevils. They wear a sweat band and a pair of $50 Nike running shoes.

The uniform for runners is very important. You never see anyone jogging in overalls, cowboy boots, or sandals. The mechanics, cowboys, and hippies have finally agreed on something. They stay out of this sport.

For the rest of the population, it is mandatory to have running shoes direct from England that were made in Korea to American specifications. The specifications are that they are to be suitable for turf, dirt, or hard surface. They must be able to transform a flabby, middleaged man into a flabby, old man. Oh sure, girls look at them when they waddle by. They are actually thinking, "There goes a flabby, old man with a young, youthful, handsome pair of shoes."

Socks at $4.95 per pair are also a must. For men, they must be white with elastic tops. For ladies, they must show the ankle and have a little tuft of brightly colored material about the size of a golf ball that shows on the back of the shoe, being careful not to hide the brand name of the shoe. That is there so men will have an excuse to look legward without embarrassment.

"Sure is a good looking pair of socks" is always a clever line for singles who are thinking doubles. It also detracts the eye from any minor defects like shin splints or torn ligaments.

A sleeveless shirt, shorts with a racing stripe, and a sweat band, about $100 total, complete the outfit. The latest craze is not running, jogging, or walking. It is stumbling, and I see lots of people taking it up. I stumble about three miles a day myself and am considered a pioneer in the field . . . or roadside . . . or under a shade tree.

But take heart, my nonathletic friends, there is a new perfume for ladies and after-shave for men called JOGGER that will give you instant credibility around the health club. Just a little splash on the face or behind the ear and you smell tired.

FUN MY FOOT

It was the strangest compulsion I've ever had: to run in a 10-kilometer "fun run." I learned a couple of things. First, that 10 kilometers is 6.2 miles which sounds a lot farther when you can comprehend the distance. Second, what I thought was a good striding run was variously described by friends as a trot, stumble, or lope.

This was not a famous event, just small town stuff, so I didn't take the competition too seriously and they all reciprocated that feeling.

Because of the tough economy, it was decided that no prizes would be given, the winners would just have their names spray painted on the side of a vacant building. The starter was a fellow with a shotgun and everyone was on their mark for a while before a goose flew over. Scared me to pieces when a shotgun blast was followed by a yell of "they're off" because the elastic in my shorts was pretty old.

Very early in the race I thought I had a good chance because a fellow way ahead of me stopped and ran to one side of the road. Endurance has always been one of my strengths. When I had nearly caught up with him, I noticed that he was leaning against a car talking to a friend who was driving by. Then he jumped back in the road like O. J. Simpson and disappeared over the horizon just behind the lead vehicle with flashing light.

However, my pace was only a little slower and would have been much better if it had not been for the annoyance of buzzards circling overhead and an ambulance that I was running too close in front of . . . my own fault.

On the last three miles I really picked up the pace; people were strung out everywhere, some missed a turn, others got lost, so you can imagine my surprise when the finish line loomed in front of me and I was ALONE. The small crowd applauded and cheered me on.

"Was I first?" I gasped.

"Hardly" came the reply.

"What was my time?" I asked.

"We don't have a sundial," they apologized.

"Did I beat anyone?"

"Not yet."

So then I investigated to see who finished ahead of me even though I was too far back to see anyone. They told me two women had come in before me.

"Where are they?" I demanded. "I wanna see those Amazons."

It was so embarrassing, a woman and her daughter. It hurts to be beaten by a woman pushing a baby carriage.

I'm having to re-evaluate this whole fitness craze. If it's true that jogging is good for you and riding is bad, why is it you never see a jogger who looks like he could whip a truck driver?

FLAP OVER FLAPJACKS

Liberal, Kansas, is on a flat plains, flat off of the beaten path, flat full of funny ideas. Years ago they decided they needed something to attract attention to their wheat production. So they held a flapjack flipping race. Now every year the major networks cover the flourful event. Liberal promptly claimed the title of "Pancake Hub of the Universe," a seemingly secure position. But believe it or not, a town in England protested, claiming they had been conducting pancake flipping races and while Liberal might be a wheel or spoke, the English town was the hub. And yes, of the entire universe.

The only sensible way to resolve this dispute was the civilized way —declare war. The two towns challenged each other to a flipoff. It's been going on every year. It is a timed race over a fixed course and results are mailed across the Atlantic to determine the winner.

"Where does this take place?" I asked.

"Only, England," replied a resident.

"That's Olny, England, isn't it?"

"Yeah, but we're so good at flipping flapjacks we call 'em Only, England."

"Who won this year?"

"We did. We win every year, that's why we're the hub of the universe."

"How can you win every year?"

"Clean living, hard training, athletic ability and only reporting our times after we get their report."

The English don't have a chance anyway, because their course is through narrow, winding streets, up and down hills while the Kansans run on the broad, flat prairie. The English were humiliated this year when their fastest runner rounded a corner and ran slap into a BBC Television truck completely blocking a street on the course. While he was unconscious, the crew ate his pancake.

"The hub of the universe within my bloody grasp," he moaned, "and me own government blocks the way."

Folks in Liberal say he has a point there, so they declared this year's contest a draw with Kansas only beating them and their government by a few inflation points.

All this came out at their annual Chamber of Commerce banquet in Liberal. Those folks know how to have a good time. When lovely, efficient Cindy Strecker went out as president and Hal

Harbuck came in, the M.C. remarked, "Hal, you have a very large skirt to fill."

Not to be outdone, Hal announced he had an award to make. Holding up a set of car keys, he reported, with a quiver in his voice, "Cindy, for your efforts in our publicity campaign, I would like to present you with the keys to a brand new automobile." A gasp was heard throughout the audience, then he put the keys away and added "I'd like to, but we can't afford it."

It must be in the air, or the water, or the pancakes. After I spoke, a fellow from Beaver, Oklahoma invited me to the World Champion Cow Chip Throwing Contest. "Cow pancakes," he said. He handed me a special invitation with the words, "Can't think of anyone more qualified than you to be invited."

DUCK THE PUCK

Hockey players are downright mean. They'll get on a fellow faster than ugly on a duck. When someone yells "Duck," you better grab a stick, preferably his, not yours. Those guys could be boxers except the game is so slow that they would have to ride motor scooters around the ring as they slugged it out. This way they take up a form of legal mugging. You see it on TV all the time.

The action in the fights that break out is so fast it's hard to catch it all. One fellow recently was said to have been injured in the fracas. Now I don't know where the fracas is but I'm sure that's a mighty painful place to be injured. The trainer apparently didn't know either because he frisked the guy all over, hunting for it. They finally sent him back in the game, I'm sure with a possible broken fracas. You've go to be mean to do that, you can bet your hockey puck.

RIPCORD GERONIMO

Skydiving gives me a falling sensation just to think about it. I never did care for any sport that you had to do exactly right the first time. The only way I want to hit the silk is to have my head drop gently on a fancy pillowcase. Getting me out of the cargo door of a C-47 would be about like trying to put a chicken through the hatch of a coop without holding his feet.

Probably everybody has some apprehension about parachuting. I approach it with the same caution as a surgeon operating on a lawyer who specializes in malpractice cases.

However, a bunch of us were hanging around the airport recently when the subject came up. A fellow who went by the name of Dutch Schmidt flew in and joined the conversation. Dutch said he was a jumpmaster during World War II and related a tale that was popular among the paratroopers.

It seems that an old pro jumpmaster was trying to calm the fears of his first time jumpers. He told them their chute would open automatically because of the line that was attached to the wire inside the aircraft. If that failed they had a safety chute that they could activate by pulling a red rip cord. A nervous recruit named Nelson Nockles asked the inevitable question, "What if that fails?"

"Well," replied the sarge, "you flap your arms to slow your descent and yell 'Geronimo.' That's a special voice activating command that triggers a safety device to make sure the second chute works. That's why we yell that in the first place."

Nelson jumped, his first chute failed and he forgot what color he was supposed to look for on his rip cord. The sarge saw him whisked from sight. Moments later he heard a thumping sound on the other side of the airplane. Through the window the sarge could see Nelson flapping his arms like a hummingbird, kicking with one foot against the side of the fuselage.

When he got the jumpmasters attention again, he yelled through the window, "What was the name of that Indian again?"

COCK-A-ROACH RACING

The latest craze is cockroach racing. What a sport! It's breaking out in dumps all over America.

Like all other sports, we have to make sure that the racing commission keeps everything clean, but in this case, sanitation could be hazardous to the athlete's health.

The sport was first started by the Romans but really spread under the influence of grease.

Initially, wild roaches were captured for a breeding program. The first mating produced some outstanding runners—about 150,000 of them. The experiment was soon disbanded because of the identification difficulty of placing a tattoo in their upper lip.

Now the emphasis has shifted to careful selection of outstanding individuals captured from dark corners and back alleys. They require special trainers who halter-break them. You know the old saying, "You can lead a roach to water but don't drink it."

For the big money boys, handlers are also necessary. Just remember never to congratulate a handler for a win by giving him a big handshake.

The racing commission uses a paper cup as a starting gate and all thoroughbreds are thrown in together. The cup is turned upside down in the center of a circle on a flat surface, all entries are bumped to the bottom and those who survive the concussion dash for the finish line which is in any direction. We can put a man on the moon but we can't make a roach run in a straight line unless he's in a sewer pipe.

The spectators gather up close to watch, and if the winner is not caught by the handler, you really see a show. It's fun to see a whole crowd doing the flamenco.

If one of them gets lost in the crowd, you see all the women examining anything with polka dots.

It's also very careless to drink beer at one of these races if it comes in a dark bottle.

Those winners, who are caught, live to race another day and are amazingly tough. If one pulls up lame on a leg, the handler just jerks it off.

Many a roach has won a race on only five legs.

If this new sport catches on, you soon may be seeing the champion's names immortalized. Names like "Roach-O-War," winner of the Kentucky Scurvy and the champion who went on to win the Freakness and the Roto-Rooter Invitational before going berserk and running into the spectators. His name? You guessed it—"I'm Crushed."

THINGS TO SAY ON THE GOLF COURSE

"Golf shot, golf shot," they scream when you hit a 300-yard drive; "Like it had eyes," when you sink a putt dead center with a downhill difficult break; or "Practice swing, practice swing" when you miss a ball completely and wind up looking like a "before" ad for a chiropractor.

It occurs to me that golfers should have a list of things to say and choose something different from hole to hole in order to give a little audible variety. Here are a few suggestions:

1. After a high pop-up drive shot:
   a) That might get you an eagle, two earthworms, and a squirrel.
   b) Who does he think he is . . . Werner Von Braun?
   c) At least it's straight down the middle, too bad it landed behind you.

d) Is that the brand that has the heat shield for re-entry?

e) That's my alcoholic shot . . . too much elbow.

2. When slicing the ball into the woods:

a) Next time, why don't you try your trick shot; the one where you hit it straight?

b) Put two dozen of those together and you'd have a perfect loaf.

c) Can't blame that damage on Dutch Elm disease.

d) That'll teach those pine bark beetles.

e) That's my blue color shot . . . I'll vent my feelings to the trees.

3. When hooking the ball out of bounds:

a) With a hook that size, you could use Moby Dick for bait.

b) That's what I get for taking lessons from an Aboriginal pro.

c) Go west young ball, go west.

d) That's my Davy Crockett shot; searching for new frontiers.

e) I would give up this game, but it is the only thing I do well.

4. When chipping around the green:

a) At least you can easily repair that ball mark. Where's the sand rake?

b) That would be a championship quality shot . . . in volleyball.

c) Did anyone ever explain the difference between a soft touch and slam dunk?

d) Well, at least we've got a good start on that mining project.

5. When lining up for a critical six-foot putt:

a) No pressure, but if you miss you win a visit from a Chicago pro named Guido.

b) Relax and just try to keep the ball low.

c) It breaks a little to the left and if you miss, we'll do the same thing to your right leg.

d) Don't worry. If you miss it, we'll still be friends . . . Of course, you'll become a spectator.

Ah, what a game. As my friend, Lynn Ramsey, says, "Golf is a good game for people who think they have their life all organized."

CRACK SHOTS 11

Confucius say, "Duck who fly upside down,
quack up."

AVIATION

I love to fly and come from a long line of aviators. Two of my great uncles were among the first men in space. Uncle Fred received his honor when his suspenders got hung on a passing fire truck. Uncle Milton became the first man in space with a cue stick in his hand because of a boiler room explosion down at the pool hall.

The aviation bug really bit me during my tour of duty in the U.S. Army. I was a helicopter mechanic in Salzburg, Austria. The pilots had a nasty habit of making you fly with the helicopter every time you worked on it. It made very conscientous mechanics. "Wait a minute, sir. Let me double check the torque on those nuts."

There were a few secluded lakes in Austria where some of the Austrian girls went to sunbathe in the nude. They would lie on the sandy beaches, their clothes piled in a neat stack beside them. Once after working on a chopper, the pilot told me to get in and off we went on a training combat mission. We swooped up a valley, over a hill, and down on to a beach. You haven't lived until you've flown sideways across a beach blowing people's clothes away.

When the other mechanics found out about this, it was amazing how maintenance procedures picked up. It seemed like something always needed attention, followed by the mandatory check ride. Years later as a college professor, I had need to draw on my aviation experiences again. Because of the pressing demands for speaking engagements, I hired a private pilot and plane to fly me to speaking engagements. Oscar Rasmussen, an ex-United airline pilot, is not only a great instructor, but still a very close friend. He inspired me to get a private pilot's license. He would let me fly in the co-pilot's seat. I thought I had it all under control. We were flying to a meeting once with two passengers in the back seat. I was at the controls, but busy telling a story to the two passengers in the rear. In the middle of my story, the engine suddenly quit. No warning, it just quit. The two passengers panicked. I did not. I suspected Oscar had a hand in this fiasco, so I calmly turned to him and screamed at the top of my lungs, "What did you do?"

He laughed heartily, then turned the fuel supply back on. We resumed normal navigation and Oscar asked if I had really been concerned. I replied, "Of course not. I knew you had something to do with that."

He said, "Yeah? Well, finish that story you started."

To this day, I haven't been able to think of what I was saying.

Not only have I flown privately all over this country, but I've been blessed with the opportunity to fly commercially all over the world. Aviators have a unique sense of humor. I was on a commercial flight to Chicago on a well-known U.S. airline. The fellow next to me was a wreck. He had never flown before. He was saying things like, "Look down there. Those people look like little ants."

I said, "They are ants, dummy. We haven't taken off yet."

Once in the air, I tried to instill the philosophy of positive thinking in my new found friend. He kept saying things like, "We're going to die, I know it. We're going to crash. Terrible things are going to happen."

I told him, "You've got to stop thinking like that. You have to start thinking positive thoughts. You know what's going to happen to you if you keep thinking negative thoughts like that? You're just gonna die all tensed up and there's nothing more painful than dying all tensed up."

Well, that kind of positive thinking seemed to bring him back to reality for the moment.

Then it happened.

We hit turbulence, we were totally engulfed in clouds, with lightening flashing in every direction, and balls of fire rolling off the wing tips. It was a very emotional time for everyone. Instead of the announcements saying, "Buckle your safety belts, please," it was, "Now I lay me down to sleep . . . ."

So, my companion turned to me and said, "Tell me the truth. We're going to crash, aren't we?"

I said, "To tell you the truth, I've been flying many years, but I don't think I've ever been in turbulence this bad. We are in a critical situation."

He said, "I knew it. I knew it. If the good Lord will get me out of this, I will give up drinking."

I said, "Well, we're in such a tough spot if He'll take both of us, I'll cut down."

He said, "I knew it. I knew it. If the good Lord will get me out of this, I will give up smoking."

I said, "Well, I never have smoked, but if He'll take both of us, I'll start big and quit early."

He replied, "I knew it. I knew it. If the good Lord will get me out of this, as far as women are concerned . . . ."

I grabbed his arm and yelled, "Wait a minute, I think I see a hole in the clouds."

Sure enough, there was a hole in the clouds and we descended into a perfectly calm day at Chicago O'Hare Airport. But the pilot, after coming through all this turbulence, apparently let his guard down and made one of the roughest landings I've ever experienced. People who didn't fly very often panicked. They were waiting for the wings to break off, the fires to break out, and sirens to start blaring. Of course, those of us who fly all the time knew exactly what was going on, why, we were hysterical.

But the pilot who was in total control and understood the situation calmed our fears with a single announcement, "Ladies and gentlemen, Air Chance Airlines has attacked Chicago . . . ."

"And Chicago has surrendered."

Although you may not be the Charles Lindbergh or Amelia Earhart type, perhaps you can relate to the following tales that allow you to experience everything from hangar flying to piloting a 747.

WING AND A PRAYER

I spend a lot of time in an airplane. In fact, when I recently figured it up on a 40-hour work week basis, it amounted to four months per year. And to think I was once described as a fellow who "really had his feet on the ground." Of course, that was when they dragged me on for my first flight. Winston Churchill was right when he said, "There are no atheists in foxholes or cockpits." I might add there are mighty few in the passenger section either. Throw in a thunderstorm, turbulence, the cough of an engine, and the team of MadLynn, Murrey, and O'Hair will be the first in line to make a confession—even to a Rabbi.

Abraham Lincoln wrote, "I can understand how a man can look down on the earth and be an atheist but it is beyond me how a man can look up at the stars and believe there is no God." Well old Abe was a tall fellow but he never looked down from 30,000 feet while looking up at the same time. It's enough to inspire a Northern Bishop to pay his dues to the Southern Baptist Convention . . . just added life insurance.

In spite of all our fears, we still fly and joke about it to ease the tension. Like the fellow who wrote the president of an airline, "Dear Sir: Your airplanes are old, your stewardesses are cold, and you're not so hot yourself."

But we've learned to depend on fast transportation and can't do without it. I saw a lady run up to a ticket counter and nervously ask about a flight. The airline rep said, "You better get on down to gate 60, that flight is boarding now."

She took off, ran about 10 paces, stopped, ran back, and asked, "Do you have anything earlier?"

THOU SHALT . . .

Tucked away in the flying manual of a 1946 piper cub were the handwritten ten commandments of an anonymous pilot. The first rule read, "Thou shalt not become airborne without checking thy fuel supply." In layman's terms, that means it's hard to play aerial leap frog when you don't have a leg to stand on.

Commandment two stated, "Thou shalt not taxi with carelessness." Airplanes handle marvelously in the air, but on a windy day, next to a pond, one makes a mighty poor substitute for a submarine . . . especially on its back.

The third warns of a potential for a mid-air: "Thou shalt ever take heed unto air traffic rules." In other words, when the controller says, "Take up heading 081 and descend to 3500 feet," you don't say, "Listen, buddy, just say, 'right or left, up or down.'"

I remember once flying a slow Cessna at night in front of a 747. I asked the controller if he wanted me to yield to the heavier traffic. He said, "No," but did ask the 747, who was trying hard to fly slow enough to stay behind me, if he had me in sight. Calmly the captain replied, "Roger, I've got him. I think he's stopped."

Number four states, "Thou shalt not make flat turns" which is roughly equivalent in auto terms to "When skidding backwards on ice, don't worry about turn signals."

Commandment five reads, "Thou shalt maintain thy air speed lest the earth rise up and smite thee." A similar relationship exists when a man gets smart with his wife.

The sixth commandment is: "Thou shalt not let thy confidence exceed thy ability." I remember making that mistake once myself when we thought one of the kids was thoroughly potty trained.

"Thou shalt make use of thy carburetor heater." This one may throw a lot of new-pilot types. Ice forms in airplane carburetors under certain conditions, causing stoppage of two things—fuel flow and normal heart beat. Properly used, heat restores both.

"Thou shalt not perform aerobatics at low altitude." Even my uncle, a non-pilot, learned that one early in life while hanging out in bars. In either case, pilot or non-pilot, aerobatics started near the ground can end up six feet under the ground.

"Thou shalt not allow indecision in thy judgment." A classic example of a Piper Cub accident occurred when a student pilot said, "I think I can make it," took off from a muddy field with a full load and flew through the wind direction indicator, powerlines, and the port-a-potty section of a construction project. The plane was bent badly but the unhurt pilot had this dumb request of the news media, "Don't tell my instructor."

The tenth commandment is the most memorable and famous: "Thou shalt know always: There are old pilots and bold pilots, but no old, bold pilots."

THE ABCs OF LIFE

On a recent airline flight from San Juan, Puerto Rico, to New York, somebody really got cute. The flight attendants are given a news video tape from CBS to show the passengers. It always arrives just before take-off and is delivered through the CBS affiliate; standard procedure in many cities.

Either some joker was trying to get even for getting his walking papers or just had a wild idea and wondered if he could get away with it. He substituted a mature audience video marked "CBS Magazine of the Air." It should have been called "The ABCs of Life."

Since the audio portion can be heard only through earphones and the flight crew never pays attention to the screen, the substitution went unnoticed by the stewardesses except for strange behavior:

Elderly women were asking for Valium. Men wearing spectacles were calling for Windex.

Magazines were not being read; they were being used as fans.

Because of a shortage, several people were sharing the same earphones.

The navigator wandered out of the cockpit for a quick cup of coffee and never returned.

Small boys had their eyes washed out with soap.

The smoke detector alarm kept going off due to strong signals received from runaway pacemakers.

Finally, somebody complained. The complaint was that there was too much glare from the windows.

When all the shades were pulled down, there were so many people blushing that many of them glowed in the dark.

A minister bowed his head and said, "Let us pray." A bachelor next to him said, "My prayers have been answered."

The crew finally suspected something because instead of saying, "Could I have a cup of coffee?," the passengers were saying, "Sit down, please. You're blocking the screen."

The final tip-off to the crew came when the spot normally reserved for the world and national news received a standing ovation.

The mistake was caught and the video removed. The airline braced itself for news coverage, scandals, complaints, and possible lawsuits. Only three letters arrived at the complaint department. The first one said that the film lacked much of a plot. The second implied that this was a sneaky way to build their frequent flyer business. The third one threatened to sue for physical damages because she was forced to watch. She had a bulkhead seat and suffered eye, ear, and neck strain.

I asked the stewardess who told me this story if the airline had suffered because of the fiasco. She said they certainly had. Ever since they have been overworked, overlooked, and overbooked.

FIRST CLASS WINDOW SEAT

Getting to North Dakota is quite a chore, getting to Williston, in the winter time, is a miracle. Out of Minot, North Dakota, my airline ticket showed that I changed to Air Kangaroo for the short hop to Williston. Since there was a line of Indians in front of the counter being frisked for tomahawks I just picked up the phone and called the agent. He had to answer.

"What time does the next flight leave for Williston?"

"Saturday," he replied.

"This is Saturday," I said. "Now, what time?"

"What time can you get here?"

"I'll be there in a few minutes, but I see that we will be on a very small plane. What's the difference between first and second class?"

"On first class you ride inside the plane. It just costs a little more."

"My ticket says 9 to 5. Isn't that an odd time to leave?"

"That's not an odd time, that's the odds that it will make it."

"Can I get a seat by a window?"

"Yes, but not by an exit. They are all taken."

This plane was a twin otter, flown by a pilot who wore an eagle feather in his hat, had his hair in braids and refused to take off until everyone had bought some turquoise. He kept announcing the special prices for Christmas gifts on the unicom.

"My people have wandered in the wilderness for 40 years to make this fine Indian jewelry. We thank the Great White Father for sending the paleface buyers," chanted the pilot.

It sure was cold riding on the wing but I made some great buys from Chief Pontius, the pilot, and his navigator, Solomon Lone Eagle.

CRACKED IN PHILADELPHIA

We are just out of Philadelphia on a small twin engine airline. A curtain separates 11 passengers from the crew of two. The curtain is not closed and since no stereo, movies or air conditioning is available, we amuse ourselves by listening to Philadelphia Center directing our flight through weather similar to that of a steam bath. Suddenly it gets interesting.

"Hello. Thank goodness I hear voices. Who is this?"

"Sir, you are transmitting on Philadelphia Central Control frequency. Please make your request brief."

"O.K. Help."

"What is your problem, sir?"

"I'm in the clouds."

"Are you instrument qualified?"

"The plane is, I'm not."

"What is your position, sir?"

"I'm a broker for Acme Grain Company."

"No sir, I mean if you are lost what was your last known position."

"The airport where I took off."

"We have your transponder code indicating you are six miles north of Bald Eagle Mountain. What are your intentions?"

". . . that mountain."

"Sir, key your mike before you speak and speak slowly. What are your intentions?"

"To S-T-A-Y A-W-A-Y from that mountain."

"We are here to help you sir. What would you like to do?"

"You gotta be kidding. I wanna land this thing."

"Yes sir. Turn to a heading of 270 for a direct approach to the nearest airport five miles away."

"You fellows get me down safe and I swear I'll start back to church. And drinking, I'll give that up. And cussing, I'll quit. And all that money I made on the Russian grain deal. Wait a minute. I see the (expletive deleted) airport."

"Good day, sir."

"If you fellows are off this Sunday drop by the house and we'll have a drink of vodka. Any time after noon. That's when we get up."

The liberty bell is not the only thing that is cracked in Philadelphia. At least we know why all the grain is going to Russia on credit. So they can make vodka out of it to sell us for cash. Grain dealers are not the only ones who are up in the air about it.

COMMUTER TRAUMAS

Flying in helicopters is great fun. About the only thing that I can think of that exceeds it would be flying on a roto-tiller. That way, rough landings can always be salvaged by planting potatoes.

I was on a commuter helicopter recently that was supposed to make my airline connection fast and efficient. The pilot got my attention when he went over his checklist. "Number 1, check. Number 2, check. Number 3 . . . huh, number 3? I never noticed that before."

When I asked what led him to become a helicopter pilot, he said it must have been his previous on-the-job training program.

"You were training to be a helicopter pilot?"

"No, I was selling mixmasters."

We bored a hole through the clouds and landed at Kansas City where I was to catch a "small airplane" to Topeka. They lost my luggage but had a unique answer for my question of "What happened to my luggage?"

"It fell out," they said.

Transferring to the airplane should be better I reasoned. A very young, nice looking girl with short blonde hair, resembling Amelia Earhart, strolled up wearing a leather jacket.

"You look like you could be our pilot," I joked.

"I am your pilot," she replied.

"Are you old enough to fly?" I asked.

"Want to see my diploma?" she shot back.

"Does the seventh grade give out diplomas now?"

"I was a civilian pilot under contract to the military during the Vietnam War."

"Yeah, which side?"

"Wanna get to Topeka?"

"I love our patriotic veterans," I smiled.

"That's more like it. Go to the ticket counter and get your boarding pass and equipment issue."

"What is 'equipment issue'?"

"Goggles and scarf."

There were five of us besides the pilot. I was jammed into a seat with so little leg room that I couldn't get my legs and feet out of the seat I was sitting in until the pilot slid her seat forward for take off. "Sorry about that," she grinned over her shoulder. "You can uncross your legs now."

"Good," I said. "I'd hate to crash and be found in this position. Friends would mistake me for a Buddhist monk."

When we landed in Topeka, I limped inside to find the final insult. The baggage department man said my luggage didn't make it. I knew it wasn't my day. He was wearing my clothes.

FOOLPROOF SCANNER

It never ceases to amaze me what people carry on a trip. One of the most interesting jobs in the country must be the security searchers at the airport. When they x-ray the luggage and see something unusual, they get to go through your suitcase, purse or whatever.

I've noticed that purses have become much larger since they stopped putting attics in homes. While on a recent trip, I saw a guard go through a purse because it set off the alarm. When they poured out the contents it was easy to see why. There were enough keys to operate a Pittsburgh smelter for months, enough molten metal to build arms for the entire country of Litchenstein, and not one of them was known to fit any existing lock in the world. There was cold cream, face cream, body lotion, foot cream, enough oil to drive the Arabs to their knees in submissive competition.

The only reason they didn't arrest this lady was that she had so much goo on her that nobody could have held on to her. They had to roll her in resin before she could stay in her seat long enough to get the safety belt snapped.

Men carry even more metal on them than women, but I think they do it on purpose because so many of the security people are women. There is something about a woman in uniform that makes her dangerously attractive, and the fellows seldom ever seem to mind being searched by the girls.

One young fellow set off the alarm, emptied his pockets but kept setting it off so an equally young and attractive uniformed young lady asked for his permission to frisk him. She did, then asked, "Do you have any concealed metal on you?"

"Only a heart of gold, kiss me."

There were 120 passengers in transit and one guy in heaven. It's amazing. He said he has spent three days being frisked at the airport. As soon as he can afford it, he's going to buy a ticket and go someplace. The girls got so fed up with him after a while that they only wished him an adequate day.

They claim that the systems are getting better. The walk-through scanner is said to be foolproof. The manufacturer even sent his brother-in-law over to test it.

All this has a purpose, so the stewardesses can tell a lot about the passengers. Anyone calmly reading a newspaper is a veteran traveler. Anyone looking out the window is a newcomer. Anyone else looking nervous, biting their nails, is either a hijacker or the pilot.

METAL DETECTOR MALFUNCTION

Going through airport security could be a lot of fun except that some old fussbudget with a poor sense of humor got the concession on screening devices. Her name is Ura Kiljoy, meanest old heifer around, and she had signs erected as you enter the metal detectors that say things like "Please, no jokes" or "We take jokes about bombs seriously."

One of these days, so help me, they're going to get me because I can't see a thing serious about those screening machines. It's like lining up to run through a car wash. People get tense because they think they can't make any kind of little joke. However, I've found that there are a few things that you can get away with so that only you recognize the joke, thereby short circuiting the system.

First, after you walk through the detector, wait until the next guy gets in it and make a high pitched beep sound. Then look at the policeman but point at him. It also helps to frown and slowly shake your head from side to side.

Secondly, look into the darkness of the conveyor where your carry-on luggage is arriving, pretend you are talking to yourself and say in a hushed but audible tone, "I thought I saw a snake." When the lady running the machine peeks in there say, "Would you hand my bags to me? It's the cobra colored luggage."

Finally, if you should have enough metal on you to accidentally set the beeper off when you pass through the detector, just grab your heart with both hands and say, "Ahhhh" while falling to the floor. When people come to your aid say, "I've complained to the company about a defective laser modulator on this machine. The rays are invisible you know."

However, about the best stunt I've seen pulled was recently when a line of people tried to go through the detector at the same time. Buzzers went off and everybody was told to stop. Then a lady turned around and slapped a man. She was red faced and mad. The guy looked puzzled, turned to the crowd and said, "I didn't do anything." Then a six year old kid spoke up, "I did it. She backed up against me and I couldn't breathe, so I bit her."

BAGGAGE TRAVELS IN CIRCLES

"I fly 100,000 miles per year promoting books," said the young publishing tycoon, "but that's nothing, my luggage flies 150,000."

The feeling is all too familiar for frequent flyers. You buy a ticket to Des Moines, your luggage has a great time in Pango-Pango. I once flew to London on a British airline, being assured by officials that my bags would at least be on the Island. They were . . . the Faulkland Islands. They came back months later covered with wool and smelling like sheep dip.

Just watch the baggage handlers sometimes and you'll see why stuff gets rerouted. Mad at the boss? Throw a piece on the wrong conveyor. Mad at the spouse? Give a karate chop to anything that reads "FRAGILE." Many of these guys flunked out of pilot school so now they practice with your luggage for their next profession . . . as a bombadier.

Sure, the ticket agent is a nice person, but did you ever notice where they send your bags? They go down into a dark place where a gorilla is kept entertained by testing the hinges and handles. You've probably seen the TV commercial.

That's only Phase I. Phase II sends bags through the G & W division . . . that's gears and wheels, then on to Phase III: the spotlessly clean loading room which doubles as a car wash.

Phase IV is actual loading onto the correct plane, also known as the fiction phase.

The person in charge of your luggage, however, is a world famous name—Idi Amin.

Ever notice that you can fly first class, coach, tourist, special coach or even inside the plane, but your luggage just goes one way? That way is through a tar pit, giant trash compactor, car wash, and Peking.

And all those slogans only refer to you, not the cargo:

"Belta is ready when you are . . . let your luggage come by bus."

"We really move our tail for you . . . call Mayflower for anything else, Buster."

"Fly the friendly skies . . . but it's every bag for itself on the ground."

"Doing what we do best . . . and don't complain, Jack, or we'll bust you in the chops."

You just can't win. I checked my matching set of luggage (two cardboard boxes) on a close connection, hoping they would make it. Later our pilot announced, "Folks, we'll be delayed up here awhile. The bad news is that a plane in front of us has had to make a wheels-up landing. The good news is that everyone got off safely . . . because they landed on your luggage."

And don't get smart, because I heard an official in charge of lost luggage say to an irate passenger who lost his cool: "Mister, at this point, only two people in the whole world care about your luggage and one of 'em is rapidly losing interest."

CONFEDERATE AIR FORCE

The Confederate Air Force, based in Harlingen, Texas, is a flying museum. Some of the relics are flown, others do the flying. All prove the old saying that, "The South shall rise again." The object of the association is to preserve aircraft from 1939 through 1946 that were used in the military. They have American, British, German, Japanese, and other fighters, bombers, etc.

Every member of this group is the same rank, Chicken Colonel, so orders of the day have been replaced by suggestions. Although they wear cowboy hats and fly the Rebel flag they have a wing in Minnesota, a tail section in North Dakota and a cockpit full of love for airplanes.

They were once invited to fly in formation over the nation's capitol. Although the general staff agreed that the capitol was Richmond, they decided to humor the blue coats and fly over D.C. (which they are convinced now stands for Dixie's collateral). The only suggestion of the day was that nobody fly under the Potomac bridge. One Chicken Colonel was almost grounded because he grinned every time the Potomac bridge restriction was mentioned.

A squadron of Zeros, Spitfires, Messerschmits, P-38's, and an old B-52 bomber thundered down on the Pentagon, did a few wingovers, made a mock attack on the Good Year blimp, wrote Robert E. Lee in smoke and bombed the lunching government crowd with magnolia blossoms. Half the crowd was ready to stop drinking. The other half was ready to start.

The half that was interested in getting high with aviation went out to drink a toast to these old, bold pilots and planes of the Confederate Air Force. Jefferson Davis would have been proud of these men who exemplified Southern Comfort with their motto, "Semper Mint Julip."

RAT NOW

As a pilot with over 3000 hours in the air, I get to hear a lot of interesting chatter on aircraft radios. Recently a fellow was bragging that he had soloed last month and was building up time rapidly. "I average one take off and three landings per flight," he reported. I have days like that myself.

This past Mother's Day found me in the air to visit mine. Calling the flight service station from the air, I checked weather enroute with a male voice. After getting a report, I jokingly wished him a happy Mother's Day. Without a second's delay I got a "Thank you" from a female voice. "My mother," he said, "I had to work today, so I invited her down."

A couple of days later, I was flying in to Lafayette, Louisiana, on a rather murky day. Low clouds and reduced visibility made the low time pilots a little nervous and I kept hearing things like "I'm coming back to the airport. Can't get through out here."

Approach Control kept having to say, "Who's coming back? What is your aircraft identification number and position."

One guy gave his number, then listed his position as "left front seat."

While all this was going on, there were some military pilots shooting instrument approaches just for practice and obviously enjoying it. Their military identification numbers were RAT 1, RAT 2, and RAT 3.

Approach, in a slack moment asked, "Where does the designation RAT come from?"

The lead pilot replied, "Stands for Reserve Air Transportation. We're in the Naval Reserve." The RAT 2 pilot quips, "Stands for lots of things . . . Ready Any Time." RAT 3 adds, "Or Rear Admiral's Toy."

While everyone is chuckling, there is a garbled message that ends with "coming back." Approach replies, "Say again . . . was that RAT 2?"

A nervous voice replies, "No, that was 23 Juliet and I want to land RAT NOW."

THE WRIGHT WAY

It is not often that one gets to witness history being discussed by those who made it, but at a meeting of the National Congress on Aerospace Education in Orlando, Florida recently I saw it happen. Two gentlemen, both in their 80s, Dr. Paul Garber, Historian Emeritus, National Air & Space Museum, and Glenn Messer, a barnstormer who was taught to fly by Orville Wright, took to the platform. Nothing fancy, they just sat around a table on stage with Dr. Garber interviewing Glenn Messer. It went like this:

"Glenn, you are a pioneer flyer, race car driver, and Hollywood stuntman. I understand you also made one of the first parachute jumps."

"Yes, jumped out of a balloon. They had the chute packed in a sort of bag under the basket. It was packed in talcum powder to keep the chute from sticking together and you just bailed out over the side. The talcum worked for you in dry weather, against you in wet weather."

"Then you graduated to airplanes?"

"Right, I had four hours of instructions, then started flying exhibitions."

"That must be some kind of record."

"No, I think the record was set by a friend of mine who had his first flight, exhibition and crash all on the same day."

"Then you went to England and joined the Royal Air Force."

"Yes, we were flying Camels in WWI. They were strange crafts to control. In order to turn right, you just sort of brushed the right rudder then gave it left rudder. If you didn't learn to do it right, it went into a right spin. Every day I would hear those Britishers say, 'Poor chap. Span in to the right.'"

"You obviously did well."

"I didn't take a chance. I took off on my first flight and flew an upward left hand spiral to about 4000 feet before I let that Camel even look to the right."

"You didn't have navigation aids did you?"

"Just landmarks. I was following a railroad one day and suddenly lost it, so I flew back to see where I went wrong. Found that the railroad went into a tunnel."

"Do you remember when we used to fly off the Polo Field?"

"Yes, but we trimmed a few branches back and thinned out part of the grandstand. They really should have stopped the game for takeoffs and landings."

And so it went for half an hour. Wing walking, flying stunts, carrying the mail, teaching, barnstorming, they did it all.

"Understand you had a unique way of handling a student pilot that froze at the controls by using a fire extinguisher. How did that work?"

"The student rode in the front of the instructor in those open cockpits. We had a fire extinguisher mounted outside between the two pilots. If a student froze up, it could be dangerous so I used the fire extinguisher to calm him down."

"How did that work specifically?"

"I jerked it loose and tapped him gently on the head, causing him to relax."

AROUND THE WORLD HANGAR STYLE

"Hangar flying" is a sport too few people have experienced. Unless you pilot a plane yourself, you may not know what the term means. Pilots know it as another way of reliving former death defying feats of heroism while hurdling through space in a flying machine. Psychologists have a word for it—lying.

I've heard some pretty good yarns while sitting in a hangar with the rest of the guys waiting for the fog to lift.

"The wind was blowing faster than my approach speed so when I tried to land, I was actually losing ground speed. Boy was I scared. Called on every bit of courage I had as an airman. I gave her full throttle, overshot the runway, cut the engine, and backed her in."

"There I was at 700 feet in a J-3 Cub when I looked down to see a diamondback rattlesnake coiled behind the right rudder. I gave it full right rudder, trapping his head between the rudder pedal and the floor. I gave it full throttle and climbed in a tight circle to the right while that rattler's tail buzzed like a Yamaha off-trail bike. When the buzzing stopped, I was at 30,000 feet, wings loaded with ice, the diamondback frozen so hard you could drive a tent peg with him. I gave it left rudder, removed the snake and broke him into 12 six-inch pieces like an icicle. Ran out of fuel. Dead-sticked it into a cow pasture. Suffering from fatigue and dehydration, I found a toolshed nearby with a supply of bottled drinks. Turned out that snake saved my life. Used his head as a bottle opener."

"That's nothing (this statement is inevitable). I was flying this experimental plane. It went into an uncontrollable spin at 10,000 feet. I had on some baggy pants, so I took 'em off and tied a knot in each leg, held 'em over my head and bailed out. Floated down and landed in the middle of a crowd at a supermarket opening. Very embarrassing."

"Because you had lost your airplane?"

"No, because I had lost my underwear."

It would also make one a bit anxious to untie knots in each pant leg during a ribbon cutting—with nobody facing the ribbon. According to the teller of this story, only three complaints were lodged. One for aerial flashing, one for eyestrain, and one request for younger skydivers.

With the cost of aviation fuel nowadays, more people should take up this new sport. Flying a 747 is child's play. Me and my buddies recently flew around the world in a 1934 hangar.

PILOTS OR PATIENTS

Oshkosh, Wisconsin, is the home of the famed EAA (Experimental Aircraft Association), so naturally us "high flyers" tend to congregate at Oshkosh. The reason they meet there is to test pilots for sobriety. If they can say "Oshkosh" plainly there is no need for a breathalyzer.

So there we were at the Wisconsin Airport Managers Association. "Skip" Becher, Jr., a corporate pilot with thousands of hours told the saddest tale I've heard—how flying nearly grounded his marriage. You see, airports have abbreviations limited to three initials: JFK, FDR, DFW stand for John F. Kennedy, New York; Franklin D. Roosevelt, Frederick, Oklahoma; Dallas-Ft. Worth in Texas.

Skip was to fly to Sturgeon Bay, Wisconsin, abbreviation SUE. He called flight service for weather but Sturgeon Bay had missed reporting on that hour. So Skip copied the telephone number in order to check direct with the airport before he took off. He dashed home to take a quick shower, told his wife he had to make this flight with a client and would be out overnight. His wife, helping him make the quick change, emptied his pockets into a fresh suit and came across a suspicious note, "SUE 897-0068." He received a thorough briefing this time and needed no notes to remember it.

This experience led Skip to study other abbreviations. A few of them include EAT (Wenatchee, Washington), ATE (Mobile, Alabama), and GAS (Galopilos, Ohio), which could have some connection with SAD (Safford, Arizona), BAD (Shreveport, Louisiana), and GAG (Gage, Oklahoma), not to mention PIE (St. Petersburg, Florida) in the SKY (Sandusky, Ohio).

Skip says it's a good thing these abbreviations are not stamped on people's forehead to get them to their destination. Imagine a portly matron wanting to book passage to Fresno, California. Her stamp would be FAT. Oh, well, we could always go to Atlanta International, ILS 9R . . . which is FUN.

One other story of note involves the Wausaw, Wisconsin Municipal Airport which has a flight service station located just a few feet from a state mental institution. The "patients" are allowed to roam at will, since the airport is in the countryside. They are always wandering into the flight service station to ask "What's the weather enroute to St. Louis?" or similar questions. The briefers finally complained to the city that they were being overworked with all these unnecessary briefings. The city manager suggested, "Why don't you just tell the 'patients' that you're not going to tell them, and just brief the pilots?"

"Because," said the briefer, "we can't tell the patients from the pilots."

PIGGYBACK OR STANDBY

I met an airline reservations agent recently on a coffee break and we got to talking about the language barrier that exists between the people who fly and those who make it possible for them to get there. "Some of them are from another planet," she said, "like the fellow who wanted to ride in the cage with his dog so he wouldn't have to buy a ticket."

One guy didn't even know where he was going. All the information he had was a nine digit zip code. When she traced down the information and told him that the zip code was from a suburb in Chicago, he said, "No, that's not it. Could you try another arrangement of the numbers?"

When an elderly gentleman was told he would have a connecting flight, he wanted to know if that meant like he had seen on television. He worried about "those piggyback planes."

A lady said she did not mind being put on standby for a flight. If they couldn't find her a seat, she would go to the gift shop and buy a little stool.

One character wanted to know the cost of a short flight. When the agent asked exactly where he wanted to go, he said, "Just around the block a time or two."

A fellow got all the details of his destination correct and then tried to pay for the flight with quarters through a pay phone.

When the agent told him she couldn't accept payment that way, he got mad because she wouldn't give him his money back.

"I don't have your money," she patiently explained. "You put it in the phone and that is something I have no control over."

"Don't give me that line, lady," he said. "I've seen the ads on TV. I know about A T & T. I know that the letters stand for Airplanes, Tickets and Telephones. Cliff Robertson wouldn't lie."

An elderly lady came to the ticket desk and said she wanted to visit her kids. She asked for a ticket to Charleston. "West Virginia or South Carolina?" inquired the agent.

"Oh, dear me, are there two of them?"

When informed there were, she said, "Well, just give me a ticket to visit my other daughter in Columbus."

"Georgia or Mississippi?"

"Never mind," she said. "Give me a ticket to see my son in Illinois."

"What town?"

"Leaping Pastures," she answered.

"We don't go there, only to Chicago and Springfield."

"That's it, Springfield. I knew it had something to do with grass."

"Are you sure that's where you want to go? We also have a Springfield, Missouri."

"Never mind," she sighed. "I'll catch a bus to Sea World. I don't want to fly to anyplace that can't stay put."

HEFTY, HEFTY

The airline stewardess was the type most men find attractive. That is, she was female. Her long blonde hair glistened in the sunlight so brightly you could hardly see the faint black roots. Her figure was like an hour glass, with sand in all the right places. The low cut uniform had a plunging neckline that was delicately decent but imaginatively wicked.

As I approached the entrance to the aircraft, she pretended not to notice me, chatting instead to the other passengers, flashing her lovely, perfectly formed teeth in a congenial smile.

Then it happened. We were close enough that I could smell the mixture of Chanel #5, face powder, and Zest soap. That's when she made her move. "Not very original" I thought as she touched my hand with hers and spoke softly so the others wouldn't hear, "Let me take your garment bag."

Clever, very clever. I wondered what her next move would be so I played along promising myself to let her down easy if things got more serious. Sure enough, she continued the conversation, ignoring the other passengers. "How far are you going?" (Careful now. Think this out properly so the answer is not misinterpreted). I gave the vague answer "Huh?" (Stalling for time. I'm a married man and she's young enough to be my sister.)

"Do you get off at the first stop. What is your seat number?"

(Boy, she's got it bad. Can't stand losing track of me. She even writes down my seat number and attaches it to my garment bag.)

Later, she finds excuses to open conversation. "Something to drink?" "Headphone set?" "Magazine?"

(Poor kid. She probably never met a real he-man all strapped down like this before. She probably has me mistaken for Robert Redford.)

I played it cool except for reading the magazine upside down, plugging the headset into the air vent and spilling coffee down the front of my pin-striped overalls.

As we landed, I was the first one at the door of the aircraft to de-plane. Naturally, she was there, a dainty hand slid softly into the crook of my arm and she whispered "Please don't leave."

"Why not?" I asked with a rakish smile.

"That's not your garment bag you're carrying. It's the garbage from first class."

No matter how tough Jonathan Winters says they are, that's the last time I'm gonna use a Hefty for a garment bag.

GIFT OF GAB

"Zip" Franklin of Lovington, New Mexico is the cornerstone of the Franklin Flying Circus foundation. Although his two sons, Jim and Steve, do most of the flying, Zip is a three ring circus all by himself. He is a philosopher and can give an opinion on almost anything as long as he can talk in the lofty gift of gab given to aviators.

Q. "What do you think of welfare?"

A. "It don't work no better on cows than it does on people. We used to fly in feed to snowbound cows. They got so used to pie in the sky that they chased every plane that flew over, ran through fences and stopped digging through the snow for a good living right under their noses. They all had stiff necks from searching the sky for 'Uncle Sugar.'"

Q. "You are a rancher and farmer. Why would a man encourage his sons to be daredevil pilots?"

A. "The daredevils are earthbound, those who flirt with danger by drinking, smoking, chasing women . . . farming. We fly airplanes. When we set out to get high we don't fool around."

Q. "You mean you fellows don't believe in drinking, smoking, or chasing women?"

A. "We don't smoke."

Q. "What do you think of air safety?"

A. "I've always stressed safety. The most dangerous times are on the ground. We had a little dog that ran out and snapped at the prop just as we fired up the plane. I heard a little 'pling' and knew what had happened. I shut down the engine and me and the boys took a look. He was unconscious and his nose had been cut clean off. The boys found his nose and I sewed it back on. That scoundrel learned respect for a plane and lived for five years after that. He would have lived for much longer except for these occasional violent thunderstorms we get around here."

Q. "He got hit by lightning?"

A. "Naw, he got caught in a violent downpour. I had made the mistake of sewing his nose on upside down and he drowned up on top of a sandstone hill."

After that much philosophy we all decided to close the hangar door. But Zip had one last opinion to share.

"You fellows better turn in soon if you're gonna fly tomorrow. Remember the old Chinese saying, 'He who flies with the Eagles by day must not hoot with the owls by night.'"

LUCKY SHOTS 12

Let a smile be your umbrella and you'll get a
mouth full of rain.

PHILOSOPHERS

A great military leader once said, "Old soldiers never die; they just fade away." Of course, old soldiers never die because it's the young soldiers who are up at the front doing the fighting. General Douglas McArthur was one of the better known philosophers of our time. Probably his most famous words were "I shall return." Philosophers have to be careful how they say things. Otherwise, people won't remember them as great philosophers. If he had said, "I'll be right back" or "See y'all later," it would not have had nearly as much historical impact.

It has been my privilege to meet some of the great philosophers of all time. Their words are covered in this chapter. I'm not talking about Aristotle, Plato, or Socrates, not even the modern day philosophers like Eric Hoffer, Lyndon Johnson, or Billy Carter. I'm talking about common people who not only say things funny, but say funny things. The philosopher Corrie Tenboom was once asked for her philosophy of life. She replied, "Fill what's empty, empty what's full, and scratch where it itches."

My colleague and close friend, Robert Henry of Auburn, Alabama, is one of the funniest men in America. He has what I call a fun philosophy. About his wife, he says, "Winning an argument from Merrilyn is about as difficult as nailing jello to a tree." Of his boys, he says, "Patrick is my oldest. A man has to have guts to name his kid Patrick Henry. We were

216

careful to sterilize everything that went in that boy's mouth as a baby. Then we relaxed. Brent shared his bowl with the dog. He's fifteen now and he's for sale." Robert is active in the conservative wing of his church. "Everybody's a Baptist in Alabama unless somebody's been messin' with 'em." But beneath the jokes is a walking, talking role model who practices what he preaches in his best known speech and philosophy of "Win with ACES," an acronym for ambition and attitude, commitment, enthusiasm, and service.

In this last chapter, you will meet people and/or philosophy that may not change your ambition, attitude, or make a great difference in your life, but I believe you will find it to be fun. As a young boy, I recall my first philosopher. He was an old Indian chief of the Choctaw tribe. Known for his wisdom and sage advice, I asked him to give me the secret of life. He coughed and wheezed and with a voice barely audible said he would tell me the secret of life if I would promise never to forget it.

"I'll never forget it," I promised. "Please tell me, chief."

The old man mustered up enough strength to prop himself up on his elbows and just as he was about to tell me, he wheezed again, "Promise you never forget."

Knowing that the end was imminent, I made a blood oath that I would never forget his words of wisdom.

With a relaxed look on his face, he uttered his last words to me. "Remember that wet birds never fly at night. Don't ever forget." And then he died.

To this day, I don't know what he meant by that, but I'll tell you one thing . . . I never have forgotten it.

A DIFFERENT HOST

Gadsden, Alabama has a hotel called the Downtowner Motor Inn. The genial host is Tom Cross who belies the slang interpretation of his last name.

Speaking at the Alabama Kiwanis Convention, I naturally wanted to have a reserved room waiting for me. Usually when you check into a hotel they have to scratch around for your records. Often the clerk never even looks up when asking, "Do you have a reservation?" After an affirmative answer he asks, "Do you swear to God you have a reservation?"

That's where Tom Cross operates differently. He wrote me a letter telling me that he would be glad to have me stay in his lovely city as long as I stayed in his lovely hotel. He even said that his limousine would be waiting at the airport to take me to town. I was the only one who got off the plane at Gadsden but the limo was there.

When I walked into the hotel I heard a big, jolly fellow ask the desk clerk, "Has Doc Blakely checked in yet?" Since I didn't see a pistol or a badge on him I confessed guilt to being the party in question.

He said, "Lawdy mercy man, we're glad to have you in Gadsden. Gimme a dollar." Then he laughed and told me how much he had heard about me, said he had alerted the restaurant help to give me my usual gourmet meals. I was offered collard greens and grits for a starter.

I was truly impressed with my own importance. My room was on the most exclusive floor, the sixth. Everyone knows that is where they put the important people. The elevators were a little strange. They had people who stayed in them and drove them for you. When you rang the elevator button it really rang and a guy yelled up the shaft, "Be right there." The longest I waited for an elevator was 15 seconds. My body traveled from the sixth floor to the lobby in three seconds. My stomach made it in five.

Meanwhile back in the lobby, I hear Tom asking, "Has Delbert Dinwiddy checked in yet?" Guess what, Delbert is as famous as I am and just important enough to stay on the best floor in the house, the seventh. Of course everybody was made to feel welcome and important. That's because of Tom's philosophy. His daddy told him years ago, "If you're gonna be a man my son be a man in full. In the land of milk and honey be the only Jersey bull."

PICK A PECK OF PACKERS

A fellow from back east recently came out to the Texas Panhandle to look over the cattle feeding business. He was doing some research for his book, "How to make a million for $9.95." Most of the feeders soon concluded, with him, that the way to do it was to sell about 100,000 head of books and stay out of the cattle business.

Even though this writer was from way back east (over around Nacogdoches) he was a "good old boy" and the gregarious Panhandlers took him around and gave him the works. The fact that the writer had an expense account from his publishing company had nothing to do with the feeders giving up their booth at McDonalds in favor of a linen cloth covered round table at Pierre's. Over filet mignon and small bottomless glasses of burgundy the cowmen explained to the tenderfoot the difference between a stockgrower, a feeder and a packer buyer.

"A stockman is the fellow who raises the cattle in the first place. He's kinda like a lovesick boy who will do anything to show off in hopes of attracting the interest of the girl of his dreams."

"Yeh," added another philosopher, "and the feeder is like the next step, a bridegroom who proposes to the girl and marries up with her for better or for worse."

"What about the packer buyer?" asked the writer.

"Well," replied a sage, "he's sort of like the preacher. He just gives a little speech about how great it's gonna be after it's too late to back out."

Optimism seems to dominate in cow country. This was evidenced by a trip to Friona by the writer and his three friends. At a local cafe the gum chewing waitress asked what kind of steak the boys wanted. By this time the scribe was burned out on beef but wary of being poisoned by importation.

"Is the seafood platter good and fresh?"

"Sure is," replied the look alike for Flo on Mel's Diner, "we fly it in every morning from Amarillo."

The bookworm was converted on the spot, born again. Rumor has it that he won't even drink now unless he can have Beefeaters gin.

THAT AIN'T HAY OR IS IT?

The talk circuit is filled with people making great speeches, promoting programs of genius, sharing the wisdom of their brilliant minds. Teddy Kennedy speaks also.

Every time I make a talk, someone wants to know where my next one will be. It happened again the other day. Everybody laughed when I told them I would be doing my part to add a little culture to the Mineola (Texas) Hay Show. They laughed at the Hay Show too, over 400 rural-urban people who get together once a year to promote agriculture. Rotary Club, Lions Club, merchants, and the Chamber of Commerce combine to judge and chemically test the quality of hay produced by locals. As the old saying goes, "You can lead a mule to water . . . but if you can get him to float on his back . . . well, then you got something." They've got something at Mineola.

One of the things they have is a wild man named Byron Leewright, auctioneer of winning hay entries. Byron is what you might call uninhibited. His style has been compared to the new natural cereals—half nuts and very flaky.

Taking a bid on one champion bale of hay from the president of one bank, then another from the president of a competitive bank, he stops the bidding to remark, "Don't just sit there folks, if we get them to bidding against each other, no tellin' what this stuff will bring."

When he asked an aide to refresh his memory on where he was in the bidding the helper told him the bid was $185. "Well, that's enough," Byron shouted, "let him have it."

The big lots are sold by the bale also but at lower levels. Byron doesn't rely totally on his helpers, he also watches the bidders. At one point, an aide corrected his chant to "$2, do I hear . . ." to "$1.90." Patiently, Byron explained to everyone, "There's a gentleman over there with two fingers in the air. Now, he either wants to be excused or I've got a $2 bid."

The auction raised several thousand dollars and as one wag put it, "That ain't hay," but it was. Everyone also agreed that Byron was a great success, lots of laughs but as with the case with most auctioneers, it would be nice to have an on-off button to control him. "Yeah," remarked an impish friend, "and make it r-e-a-l hard to turn on."

BIG BASH—SMALL TOWN

Silsbee, Texas has one of the greatest social functions I've ever attended. They call it the annual chamber of commerce bash. It starts about 4 P.M. on a 40 acre pine farm where white jacketed waiters pass among the pine cones dishing out such delicacies as Swedish meatballs, cheese dips, corn fritters and soft meal hot tamales. And salt, lots of salt so a proper thirst can be developed to take advantage of liquid refreshments. Some fellows showed up with their own salt block and licked so much that those who wore wire rimmed glasses had them rusted right off their eyes.

I was given a royal tour of the town prior to the banquet at the high school cafeteria. It was a very moving experience. As soon as I finished speaking everybody got up and left.

But they have the right idea about putting on a good show. They advertise it as a fun time, and people come from as far away as Kountze, Evadale, Buna, and Fred. Tickets to the banquet are limited, and they are always sold out long before the day of the shindig so that a waiting list develops that is longer than a bridegroom's expectations. That's good salesmanship because there is nothing that people want to go to more than something they can't get into.

The economy of the town is built around timber because timber is built around the town. Pine trees are big business, and real estate prices are measured not in dollars but in board feet. Out near the edge of town a plump, middle aged, gray-haired woman shuffled out in her houseshoes and nightgown to check the mail box as we drove by on the tour. A citizen leaned up from the back seat of our car and said, "See that woman there? I worship the ground she walks on." Then he added, "She's got some property to the east of here that I'd love to have too."

The town is so well off that a new doctor just moved in to the city who is a cholesterol specialist. He takes the fat out of his patient's wallet. When you check in the hospital they exchange a nightgown for your chain saw, spray you for termites and check you for woodpeckers. These lumberjacks are so well heeled that the doctor has a cash register at the checkout desk. The patient lays down on a conveyer belt and the medic adds up what he did to him as he passes by.

Silsbee has money, as evidenced by the number of banks and saving institutions there. My friend, David Stanley, president of First Savings Association of South East Texas, moved in here just about three years ago because it looked like it had potential. He has already outgrown his original facility and plans to buy a building from a bank who outgrew their facilities.

Even in spite of all this success the townspeople have kept their country style, easy going manner. David met me at the Silsbee International airport and Loblolly Pine Farm. They have a dirt strip with a nice sign on the telephone booth that says "Welcome to Silsbee, Silsbee Chamber of Commerce." But they are modern. When I left that night they had the runway lighted for me. About every twenty yards was a fruit jar filled with lightning bugs. I'll think about all my new found friends everytime I hear a cash register ring or smell creosote.

LONELY HEARTS TAKE HEED

I've always wondered why someone didn't start a real original chain letter. I'd like to do it myself but the postal rates on chain would make it prohibitive. But every once in a while some genius comes up with a linkable chain letter. The following came yesterday:

Dear Doc:

I started this letter, a year or so ago, to bring a little happiness and joy to the hearts of tired, overworked, unappreciated, common men. Naturally, you came to mind.

You will promptly perceive that, unlike most chain letters, this does not cost you anything. You simply pick out five of your friends who seem equally common and send them a copy of this letter. You send your wife to the man whose name appears at the top of the enclosed list and add your name to the bottom. Within four weeks, when your name comes up you will receive 1,416 women and some of them are bound to be knockouts.

Beware that the chain is not broken. Pierre LePew of Alberta, Canada, broke the chain and froze to death during an energy shortage.

His neighbor, Jacque LuKey, kept the chain intact and was chased through a blizzard by his irate wife, thereby keeping both their temperatures to the boiling point. Clinton Higginbottom of Richmond, Virginia broke the chain and the next day his pacemaker had to be recharged because of inactivity. Although a jumper cable from an electric typewriter got his heart started again, he has never been quite the same. R. Nixon, most recently of California, broke the chain and got his own wife back on top of all his other troubles.

As an added bonus, if you act now before the postal rates go up, you will also receive green stamps for acting so promptly, and an insurance policy with a double indemnity clause for having the nerve to act at all.

I've got to go now. The doorbells are ringing. All of them. My name just came up.

Cordially yours,
Richard Burton

"But Richard Burton is dead" you say? Maybe he broke the chain. Maybe he didn't but in either case what a way to go.

NICE TREADS

I never thought of it this way but a tire salesman told me he could tell what kind of personality people have by looking at their tires.

The even tempered person will have tires that wear uniformly. He's the one who makes the 40,000 miles as advertised and when he finally buys a new set the old ones are so thin that they can double as a football bladder. You'll starve to death trading with him.

The nervous guy stops and starts quick, never rotates anything except his nerves and has tires that look like they entered the Baja 500 and lost. His name is spoken reverently by the tire salesmen's children in their nightly prayers.

The tightwad always drives 20 miles under the speed limit, raises himself in the seat when running over a pebble in the road, has dry rot cracks that appear like spider webs on his blackwalls and air that dates back to World War II. He's the only guy around who can wear a tire out from the inside. They pray for him, too—to run over a land mine.

The hot rodder peels rubber by throwing his car in gear and his brains in neutral. He rotates his tires—on top of the pavement—and squeals his way into the hall of shame, which is usually located in a local body shop. Tire salesmen whistle and grin every time they hear the musical strains of the Firestone Quartet.

Tire salesmen are dedicated professionals who notice things that a commoner would miss. Sophia Loren drove into a Goodyear center to have her tires checked on her Rolls Royce. As she walked away the professional was heard to say, "Now there's a real tribute to proper balance, even wear, and just the right inflation."

A customer muttered, "Yeah, but her tires are a mess."

ARMED AND DANGEROUS

I don't know what it is about me that attracts strange people but if one is in the area he will seek me out like a moth seeks a flame, a bat seeks a cave, a Dallas Cowboy seeks a new contract.

Minding my own business recently at a Las Vegas arm wrestling contest, this small but tough looking character challenged me. Being semi-macho, I let my ego get the best of me, came out of the audience and agreed to an exhibition. I had watched the others get themselves braced, wrap a leg around the braces on the table, so I gave it my best. It was very much like playing Russian roulette with a single shot pistol.

Bones cracked, joints popped, and there was this awful tearing sound like a tendon being ripped from raw bone. And that was just getting out of my seat.

Once I got myself into position with everything I could get wrapped around something, I nodded my head signifying I was ready. I learned a great deal from that experience, mainly how rope is made from hemp.

When I woke up, they told me it was one of the best shows they had seen since the Flamenco dance troup tried to corral a family of cockroaches.

The most important thing to remember about arm wrestling is the grip. One should grasp the opponent where the most leverage is obtained. If you are quick enough, I would suggest the throat.

The next most important things to remember are to say your prayers and memorize the numbers 911.

It's a good thing I didn't arm wrestle with both arms because I needed one to get out of bed with the next morning. Actually I needed three.

After a hot shower, I loosened up a little and was greatly encouraged when I finally managed to reach my head with a comb. Even my hair was in pain.

When I got dressed and walked through the lobby of Circus-Circus, I was mighty thankful that all of this took place there. I had to walk like Cheetah dragging my suitcase but nobody seemed to notice except this guy in a loincloth.

So take warning, folks. If you are challenged at an arm wrestling exhibition contest by some wiry, 120-pound youngster, swallow your pride and don't accept. It's a trap. Don't trust her.

WAY THE COOKIE CRUMBLES

Regional Sales Managers can be pretty tough cookies. Ted Sokol of Omaha was one of those. He recently retired from Archway Cookies, who make the tender kind, and, for my money, the best. Ted adds special ingredients to his sales presentations, enough laughing gas to fuel a hot air balloon to 38,000 feet.

"Cookies are healthy food," exclaims Sokol. "They don't have any bones in them."

"A cookie won't catch fire and explode on take off."

"They are always in style, never clash with anything you're wearing. If you have a few freckles, you can coordinate with chocolate chip cookies even if you're naked. I love cookies."

However, Ted recently retired and attended an Archway meeting in his entirely new capacity for the first time. He couldn't stand it. At the close of one presentation, he asked to say a few words. The ingredients were a recipe for a half-baked philosophy of life. "I wanted to advertise a little here today. Since my retirement, I've become a consultant. That's a fellow who knows more and more about less and less until he knows absolutely everything about nothing."

"My consulting hours are from 2 to 4 on Monday and Friday. The reason for those short hours is that I didn't realize my wife was going to retire when I did.

"By the time I get through with all my chores and fix my own breakfast, it's time to start lunch and drive her to her bridge club meeting. They get so serious about it sometimes they even remember to play cards.

"In the evenings, I have to devote my time to my collection of precious metals. I pick up aluminum cans on roadsides.

"Tuesdays, Wednesdays, and Thursdays I babysit the grandkids and practice aerobic yelling.

"I'm so busy that I've sold everything but my putter, taken a time management course, and switched to miniature golf.

"So, even if you don't need a consultant, let me give you some free advice. You should seriously think about retiring.

"I have and I've decided that if any of you create an opening, I'm ready to go back to work."

DEALER'S CHOICE

Speaking to the Montana Automobile Dealers Association in Missoula was an accelerating experience for me. The market may be depressed elsewhere, but Montana dealers say they get exhausted hearing about it. They have gotten creative to deal with the market.

One fellow sold a car that he didn't have, then called his buddy dealer in a nearby town and talked him out of the model he needed at cost. Only thing was that this car already had the name of the wrong dealer on the trunk. So, being a good advertising man, he redrilled the holes, changed out the name, repainted the trunk . . . and charged his buddy $80 for the job.

"I let you have the car at my cost," complained his friend long distance.

"So, what's the problem? I changed out the name and only charged you my cost," he replied.

At the convention three dealers got to arguing about who represented the finest line of automobiles. In the parking lot outside the Red Lion Motor Inn, a dealer drove into the makeshift show arena in a sparkling powder blue Cadillac complete with power steering, power windows, power upholstery.

The proud dealer proudly produced a bottle of champagne, cracked the bottle lightly on the bumper, sprinkled a bit on the hood and proclaimed, "I christen thee George Washington, first and foremost name of quality in America."

Next came a Lincoln dealer with his new model featuring whitewall tires even on the inside. He smiled broadly, pulled a fifth of Cutty Sark from a velvet bag, cracked it open with a mighty whack on the bumper, poured it over the hood and proudly announced, "I christen thee Abraham Lincoln, honest, trustworthy, and most admired name in America."

Lastly, a dealer in jump suit and crash helmet roared into the ring: plain black tires, no hubcaps, plain vanilla. He slid sideways in front of the reviewing stand, crawled through the open window, cracked a bottle of Coors beer over the hood ornament and babbled, "I christen thee, Teddy Roosevelt . . . you rough ridin' son-of-a-gun."

MAKING OF A COWBOY

It used to be that being a cowboy was easy. All you had to do was buy a $40 saddle, a $100 Stetson, a $75 pair of boots and figure out how to pay for it out of $20-a-month wages. Of course, the overhead was sky-high too, except when it rained; then, you could sleep under the chuckwagon.

You froze in the winter, burned in the summer and alternated between choking on trail dust or sourdough. You rode a different horse every day; the only constant factor was the uncertainty of his movements at life-threatening moments like a tumbleweed making an approach within sight of the horizon.

Once a month, you had to take a bath and go to town, so you could look at all the things that you'd never have money enough to buy. That was back when Roebuck was still a partner of Sears, and the ladies' underwear section still had the raciest illustrations around.

Cowboys cut each other's hair, with a bowl or camp pot serving to protect the ears from sheep shears. The honky-tonk was the favorite watering hole where "hands" gathered to listen to country-western music and drink Jack Daniels, Jim Beam and the national beer of Texas. The juke box had lights that blinked and flashed inside red, yellow, and green transparent panels. It was hypnotic, the way that atmosphere could remove the aches from joints jarred to stiffness from a thousand broncs long since gone to glory. Those fallen angels used to hang around the nickelodeons peering into the tiny list of the latest Hank Williams tunes. A cowboy would only glance at "her" for about a solid hour before getting up the nerve to ask her to dance. Then together they would "'take the cure" out on the dance floor. Yes sir, Lone Star beer and San Antonio Rose have loosened up more aches and pains than aspirin.

Then before the money ran completely out, any self-respecting cowboy got in a fist fight and managed to get himself thrown out before he got serious about this sweet, lovely girl whose husband didn't understand her. With his spurs a-jingling, he crawled into the cab of a 2½ ton truck and stopped by the cafe for breakfast before sunup.

Wanting to impress the waitress with his newly acquired macho image, at 4 A.M., he looks at her with a rakish grin and says, "Darlin', let me have two headlights and a side of fenders."

"What's that, cowboy?"

"Eggs and bacon, you sweet, innocent thang."

She returns in a moment with a bowl of leftover hash. "Where's my headlights and fenders?" he demands.

That's when she whispers in his ear with a sexy voice. "Thought you'd want to gas up first."

Then it was back to the ranch where you had 30 days to come up with something clever you could have said . . . cowboy.

DUCK AND DODGE

Burlesque is a form of humor which has all but died out in this country. For those of you who never got to see it, burlesque was a mixture of comics in baggy clothes and girls in skin-tight outfits. "I never saw skin that tight," remarked a paying customer. "Or knew that girls had that much of it."

It was this slight risque atmosphere that drew so many young men to stand tall, lower their voice, and lie about their age. You had to be 16 before you could legally purchase a ticket. A father once reprimanded his 14-year-old son about sneaking into the burlesque show because "you might see something you shouldn't." The kid sneaked in anyway and sure enough he saw what he should not have . . . his father.

However, the real thrill of burlesque was the comics. Think of a live production in your hometown by the Hee Haw cast and you'll get the picture. Someone once said, "Any joke is okay in burlesque if you're knowledgeable in poultry and automobiles. Just remember 'Duck and Dodge.'"

Here are a few lines that a modern burlesque might throw out. Please, no tomatoes.

I'll tell you how bad the smog is around here. I know an artist who paints what he sees. Hasn't painted in three years!

Most experts feel the Red Chinese don't have an effective means of delivery. We have a Post Office with the same problem.

They say football has taken over as our national pasttime—and what the Houston Oilers play is pretty popular too!

They talk about American efficiency, yet the secretary always answers the phone, and most of the time it's for her boss.

The trouble with women in the business world, if you treat them like men, they get mad. And if you treat them like women, your wife gets mad.

I could tell this was a rich farming community. You don't often see whitewall tires on a manure spreader.

Fein and Klein were sitting on a park bench. "I'm afraid to fly. Those airplanes ain't too safe!"

"Don't be a baby," said Klein. "Didn't you read last week there was a big train crash and 300 people were killed."

"Three hundred people on a train—what happened?"

"An airplane fell on it!"

One evening last summer during a particularly violent thunderstorm, a mother was tucking her small boy into bed.

She was about to turn off the light when he asked with a tremor in his voice, "Mommy, will you sleep with me tonight?"

The mother smiled and gave him a reassuring hug. "I can't do that dear. I have to sleep in Daddy's room."

A long silence was broken at last by a shaken little voice saying, "The big sissy!"

So much for burlesque. It's fun to look back at the old jokes.

And the skintights? Gone, but not the tight skin. Just watch cable television.

COWTOWN TO WALL STREET

Two cattlemen in the lobby of the First Bank and Bust of downtown Cowtown were economizing by drinking that free coffee while they read day-old copies of the Wall Street Journal and filled their pockets with lump sugar. Cattlemen always look at both sides of a problem, sort of a good news-bad news philosophy with a country twist.

"This is the worst market there could be, ain't it?"

"No, it's the best market . . . if you're buyin'."

"This is sure no time to have a note due on cows that you borrowed money on to buy last year, is it?"

"No, it's a good time, cause there ain't a dang thing they can do about it."

When the Bank President strolled by, one of the cowmen called him over and with a big grin whispered in his ear: "It came a hard, cold rain out at my place last night. You better get your boots on and go feed your cows."

Which just goes to show that we're all in this thing together, from Cowtown to Wall Street. If we can keep our sense of humor while all about us others are losing their heads . . . we probably don't completely understand the situation. Good news, bad news, it depends on your attitude.

Success depends on which side of the coin we choose. Heads we win, tails we lose.

OUTHOUSE TREND SETTERS

The clothing industry must be a high class business, right? Advertising must be done in a serious manner, right? Names must be chosen carefully, right?

Well, of course. Everybody knows that millions are spent each year on naming products or even the chain stores. Safeway sure wouldn't have chosen Dangerpath, Neiman-Marcus wouldn't have selected Hank's Haberdashery, and Bottom Dollar would have frowned on Higher Than Heck.

So, armed with all this information, a young fellow named Carroll Jones set out to open a clothing business. It was a modest operation based on sharp buying of quality merchandise: overruns, irregulars, but good stuff. The price was sometimes half the regular retail market. Guess what he named his business: OUTHOUSE OUTLETS, INC. People laughed all the way to the store and he laughed with them. All the way to the bank.

There are now over 30 of these stores and they are growing. Inside most of them they have little outhouses, with a quarter moon cut in the door, where you try on the merchandise. Some oldtimers bring their grandkids down just to point with pride and say, "There, that's what they used to look like." Many a kid has bought a shirt just so they could experience the thrill of resting in an outhouse, flipping through the mail order catalog and peeking out through a quarter moon slit as the rest of the world goes by.

My friend Dr. Charles Jarvis says that's perfectly understandable, "We are so progressive we forget how simple things can be. We moved all the plumbing indoors. Now, we cook outside. That's progress?"

While the outhouse may be a return to the simple life it does seem strange now to see everybody driving there.

The folks who own the stores at the local level have to have a sense of humor but they are hard workers, happy and successful. At a recent business meeting where I was on their program I overheard comments like this:

"If you want to find your competitor, look for someplace warm. He'll be asleep there."

"I tell them my business has a different style—tasteless."

"Long dresses pick up germs. You ought to see what short dresses will pick up."

And when I asked the Chairman of the Board how he felt about his success he replied, "I feel more like I do now than I did a while ago."

Outhouse apparently feels like Fred Allen did when he said, "It's bad to suppress laughter because it goes back down and spreads the hips."

COMPARED TO WHAT?

There is an old story about a man who was asked the question, "How's your wife?" His answer was, "Compared to what?"

That got me to thinking about other clever answers that could be used for questions that are asked. It is an art to answer a question with a question. Lawyers use this art all the time. There is a name for it. Ask any lawyer's client who lost his case and he'll tell you the name, no questions asked.

However, here are some questions for snappy comebacks to the original question.

"Why do you always question me?" "Do I?"

"What can I do for you?" "Have you thought of leaving your body to science?"

"Will any others be seated at your table?" "Who did you have in mind?"

"Why am I always broke?" "Who did you marry?"

"When will the postal service improve?" "What postal service?"

"How long will you love me?" "What time is it?"

"Is that the truth?" "Would I lie to you?"

A word of advice in playing this game: Don't ever ask the first question because there are some who will flagrantly disregard the rules and answer a question with an answer. For instance, if you ask, "How are you?" there are some people who will tell you much more than you wanted to know. Few can question that, can they?

COUCH POTATOES

They say there's a new trend developing in the United States. People are staying at home more. Uncle Fred was way ahead of his time in that regard. Aunt Ida kept him chained to a chair.

Now people are doing it on purpose. Couch potatoes, they are called. They can spend their entire life in a recliner and watch satellite TV for 24 hours a day. A thunderstorm knocked out the power in our house and one of my kids swore he could still see faint images of cartoons on the screen. When the electricity came back on an hour later, he was still gazing into the microwave.

The latest thing out is a Couch Potato doll. The potato sits in its own tiny couch with a cola and a bag of chips. This should stimulate sales of potatoes like the pet rock helped out the gravel industry, right? Wrong, the "potatoes" are made of dark beige nylon. It's a plot to drive up the price of panty hose.

I figure women are mad at the guys for all those years they had to wear potato sacks.

The couch potato is no myth, however. Nearly every home in America has at least one recliner chair where someone is on an experimental diet of pizza, beer, and TV. Know what's the favorite program of couch potatoes? You guessed it—Jake and the Fat Man.

I know a couple who bought a double recliner so they could put a little romance back in their marriage. They both gained so much weight that one night it was all one of them could do during the emergency. She finally managed to get one arm out far enough to call the fire department for the jaws of life.

Now they have two double recliners and only occasionally get romantic. The other night, he passionately said to her, during a commercial, "Sweetheart, how would you like to have another litter?"

Out in California (where else?) there is even a Couch Potato Club. Anyone from Idaho gets free membership and there is a foreign chapter in Paris. The French Fried Chapter, of course.

A newsletter is published by the originator of the Couch Potato idea, Robert Armstrong, a cartoonist from Dixon, California. It's called The Tuber. Obviously, the movement has gone underground.

But the movement has spread like fat cells through the Rotary Club and now even high-class folks admit to being a couch potato. However, we prefer to call it Transcendental Vegetation.

ART OF COMMUNICATION

American sayings are strange forms of communication. If you want to illustrate how attractive a girl is, you could say "Yahoo, wow, man o' man, she's a doll", but that would be crude; so the semi-crude say something like "Her lips are painted to look like she's always whistlin'." That may not be entirely complimentary because another saying is "A whistlin' woman and a crowin' hen, both will come to a no good end."

What stimulated this column was the onslaught of hot weather. I recently got in a friend's car that had been sitting in the sun. As he opened the door, he exclaimed "Boy, that's hotter than a pot of collards." A fellow who tells those kind of tales is often a big mouth and others might describe him by saying "He could bite through a side of bacon without greasing a gum." If he's not too bright, they say, "He must have been hit with a wet cob when he was young." If he puts on a suit but normally wears overalls, they say "He's dressed up like a dirt road dandy."

Public officials have especially affectionate descriptions. The mayor becomes the "Head Tush Hog," the city council is said to be "ridin' a gravy train with biscuit wheels," and a tough sheriff is said to "carry a broom handle wrapped in a *Baptist Standard.*" The politician who gets involved in some scandal is described as "so crooked he could sleep in the shade of a corkscrew."

An honest but poor, struggling businessman is referred to as "too poor to paint and too proud to whitewash." A mercenary merchant is described as one who "would kill a flea for the hide and tallow." If he was once poor, but success changed him for the worse, they say "He was all right til he got two pair of britches." If he's stingy, the words are "he wouldn't give you an inch of cordwood or an ounce of corn shucks," which naturally makes him "as sorry as homemade soap" and he "ought to be hung by the neck til honest."

A self-centered person is "as independent as a hog on ice" and a person who is habit-bound to a certain practice can be counted on to do it "as regular as a goose goes barefoot." He's "gonna do it, he doesn't care if syrup goes to a dollar a sop."

Of course, I should not cast any aspersions on my fellowpersons. I used to say fellowman, but that was before I got educated by a lady who described me as "one who's brain, if implanted in a bumblebee would make it fly backwards."

I didn't think much about that until I had somebody explain it to me. But what really got to me was when she described me as being such a poor businessman that I "couldn't run a watermelon stand if you gave him the melons and the Highway Patrol flagged the traffic."

I'm not gonna say how slow her mind worked, but I have noticed that every time she reads a stop sign, her lips move.

FLEAS, FUN, FLAK, AND FAKE

In a recent TV show there was a feature on a flea spray for dogs. This particular product got rid of the fleas as advertised. Unfortunately it got rid of the dog, the neighbor's dog, and the nearest fire hydrant.

The company says the ingredients are not harmful except to certain sensitive pets but owners began to suspect something when whole flower beds died and their car tires glowed in the dark.

Of course the lawyers got on it right away and started to sue everyone in sight. Animal rights, professional courtesy I suppose.

I mentioned this controversy to a friend and he suggested that research on this product should have been more thorough. "Should have used law students for research instead of white mice," he said. "Why is that?" I asked. "Because," he replied, "there are more of them, they would be easily replaced, and there are some things even a rat won't do."

In a similar life or death matter, a fellow went to his doctor feeling poorly. The doctor told him he had only one day to live. He decided to make the most of it, went home, told his wife about it. They invited friends over, had a great farewell party, stayed up late and celebrated a great life even though it was to be cut short. When the crowd was gone and they had retired, he tried to hold her close but she turned away. "I'm sorry," she said. "I have to get some rest."

"Have a heart," he pleaded.

"Oh sure," she said. "That's easy for you to say. You don't have to get up in the morning."

Funny how danger can be exciting, humorous, and threatening all at the same time. A fellow told his wife he was going hunting but he wanted her to pack his silk pajamas so he could be comfortable in his sleeping bag. He was gone two weeks, returned wearing hunting boots and camouflage clothing. "I thought I asked you to pack my silk pajamas," he told her. "I did," she replied. "Well, I couldn't find them. Where did you put them?" "In your gun case," she answered.

Whether it is man or beast, life can be cut short in a variety of ways. Like a friend of mine says, "The old must, the young may, and the wisest knows not when." That philosophy does not hold true if you are wise enough, however. A sign in a Louisiana quick stop "Shop & Rob" store has a sign that reads: "Shoplifters will be shot. Survivors will be shot again."

FOR HEAVENS SAKE

Someday it will all be clear to us I suppose, but right now, it's pretty difficult to understand about heaven and how some folks are going to get in on it. For those who claim to have no questions about the process, I have an answer to match the question.

It may be like the autumn leaves hanging on a tree. Two leaves were talking one day. "Where do they go when they fall?" asked one. "Some say one place, some another, but not one has ever come back to tell his story," replied the other.

Then one day the last leaf was left alone. The icy winds blew and finally, its grip was loosened. As it came to rest with those who had gone before, suddenly all the mystery was gone and death to one world was but life in another.

"Ah, the meek shall inherit the earth . . . seems so simple. Why couldn't I see that before?" asked the newcomer. "Boy, it sure is hot here in heaven."

"You ain't in heaven," cried out a host of lost leaves. "You're in a forest fire."

"Many will be called, but few will be chosen," said the Salvation Army Major to a skidrow bum, as the scene changed to the more earthly world. "Don't gimme that," replied the sinful stranger, "You just tell me how to get to the nearest bar."

"The road to hell is paved with sin," said the Major.

"I always suspected those shifty-eyed contractors myself. How far is it to Dallas?"

"250 miles."

"How far is it back?"

"250 miles."

"Not necessarily."

"How could it be otherwise, brother?"

"How long is it from Christmas to Thanksgiving?"

"About 10 months."

"How long from Thanksgiving to Christmas?"

That's when the Major explained to him the power of miracles. "I don't get it," said the drunk.

"Turn around and bend over," said the Major. When the wino obliged, the servant of the Lord smote him with a heavy foot.

"Oww, that hurt," said the sinner.

"Yes," explained the saintly teacher, "if it had not . . . that would have been a miracle." A small puff of wind swirled by and with it last year's leaves, punctuating the miracle of another spring—new life . . . as old as time.

THE LAST SHOT

I was drafted. I resisted, but they insisted.
We won by insistence . . . or was it persistence
that brought us to the end.

Epilogue

Do little things, like fingernails on a blackboard, annoy you? Well, I have several that get under my skin and I've compiled a list:

- It's annoying when I go to the doctor with an ingrown toenail and he gags.

- I also don't care for nurses who close their eyes when giving me a shot.

- Why is it that businesses downtown will have double swinging doors and always have the one locked that you choose to push?

- I'd like to take a sledgehammer to those currency changers that decide for you how wrinkled a perfectly legal dollar bill can be.

- Water fountains are the reason I had to give up water altogether. Just as I made adjustments from the stream hitting my right eye, left nostril, or forehead, the thing dies completely and you can't suck a drop out of it without collapsing a lung.

- That little red strip on a band-aid drives me nuts. When it breaks, you understand why. It is trying to cut through a covering that cannot be torn, mutilated, or pierced by a .357 magnum.

- There are certain kinds of bugs found on freeways that fill up with grease from the local fast food places and make Kamikazi attacks at eye level only on the driver's side of the windshield. The only ones able to handle emergencies of this sort, as you have probably seen, are experienced rural mail carriers.

- It bothers me when a busload of school kids pulls alongside my car and, though I can't prove it, I know they're laughing at me.

- I hate it when one bumper guard is missing from the underside of a toilet seat.

- When seated at any banquet table, why do they place me at the only spot where there is a table leg, an uneven abutment of two tables, and a crack in the platform riser?

- It makes me nervous to eat in a very expensive restaurant, feel under the table, and find gum.

- I can find no earthly reason why people eat a watermelon from the center out and a steak just the opposite.

- Has anybody ever thought of the danger of a head on collision with a vehicle bearing down on you with flashing lights and a sign on the front that reads "ECNALUBMA?"

- God forbid this should ever happen to you, on an oversold, 4-hour flight there is one middle seat left . . . it annoys me that I can buy the seat, but not the right to either of the arm rests.

- I'm really annoyed with people who pick up a copy of *Shoot Luke* and read this page first hoping to get a summary of the most hilarious stuff imaginable.

Remember?
You don't?
That reminds me. What did I do with that list?
Dang those pigeons. The air is full of 'em.

More Doc Blakely Programs and Books

To Teach You

How To Use Humor Effectively.

TAPES

☐ **The Ten Second Executive Humorist**   **$60**

> In this album, Doc Blakely teaches you how to use the highest, most effective form of communication—humor. These tapes are not intended to make you a professional humorist. They will teach you how to think like one and use the tricks of the trade . . . 10 seconds at a time. 6 Tape set.

☐ **The Executive Treasury of Humor**   **$130**

> Edited and presented by Arnold "Nick" Carter, Vice President of Communications, Nightingale-Conant Corporation. Featuring Doc Blakely and an all-star team of eleven more of America's premier platform performers at their very best. They'll make you laugh and they'll make you think! Two volume set. 12 tapes.

☐ **Words in Stone or**
Don't Chisel Your Way Through Life   **$10**

> This talk was inspired by the speaking circuit. Traveling all over the U.S., Doc chanced to see numerous monuments with great words of wisdom carved in them. Some are wise, some foolish, and some just plain funny. Single tape.

☐ **To Soar With Eagles**   **$10**

> This talk was inspired by personal experiences in learning to fly. We all face great challenges and have to rise above them using the principles accented with humor in this talk. Single tape.

☐ **Livin' On Love And Laughter**   **$10**

> This talk is in two parts. The ingredients of love are exposed from a surprising source and laughter is added to round out the philosophy. Single tape.

Order Toll Free 1-800-346-3831

☐ Accent On Laughter $10

This talk revolves around accents (dialects) including those of the English, Irish, Scottish, German, Italian, Scandinavian, French, and others. This, Doc's most requested talk, puts the accent on sales, professionalism and success. Single tape.

BOOKS

☐ Doc Blakely's Handbook of Wit and Pungent Humor
$20

A gold mine of 1,250 hilarious jokes, tall tales, and precious nuggets of humor. This ready-to-use material can be easily modified to fit countless situations. Hardback.

☐ Doc Blakely's Push Button Wit $20

Contains 1,450 choice one-liners, jokes and quips. Jokes are categorized, alphabetized and indexed for rapid retrieval. In addition, you'll find over 100 tips on how to use humor. Hardback.

☐ How The Platform Professionals Keep 'Em Laughin'
$20

Now any speaker can utilize the techniques that made four of America's top professional humorists so popular on the speaking circuit that they were literally forced into new careers. Doc Blakely, Joe Griffith, Robert Henry and Jeanne Robertson forge a powerful link between a meaningful and an entertaining address. Over 2,000 jokes and one-liners plus 72 pages on philosophy of humor in the speech foundation. Hardback.

_____ QUANTITY   TOTAL _____

Name_____

Company Name_____

Address_____

City_____ State_____ Zip_____

Shipping and
Handling $3.00 _____

Texas Residents
Add 7.5% Sales Tax_____

Total_____

Please charge my: ☐ Visa ☐ MasterCard ☐ American Express

Account Number: _____Exp. Date: _____

Signature: _____ Phone _____ ☐ Check Enclosed

Complete and return to:
Doc Blakely, 3404 Fairway Drive, Wharton, Texas 77488.